CATHOLIC HERMENEUTICS TODAY

Catholic Hermeneutics Today

CRITICAL ESSAYS

Benedict Thomas Viviano, OP

CASCADE *Books* • Eugene, Oregon

CATHOLIC HERMENEUTICS TODAY
Critical Essays

Copyright © 2014 Benedict Thomas Viviano OP. All rights reserved. Except for brief quotations in critical publications or reviews, no part of this book may be reproduced in any manner without prior written permission from the publisher. Write: Permissions, Wipf and Stock Publishers, 199 W. 8th Ave., Suite 3, Eugene, OR 97401.

Cascade Books
An Imprint of Wipf and Stock Publishers
199 W. 8th Ave., Suite 3
Eugene, OR 97401

www.wipfandstock.com

ISBN 13: 978-1-62564-418-3

Cataloging-in-Publication data:

Viviano, Bendict.

    Catholic hermeneutics today : critical essays / Benedict Thomas Viviano OP.

    xvi + 250 p. ; 23 cm—Includes bibliographical references and indexes.

    ISBN 13: 978-1-62564-418-3

    1. Bible—Hermeneutics. 2. Hermeneutic—Religious aspects. 3. Bible. Matthew—Criticism, interpretation, etc. 3. Bible—Study and teaching—Catholic Church. I. Title.

BS587 V58 2014

Manufactured in the U.S.A.

First Occasions of Presentation or Publication

1. The Historical-Critical Method in Modern Biblical Studies: Yes or No?" is previously unpublished and was presented at the Ecole Biblique in Jerusalem at the first international meeting of Dominican biblical scholars in 1999.

2. "The Normativity of Scripture and Tradition in Recent Catholic Theology," first appeared in *Scripture's Doctrine and Theology's Bible: How the New Testament Shapes Dogmatics*, edited by Markus Bockmuehl and Alan J. Torrance (Grand Rapids: Baker, 2008), 125–40.

3. "The Future of Catholic Biblical Scholarship: A Review Article" is a review of Luke Timothy Johnson and William S. Kurz and was first published in *Review of Biblical Literature* 2003.

4. "The Revewal of Biblical Studies in France 1934–1954" first appeared in *Ressourcement: A Movement for Renewal in Twentieth-century Catholic Theology*, edited by Gabriel Flynn and Paul D. Murray (Oxford: Oxford University Press, 2012), 305–17.

5. "American Catholic New Testament Scholarship" was a lecture given at Oxford, 27 November 2008.

6. "The Dictatorship of Relativism and the Right to a Non-Oppressive Public Religious Culture" is previously unpublished and was given at a meeting of the Ecumentical Christian Research Fraternity in Israel, Jerusalem 2005.

7. "The Dogma of the Prophetless Time in Judaism: Does Prophecy Cease with Christ for Christians? Some Explorations" first appeared in *L'Ecrit et l'Esprit: Etudes d'histoire du texte et de theologie biblique en hommage a Adrian Schenker*, edited by Dieter Boehler, I. Himbaza, and P. Hugo, Orbis Biblicus et Orientalis 214 (Fribourg: Academic Press, 2005), 418–31.

FIRST OCCASIONS OF PRESENTATION OR PUBLICATION

8. "The New Testament between Scylla and Charibdis: Matthew and Inter-Religious Dialogue" was presented as my farewell lecture, 4 December 2008, and published in French as "Le Nouveau Testament entre Charybde en Scylla: Matthieu et le dialogue interreligiuex," *Freiburger Zeitschrift für Philosophie und Theologie* 56 (2009) 390–402.

9. "Eschatology and the Historical Jesus" first appeared in the *Oxford Handbook of Eschatology*, edited by Jerry L. Walls, Oxford Handbooks (Oxford: Oxford University Press, 2008), 73–90.

10. "The Adoration of the Magi: Matthew 2:1–23 and Theological Aesthetics," first appeared in *Revue Biblique* 115 (2008) 546–67.

11. "The Christian and the State," first appeared in *The Reception of Paulinism in Acts = Réception du Paulinisme dans les Actes des apôtres*, edited by Daniel Marguerat, BETL 229 (Leuven: Peeters, 2009), 227–38.

12. "Apocalypse and Culture" first appeared as "Apocalypse et Culture: L'interprétation de 1 Co 15,20–28 dans l'exégèse protestante allemande de 1870 à 1960," in *Mysterium Regni, Ministerium Verbi (Mc 4,11;): Scritti in onore di mons. Vittorio Fusco*, edited by Ettore Franco, Supplementi alla Rivista Biblica 38 (Bologna: EDB, 2000), 739–56.

13. "Hakeldama, The Potter's Field, and the Suicide of Judas (Matt 27:3–10; Acts 1:16–20)" appeared in the studies in honor of Max Küchler, *Jerusalem und die Länder: Ikonographie, Topographie, Theologie: Festschrift für Max Küchler zum 65. Geburtstag*, edited by Gerd Theissen, Hans Ulrich Steymans, Siegfried Ostermann, Matthias Schmidt, Andrea Moresino-Zipper, NTOA 70 (Göttingen: Vandenhoeck & Ruprecht, 2009), 203–10.

14. "A Woman's Quest for Wisdom and the Adoration of the Magi," first appeared in *The Gospel of Matthew at the Crossroads of Early Christianity*, edited by Donald Senior, BETL 243 (Leuven: Peeters, 2011), 683–700.

15. "Making Sense of the Matthean Genealogy: Matthew 1:17 and the Theology of History," first appeared in *New Perspectives on the Nativity*, edited by Jeremy Corley (London: T. & T. Clark, 2009), 91–109.

Contents

List of First Occasions of Presentations or Publication | v

Introduction | ix

1. The Historical-Critical Method in Modern Biblical Studies: Yes or No? | 1

2. The Normativity of Scripture and Tradition in Recent Catholic Theology | 14

3. Review of *The Future of Catholic Biblical Scholarship: A Constructive Conversation* | 29

4. The Renewal of Biblical Studies in France 1934–1954 as an Element in Theological *Ressourcement* | 34

5. American Catholic New Testament Scholarship | 45

6. The Dictatorship of Relativism and the Right to a Non-Oppressive Public Religious Culture | 56

7. The Dogma of the Prophetless Time in Judaism: Does Prophecy Cease with Christ for Christians? Some Explorations | 73

8. The New Testament between Scylla and Charybdis: Matthew and Interreligious Dialogue | 86

9. Eschatology and the Quest for the Historical Jesus | 101

10. The Adoration of the Magi: Matthew 2:1–23 and Theological Aesthetics | 122

CONTENTS

11. The Christian and the State in Acts and Paul
(Acts 25:16 and Rom 13:1–7): Roman Fairness Then and Now | 142

12. Apocalypse and Culture: The Interpretation of 1 Cor 15:20–28 in German Protestant Exegesis in the Period 1870–1960; A Hypothesis in the Sociology of Exegesis | 154

13. Hakeldama, the Potter's Field, and the Suicide of Judas
(Matt 27:1–10; Acts 1:16–20) | 175

14. A Woman's Quest for Wisdom and the Adoration of the Magi as Part of Matthew's Program of Solomonic Sapiential Messianism | 183

15. Matthew 1:17 and the Theology of History:
Making Sense of the Matthean Genealogy | 201

Acknowledgments | 223

Abbreviations | 225

Index of Names | 231

Index of Scripture and Other Ancient Sources | 237

Introduction

HERMENEUTICS IS AN ACADEMIC term which refers to the science or art of interpretation. In the present context it refers to the art of interpreting the Sacred Scriptures of Christians, the Bible. The word hermeneutics has sometimes been thought to be related to the Greek god Hermes, the messenger of the Olympian gods, the master of communication and of boundaries (and boundary crossings).

The present author is surprised to be publishing a collection of his essays on biblical hermeneutics. He has long thought that hermeneutics is a gaseous mode of discourse used to avoid the plain sense of the Scriptures. Hermeneutics is a waste of time, I thought. It certainly can be. Yet over the years invitations come even to this skeptic to address one or another aspect of biblical hermeneutics. The essays that are the result have accumulated and perhaps they can be of interest to a wider audience in book form. This is especially true in the climate of polemical debate in which we currently live, debates over such polarities as the hermeneutics of suspicion versus the hermeneutics of loving sympathy or at least of respect. (It was Paul Ricoeur who pointed to the masters of suspicion: Marx, Nietzsche, Freud.) It was Pope Benedict XVI who emphasized the difference between the hermeneutics of continuity and the hermeneutics of rupture in regard to the interpretation of the second Vatican Council. Hermeneutics has been a lively area of theological discourse, whether we regret it or rejoice in it. It should be obvious that if you want to understand something or someone, you need to do both: try to be loving and sympathetic, but also to have a critical awareness of problems.

In pre-modern times there was an authoritative text and a largely stable tradition of interpretation of the text, whether the Bible or Homer or Roman law. There were however some major breaks in the tradition, for example, the rise of Christianity and with it the New Testament. Paul himself evoked allegory (Gal 4:24), a technique developed in Alexandria, first

INTRODUCTION

for Homer, then for the Greek translation of the Hebrew Bible. Paul also distinguished between the spirit and the letter (2 Cor 3:6). Jesus taught in parables, which by their fictional nature invite interpretation and application. (That the parables sometimes allude to real history is a side point.) The rabbis developed lists of *middoth* or rules of interpretation which they used to develop their *midrashim* (collections of interpretations, sometimes of whole biblical books). There were both narrative and legal *midrashim*. One began to sense that the realm of interpretation was infinite. There could not be a single, simple right reading.[1]

These problematic developments contrast with a naïve, direct identification of the self with the text. A young believer who picks up the Bible without much preparation has such an experience. For example, such a person could pick up a modern translation of the gospels and think: this is a true narrative; it really happened this way; here in the Sermon on the Mount wisdom about life is to be found. No interpretative buffer is needed. Some of the great saints got their start in this way, for example St Anthony of the Desert or St Francis of Assisi. Luther too had his tower experience with Rom 1:16-17; 3:21-31 (although he had already read St Augustine). This fresh, direct contact with the text is primary and can be wonderful and transforming. It should not be choked off by too much interpretative overlay. Yet with the best will in the world and with the most pure and naïve and godly access to the Word, one cannot conceal for example a massive contradiction between Galatians 1-4 and Matthew 5-7, esp. Matt 5:17-20, Either you admit that there is a problem or you are a liar, to yourself and to others. You can twist and bend the word, but the problem remains. It is this experience of inner-biblical conflict and contradiction that is the most convincing and legitimate wellspring of hermeneutical theory. St Jerome said that the conflict between Peter and Paul in Galatians 2:11-14 was only apparent; they were play-acting. St Augustine said that the fact of conflict must be admitted. God's word is not served by human lies.

Once the Middle Ages had recovered Aristotle's logical works, Abelard began a more modern approach to theology with his work: *Sic et Non* (yes and no). In this work he collected apparently contradictiory statements in the Bible and in tradition. This is one of the starting points of the scholastic

---

1. See Karl Lehmann, "Hermeneutics," in *Sacramentum Mundi*, vol. III (New York: Herder, 1969), pp. 23-27; Kendrick Grobel, "Interpretation, History and Principles of," in *Interpreter's Dictionary of the Bible* (Nashville: Abingdon, 1962), 2:718-24; J. Weingreen, G. Vermes, D. Hay, K.P. Bland, V. P. Furnish, S.B. Hoenig, G. A. C. Hadfield, E. A. Achtemeier, "Interpretation, History of," in *IDB Supplementary Volume* (Nashville: Abingdon, 1976), 436-56. Hildebrand Hoepfl and Louis Leloir, *Introductio Generalis in Sacram Scripturam* (Naples: M. D'Auria, 1958), 403-503, De hermeneutica.

method in theology. The major works of St Thomas Aquinas are organized as questions for debate, with objections and answers to questions (*sed contra*). These works arise out of the scholastic disputations in the universities. The medieval schools also developed a technique called *reverenter exponere* (to expound reverently). For example, it was not considered polite or correct behavior to disagree with St Augustine directly. So you interpreted him to say just about the opposite of what he had intended to say.

Two other major crises caused breaks in the tradition of interpretation, the Reformation and then the Enlightenment. Parts of both movements involved an approach to the sacred texts which emphasized their historical origins: date, human author or authors, the use of sources, place of composition, connection with non-biblical literature of the time of composition. The Bible was to be read as any other ancient book. A gap opened up between the Bible and the contemporary reader.

Romanticism, especially the hermeneutics of Schleiermacher, attempted a bridge over the gap between past and present, a leap through disciplined historical imagination. This project is called *Einfuehlen*, literally sympathy or empathy. Through close reading and the use of comparative material, one searched for the intention of the human author. For believers, it was this intention which God had inspired. This project could be accused of speculative subjectivity. More modern critics reject the importance of the intention of the original human author, either because one is never quite sure that one has reached it, or because the text is greater than the intention of the author. The text can acquire other meanings, not intended by the original author, but meanings legitimate in themselves and possibly willed by the Holy Spirit.

Postwar continental philosophy (Heidegger and his former student Gadamer) emphasized certain themes such as the reality of a prior understanding (*Vorverständnis*) that the sacred author brings to the text and that the modern reader brings to the text. They emphasized the historicity of truth, that truth is marked by the era in which it is written down. Gadamer spoke of a fusion or merging of horizons between the ancient author and the modern interpreter. The importance of language makes exact philology of central significance. The price of the transfer from one language to another (translation) must be weighed, for example, the shift from Hebrew and Aramaic to Greek and then Latin. The text both conceals and reveals the sacred realities of which it speaks. Debate rages over whether an objective interpretation is even possible. Are we all only trapped in our inescapable subjectivity? Moreover, critics like Harold Bloom speak of a "strong re-reading" of a text, an act of power which imposes a quite arresting interpretation on the text, even it it does a certain violence to the text.

INTRODUCTION

This book is entitled *Catholic Hermeneutics Today*. What does "Catholic" mean here? First of all, it means that the essays are written from within the Roman Catholic Church, by a (white male) Catholic priest in the Dominican tradition (from the United States). Catholic here means that this book presupposes the whole long tradition of the Church east and west, north and south. Its author does not pretend to have mastered all of that tradition in detail. What he does know of it will emerge in the different essays. It goes without saying that Catholic here includes the papal teachings on the Bible and its interpretation, from the end of the nineteenth century (Leo XIII) till today, especially the encyclical *Divino Afflante Spiritu* of 1943 and the Constitution on Divine Revelation, fiercely fought over at the Second Vatican Council, voted on and approved by nearly 3,000 bishops, including of course the bishop of Rome. To some extent this constitution is once again being fought over, something I did not expect once it had been approved in 1965. The Bible is accepted in the present work as the inspired Word of God, containing at times divine revelation, with all the provisos and cautions contained in the Constitution and in subsequent documents of the Pontifical Biblical Commission.[2] The Bible is accepted as the unnormed norm of theological teaching, as in Thomas Aquinas (*Summa theol.*, I., q. 1). Catholic here is not intended as a sectarian badge, but as an ecclesial placement.

Catholic hermeneutics as it is understood here does not exclude insights from Anglican, Methodist, Lutheran, Reformed, Baptist, or Orthodox scholars. It is consciously and ardently ecumenical. It also includes insight from ancient rabbis and modern Jewish scholars. This work does not, however, accept that the Bible can be reduced to anthropology (as with Bultmann) or can substitute a personal life decision for the concrete biblical content. Catholic tradition ought not to skip over or blur the original claims of the gospel and its truth, both in ethical action and in dogmatic coherence. The proclamation and the interpretation of the Scriptures in the liturgy is the primary context for hermeneutics, but these liturgical practices do not exclude, rather they ideally include, quiet study of the text, with the raising of critical questions as one prepares for the liturgy. The biblical miracles, from the first day of creation and the crossing of the Reed Sea to Jesus walking on the water[AQ: sea?] and raising the dead, have been both a stumbling block and a source of hope and joy from the day they were written down. Miracles are closely connected with prayer, with faith in God, and with hope. They have always been both an indispensible part of the biblical record and an embarrassment. That record does not expect us to unravel the

---

2. M. J. Zia, *What Are They Saying about Biblical Inspiration?* (New York: Paulist, 2011).

INTRODUCTION

miracles or to explain them away, but to wrestle with the truths that they express. The miraculous too is one of the challenges to Catholic hermeneutics, which can in this regard be dismissed as primitive supernaturalism if one is so minded. The miraculous remains part of the whole biblical enterprise, to be approached respectfully but also with critical awareness and a sense of proportion (Ps 77:19; 1 Cor 13:2b). Paul fights against childishness (1 Cor 13:11).

The fifteen essays in this book try to address various aspects of this immense territory, whether as illustrations or as clarifications. The first addresses the fundamental methodological issue. The historical-critical method has dominated the field in the academy for two hundred years. Just when it has seemed to triumph in all the churches, there arose an explosion of non-historical or ahistorical methods, whether literary-rhetorical or devotional. This issue had to be the first discussed.

An old ecumenical issue is the role of church tradition in the interpretation of Scripture, and even more pointedly, tradition as an independent source of divine revelation, implying that Scripture is not sufficient for salvation. Tradition is the object of chapter 2 here.

The third essay is a review of a book that tried to undermine the adequacy of the historical-critical method and tried to insinuate that the heroes of the Catholic biblical movement like Lagrange had suffered in vain. This required a word of protest.

The next two essays review the biblical renewal movement in France and the United States. They are case studies of hermeneutics in practice.

Those who resist the historical-critical method fault it for leading to doctrinal relativism. There are real dangers here and they invite wrestling with the problem of relativism even if no perfect solution is available in this epoch.

Biblical hermeneutics deals with what believers regard as divine revelation. Is the offer of divine revelation an offer that has ceased or not? This is an eminently theological question, posed in the Bible itself. The Bible offers several answers. The seventh essay here presents the options and tilts toward one of the options, mindful of the dangers in any decision.

The uniqueness of biblical revelation becomes a problem more than ever today as the members of other major world religions move to the West and as modern communications draw people together across the globe. The gospel according to Matthew is presented as a central document of Christian revelation that also speaks to Jews and Muslims.

The ninth chapter deals with the fundamental issue of the eschatology of the historical Jesus. His central message was the soon-to-arrive Kingdom of God. This message continues to be a subject of contention to this day.

INTRODUCTION

Does it involve Jesus in an error of dating? Does it have leftist political implications? Who was Jesus that he should occupy such a central position in the religious faith of so many? This essay is a handbook survey of the debate over the last few centuries.

In the last decades a new theological movement or trend has emerged, called theological aesthetics. It shifts the emphasis away from truth and goodness to beauty. It has aroused enormous interest. Yet it has also been blamed for fostering the abuse of children and the wasting of church finances on the wrong priorities. Essay 10 tries to find light on this question from the Bible itself, especially Matthew 2.

The handling of wayward theologians and other complex cases can also be helped by biblical principles such as that stated in Acts 25:16 and related texts. Good trial procedures are a part of the administration of justice and can also guide the interpretation of Scripture.

The interpretation of Scripture is influenced by the social and political circumstances of the interpreter. Chapter 12 explores a case study in North Germany, which has ecumenical implications.

The thirteenth chapter illustrates the role of topography in the story of the death of Judas in Matthew 27 and also the differing biblical perspectives on the painful subject of suicide.

The major new sensitivity to the presence of feminist dimensions to the biblical text, often earlier ignored or passed over in silence or even deliberately suppressed, is visible in the essay on the queen of Sheba and the Magi.

The New Testament begins with one of the dullest, most off-putting pages in the Bible, the genealogy in Matthew 1:1–18. Yet when read sympathetically this text provides the basis for an entire theology of history.

Because the essays were often originally published in different countries with different rules for format and footnoting, the reader will not find perfect uniformity in these areas. The hope is however that the interested student will still be able to find the reference and that is after all the goal of the footnote.

The reader will also notice some overlapping of theme and thesis. In this way a coherent case for a certain type of Catholic hermeneutics can be made, an interpretative practice which is rooted in the historical church as well as in historical-critical methodology.

The abundance of interpretations available today is such that it can induce a certain nausea. The reader fears dizziness, the hopelessness of any stable meaning. The collection of interpretations of Matthew's gospel, such as has been collected by Ulrich Luz in his three-volume commentary, can be exploited to induce hermeneutical nihilism: every interpetation is just as justified as any other. Anything goes. We should be grateful for hermeneutical pluralism, but we do not need to embrace a "Will Rogers" hermeneutical pluralism. (Will Rogers was an American rural sage who said: "I never met a man I did not like.") Scholars should not be blamed if the biblical text is rich. That is why it has nourished and delighted and troubled believing people for so long.

The quest for objectivity need not be abandoned, even if it is a goal which can only be reached asymptotically until the Parousia. We can be helped by recognizing our own prejudices and desires, and then those of other interpreters. The normal prejudices I have found are usually easy to identify: dislike of law, ceremonial ritual, detailed ethics, Jews, mysticism, philosophy-speculation-reason, clear church order, peace, nature; alternatively, a too great interest in aesthetics or sacraments or a too great love of war. A sign of a search for truth or objectivity in an author is the willingness to make concessions to the other side of a confessionally or nationally disputed issue. Harnack and Weiss were good at this, as the reader will discover.[3]

St Louis and Vienna
31 October 2013 Reformation Day and 1 November All Saints

---

3. Some recent works in the area which have come to my attention are: Christopher Seitz, *Word without End: The Old Testament as Abiding Theological Witness* (Grand Rapids: Eerdmans, 1998); K. L. Sparks, *Sacred Word, Broken Word: Biblical Authority and the Dark Side of Scripture* (Grand Rapids: Eerdmans, 2012); M. W. Elliott, *The Heart of Biblical Theology: Providence Experienced* (Surrey, UK: Ashgate, 2012); Marius Reiser, *Bibelkritik und Auslegung der Heiligen Schrift* (Tübingen: Mohr/Siebeck, 2007); Oda Wischmeyer, ed., *Lexikon der Bibelhermeneutik* (Berlin: de Gruyter, 2009).

1

The Historical-Critical Method in Modern Biblical Studies

Yes or No?

SUMMARY

This conference presents an enthusiastic endorsement of the historical-critical method as the most appropriate method for the study of the Bible in an academic context and to some extent in the church. But this endorsement is subject to certain conditions. (1) The method must be understood as inclusive of all the particular methods used in the study of ancient texts: text-criticism, source-, form-, and redaction-criticism , literary analysis, sociological analysis, comparative religious analysis. (2) The method stands midway between a purely edifying approach and an aspiration to mathematical-physical rigor inappropriate to the subject matter of the Bible. Its model is rather the judicial discrimination/weighing of evidence, i.e., degrees of probability. And for the instruction of judges there is much material in the Bible itself (e.g., Deuteronomy 15). (To derive the essence of the historical-critical method from the Bible itself is the most original aspect of the essay). (3) to the extent that the historical-critical method prevails in the *church*, it must assume the additional burden of the various tasks formerly provided by pre-critical approaches to the Bible: it must assume the additional burden of the various tasks formerly provided by pre-critical approaches to the

Bible: it must become a helpful guide to theology, catechesis, preaching, liberation from oppression, personal prayer, faith itself (Walter Wink, *The Bible in Human Transformation*, Philadelphia, 1973). These additional tasks transform the method itself, but should never cause it to deviate from its goals of historical truth and the literal sense. It must not be forgotten that the Bible itself poses problems that invite comparison and critical analyses, esp. the multiple versions provided of the same event.

THE CULTURAL CONTEXT IN WHICH THE METHOD AROSE

The historical-critical method of studying the Bible has become an unavoidable necessity in the dialogue between Christian faith and advanced Western culture in the epoch which began around 1800. By then the historical turn which Western civilization had already begun to take in the previous decades was becoming the dominant mode of cultural discourse. This historical turn affected both the forces of the philosophical Enlightenment and of the Counter-Enlightenment. Montesquieu, Vico, and Herder vied with Voltaire and Gibbon and prepared the way for Hegel, Newman, and Darwin.

The rationalism of the Enlightenment has been the greatest challenge to supernatural Christian faith since Celsus in the second century. It excluded the possibility of miracles a priori as an illegitimate violation of natural law by the very Creator of the laws of nature. And it excluded the possibility of divine revelation or communication a priori as a violation of human dignity and autonomy (Kant). Voltaire made a mockery of biblical revelation. This was further reflected in his anti-Judaism and anti-Christianity, a revival of ancient pagan critiques.

Montesquieu by contrast prepared the way for a peaceful emancipation of the Jews at the French Revolution, but he also used the method of comparative religion to present Christianity in an unfavorable light. For him as a male and as a libertine, Islam represented a form of sexual liberation from the ethics of the gospels and Paul. This was the message of his *Persian Letters*. Vico and Herder tried to renew a Christian philosophy of history that would integrate a flood of new data (the recovery of Tacitus, Homer, Irenaeus at the Renaissance, for example) and give a respectful attention to the multitude of newly transcribed oral folk traditions and epic poems. The Brothers Grimm gave a further impetus to this kind of work among the Baltic and Slavic peoples, and Elias Loennrot among the Finns. Herder himself applied this approach to biblical poetry. But the work of Herder was too diffuse. It required a Hegel to achieve a synthesis of the work of Vico and Herder in a Christian philosophy of history inspired by the gospel according to John and therewith to offer the greatest initial Christian attempt to address and to master the challenge of Enlightenment rationalism.

Why was this historical turn important, relevant to biblical studies, and helpful in the Christian and Jewish believers' response to the criticisms made against biblical faith by the rationalists? The turn was important, relevant, and helpful because on the one hand much of the Bible expressed itself in a historical, narrative mode. This created for the rationalists (especially Lessing) the scandal of historical particularity. Why should we care about individual persons long dead, like Abraham, Moses or David, Sarah, Zipporah or Bathsheba? When this particularity was elevated in the Bible to a level of principle in the doctrine of election (chosen individuals, chosen people) the scandal only worsened. Why? Because on the other hand the Enlightenment took as its model for all valid, legitimate knowing mathematical laws, laws that were universal and immutable. Hence, "all statements with claims to truth must be public, communicable, testable—capable of verification or falsification by methods open to and accepted by any rational investigator." Thus the only legitimate knowledge was knowledge derived from the mathematico-physical sciences. To such a mind, most of the Bible made no sense. Only the wisdom books were exempt from contempt. Of the biblical authors, only Qoheleth counted as a *philosophe*.

Western civilization and Christian faith were on a collision course. The philosophers of history (Vico, Herder, Hegel, etc.) came to the rescue by realizing that the mathematico-physical model of knowing was too narrow to account for the totality of human life and experience. Particular historical events could at times have universal, irreversible consequences (the Exodus, Marathon, the Crucifixion, Waterloo). The impasse between rationalism and faith could be broken by the historical model of knowing. But this meant further that a purely devotional, spiritual, edifying, or allegorical reading of the Bible, which had become customary in the church, for pastoral reasons, and which took the complete historicity of the biblical narratives for granted, without examination or criticism, was no longer adequate or sufficient in educated circles. (St. Thomas for example usually presupposes historicity in his use of the Bible but sometimes also defends it with arguments.)

A historical, critically historical method had become indispensable, an absolute necessity, if the Bible were to be rescued from the rationalists, its educated despisers, even if this meant offending the *devots*.

Concretely, this meant that, at least initially, as a first step, the historical parts of the Bible had to be read as one read Herodotus and Thucydides; the prophets and psalmists read as one read other ancient poets, Hesiod and Sophocles; the biblical laws as comparable to those of Solon and the early

Romans; biblical wisdom as one read the Stoics and Epicureans. Historical analogy must prevail. Comparisons must be made with the world outside the Bible. Only then could the Bible begin to be understood in its original context. Only then could its proper contribution be appreciated, its religious and salvific value be seen in its full splendor, its dangers avoided. Only then could the mockers be silenced, indeed, intrigued and, God willing, converted to a better mind. The real risks involved were outweighed by the hoped-for advantages.

Another aspect of the cultural context in which the historical-critical method became a historical necessity in the study of the Bible was the political one. I refer to a growing dissatisfaction in Europe and the Americas with government by a hereditary aristocracy and absolute monarchs. Against these arose the esteem for parliamentary and eventually egalitarian democracy as well as for representative government. This political context is typified by the revolutions in America and France, the Reform Bills in Britain, the unification of Italy and of Germany, the fall of the four empires in 1918: Austrian, Prussian, Russian, and Ottoman. From a Catholic point of view it must be said that the Holy See showed little positive interest in the rise of parliamentary democracy until Christmas 1944.

No group in the church was more helpful in enabling the Episcopal and papal magisterial to face up to the new cultural and political challenges than certain, mainly French, provinces of the Dominican order. I refer of course first of all to Henri-Dominique Lacordaire (1802–1861). He, by his heroic fidelity after the condemnation by *Mirari vos* (1832) of the newspaper *L'Avenir*, more than any other single individual, but of course with many allies (Montalembert), enabled the church eventually to accept and then to embrace positively this form of government, first in civil society (1944), and then, to some extent, in the ecclesial society (1965), helped by the long experience of the Dominican constitutions, the mother of the mother of parliaments. Lacordaire did this at a time when leaders of other major orders, Benedictine, Jesuit, Augustinian of the Assumption, were deeply compromised in the hopeless tasks of monarchical restoration politics.

Before Lacordaire died in 1861, his spiritual successor, the future Marie-Joseph Lagrange, was born (1855). It was his task to apply the historical-critical method to the Bible in the Catholic church, as you know well enough. It is important here to underline that he chose to accomplish this delicate task, which he did with heroic fidelity during the long years (1903–1938) when he labored under suspicion of modernism, in the Dominican order, in a province which still kept alive the spirit of political liberalism given it by Lacordaire. Lagrange made this choice consciously, because he knew that he needed the conditions of minimum psychological freedom in order to do honest work.

In his turn, Lagrange was the direct inspiration for M.-D. Chenu and Y.-M. Congar, who modeled their historical-critical reading of St. Thomas Aquinas on how Lagrange had tried to read the Bible. These four men together gave us some of the most important impulses that received their acknowledgment in the Second Vatican Council, including their ecumenical openness and their concern for the urban masses alienated from the church. The point here is that the historical-critical method applied to both Scripture and tradition, in a context of increasing political freedom, was the instrument of theological and pastoral renewal in the church.

Thus far we have argued from the broader cultural context for the necessity of a new approach to the Bible after 1800. But that is not the only reason a new approach was needed. The uninformed might imagine for instance that a new approach to Genesis 1–3, the creation stories, was imposed by new scientific data and theories on the antiquity of the planet earth (fossils, paleontology) and on the evolution of species. And it is true that a reading of Darwin did shatter a certain naïve British-American Protestant manner of reading those chapters of Genesis. (A reader of St. Thomas' questions on the Hexaemeron, *S. T.* I, qq. 65–74, would have had little difficulty with Darwin.) But the natural sciences were at best a remote cause or impetus to the new approach to the Bible. The proximate factors came from the opening up of the Near East to archaeological and philological exploration, discovery, and decipherment. The decryption of first the Rosetta stone, the Bisitun (Behistun) inscription, then the discovery of Hammurabi's and other ancient law codes, with their parallels to the Mosaic legislation, treaty forms that provided models for Deuteronomic and other covenants, the Gilgamesh epic with its parallels to the Noah story (Genesis 5–9), then later the royal archives of Ugarit with their parallels to the Psalms, Daniel and the Book of Revelation, as well as the Dead Sea Scrolls—all of this required a great development of biblical studies which went beyond the traditional methods. The new approaches came to be given the comprehensive name "the historical-critical method." In reality of course this simple designation referred to a wide variety of quite different types of criticism, as we shall see.

Pere Lagrange was primarily moved, when he began his work, by the challenges from Hammurabi's Code, the *editio princeps* of which was published by his Dominican confrere Vincent Scheil, by other Assyriological texts, and by the literary analyses and redatings of the traditions in the Pentateuch, which had recently been synthesized and radicalized by Wellhausen. Lagrange was shaken by his own efforts to trace the route of the Exodus in the Sinai peninsula. The improbabilities of the biblical narrative struck him with such force that he could never return to the naïve approach. Later, Lagrange's gifted younger colleague, Paul-Edouard Dhorme, was one of three who cracked the Ugaritic language in 1928. This opened up another whole field of research, which is far from having been exhausted.

A BRIEF HISTORY OF THE RISE OF THE HISTORICAL-CRITICAL METHOD

It is important here first of all to understand why the historical-critical method met with such resistance for so long from the church, that is, from certain centers of believing Christians, Catholic, Lutheran, Calvinist, and Eastern Orthodox. The origins of historical criticism as applied to the Bible is traced to several major figures of the seventeenth century: Benedict Spinoza, Hugo Grotius, and Thomas Hobbes. Spinoza (1632–1677) was a Jew who had been excommunicated from the synagogue when he was 24 years old because of his rationalist denial of the supernatural element in the Hebrew Bible. He later held, in his *Tractatus Theologico-Poloticus,* that the Bible "is in parts imperfect, corrupt, erroneous, and inconsistent with itself, and that we possess but fragments of it" (1670). In effect he denied the miracles. Grotius (1583–2645) was a Dutch Arminian, that is, in the eyes of the dominant five-point Calvinism of the Synod of Dort (Dordrecht) a heretic. Hobbes (1588–1679) was a sort of radical Anglican who supported state authority from a rather cynical viewpoint, against independent church leadership. In general, their motives were powerfully affected by the worst of the religious wars flowing from the Reformation, culminating in the Thirty Years War (1618–1648). In regard to the Bible, Hobbes held, for example, that the Pentateuch cannot have been written by Moses, but must have been composed long after his death, and the same is true of the books of Joshua, Judges, and Samuel; the Song of Songs and Ecclesiastes were not written by Solomon, and so on. On the other hand, Hobbes could affirm that Moses wrote everything in the Pentateuch "which he is said to have written." For Hobbes, this includes the "book of the Law" in Deuteronomy 11–27, especially because it legislates that the king takes a copy of the Law from the priests. This is important for Hobbes because it provides a biblical basis for the royal supremacy in religious matters, in opposition to the papacy and to the sects.

Whatever the intentions of this trio, whether they were noble or ignoble (the three remain controversial to this day), the fact remains that at the time they were rejected by orthodox believers as going beyond the permitted limits of theological discussion. Thus the historical-critical method was from the outset associated with authors perceived as hostile to the faith. The method shared in their bad reputation.

It is important to keep in mind that none of these three founding figures was German. It is a common but erroneous and unjust accusation that Germans were to blame for the rise of the method. In reality, the German Protestants entered the discussion relatively late. Men like J. D. Michaelis (1717-1791) and J. G. Eichhorn (1752-1827) simply attempted to bring some order and sober professional discernment of what was sound and what was careless and inaccurate in the work of the amateur pioneers. The German professors did their work at the end of the eighteenth and the beginning of the nineteenth centuries; they thus inherited the equally professional labors of the Oratorian priest Richard Simon (1638-1712) and the Anglican bishop Robert Lowth (1710-1787) among many others. It is true however that they began the process of introducing the sounder results of the method into the textbooks (introductions to the Bible) for use in the theological faculties. The integration of the method into the life of the church began with them.

From a Catholic point of view, the following generalization, made by Norbert Lohfink SJ, in the light of the complex background just sketched, is helpful. He writes:

> The situation was perhaps never so uncomfortable as in the first decades of our century; for in the previous century most Catholic biblical scholars were still in good faith in their rejection of historical-critical research. That was now no longer the case. Whoever did not want to do violence to his conscience had to go into the scholarly underground. Secret teachings were formed that dared not show their face in the Catholic public sphere, not even among normal students of theology.

This is a good description for the situation from about 1907 (*Pascendi, Lamentabili*, the decrees of the biblical Commission, *Spiritus Paraclitus*, the monitum of Rafael Cardinal Merry del Wal) until 1943, the encyclical *Divino Afflante Spiritu* of Pius XII, behind whom stood Jacques Voste OP, Augustin Bea SJ, and Jean Guitton, but especially M.-J. Lagrange. In 1903 Lagrange had pleaded in Toulouse for a recognition of literary genres other than positivist historiography in Genesis 1-11 and elsewhere in the Bible. After forty years of indecision the Holy See endorsed the recognition of these other genres (*genera litteraria*) in that encyclical. The era of bad faith was over.

This breakthrough inaugurated a new era of Catholic biblical scholarship in which the critical methods were gradually assimilated into classroom teaching and new series of commentaries. These remain incomplete, especially in the Old Testament, and much work remains to be done.

From a magisterial point of view, the first step of 1943 was followed up by the discreet deauthorization of the decrees of the Biblical Commission (1957), then by a more nuanced position on the nature of the historicity of the gospels (1964), and by the dogmatic constitution of the Second Vatican Council, *Dei Verbum* (1965). In its paragraph 11, it limited the inerrancy of the Scriptures to the matters which were written "for the sake of our salvation" (*nostrae salutis causa*). With this statement, a full use of the historical-critical method in the study of the Bible was made possible.

SOME GENERAL PRINCIPLES OF THE METHOD AS CONTAINED IN THE BIBLE ITSELF

In the patristic and medieval periods the Bible was primarily read in the church and in the synagogue. And the church read it as the basis of dogmatic development and debate. But the church also used it as a book of prayers (the Psalms and Old Testament canticles, the hymns in Luke 1 and 2), of liturgy, and as the basis for personal meditation and contemplation, that is, as a book of edification.

As such the book was treated with reverence and respect. The gospel book especially was incensed and kissed and carried in procession. It therefore was offensive when scholars began to treat the Bible coldly, seemingly without respect, as though it were like any other book. It was interrogated in a spirit of independent judgment. When a method derived from the mathematico-physical sciences began to be applied rigorously to the Bible, believers understandably began to sense that an error was being committed.

The proposal of the historical-critical method when well used is to find a middle path between two extremes: on the one hand, the Bible is not only a book of edification. Sometimes an external reverence is accompanied by a real neglect of its internal, substantive content. How often has one attended a solemn liturgy in which after the ceremonial reading of the Scriptures they are totally ignored in the empty sermon which follows? Sometimes an initial irreverence is the basis for a more serious reverence and respect.

On the other hand, one should not read the Bible with principles that are utterly foreign to its composition. A historical reading must weigh evidence for and against a historical assertion. In this it resemble the method used in courts of law, the rules of evidence.

History is a human science that often fails to reach certitude. Perhaps the best analogy to historical judgments and reconstructions of the past would be the judicial process: the police and the lawyers gather evidence, they interrogate witnesses and analyze documents. Then they present their case to judge and jury. A verdict is rendered. Their verdict is not guaranteed truth, certitude, infallibility. Yet ordinarily, in a free society, this system works well and is found generally acceptable.

The Bible offers many rules to judges that could contribute to the development of a historical-critical ability to gather and to weigh the evidence in order to come to a historical judgment. Perhaps the most frequent rule is the exhortation to impartiality: "You shall not render an unjust judgment; you shall not be partial to the poor or defer to the great; with justice you shall judge your neighbor" (Lev 19:15). "You must not be partial in judging; hear out the small and the great alike; you shall not be intimidated by anyone, for the judgment is God's" (Deut 1:17). The judge is to seek the truth of the matter without regard to his own economic interests, e.g., the possibility of a bribe or "kickback."

The pursuit of truth is a basic human and religious value: John 8:32; Matt 5:37; Oswald Loretz; the motto of the Dominican order, motto of Harvard University. In religious contexts truth primarily refers to the truth of salvation, the basic relationship between God and humankind, basic religious convictions and values. In the gospel according to John, the truth is essentially christological: Jesus as the Christ, the only begotten God, is the truth in person (John 14:6; 8:31-32). But a critical concern for the facticity of certain narratives (e.g., the crossing of the Sea of Reeds dry-shod, Jesus walking on the water, the raising of Lazarus) is a comparatively late preoccupation (seventeenth-eighteenth centuries) and in many societies an expendable luxury. It is a product of the scientific, technological west and is bound up with the theological discussion of miracles and the supernatural and divine power/causality/intervention and the efficacy of prayer. That is, this concern for historical facticity touches very basic religious themes and values. Thus it is easy to understand why such a concern has caused anxiety and crisis in all the western religious traditions: e.g., fundamentalism in American Protestantism, antimodernist witchhunts in Roman Catholicism, *fatwahs* (an Islamic judicial opinion, which in some cases can leed to the death penalty) in Islam, the excommunication of Tolstoy by the Russian Orthodox Church shortly before his death in 1910. The substance of the faith seems to be in question.

It is therefore important to see that such questions and concerns are not simply imposed on the Bible from outside, but are present in the Bible itself (e.g., multiple versions of the creation story, of the crossing of the Sea of Reeds, of the multiplication of the loaves and fishes). Moreover, principles for the solution of these questions are present in the Bible itself. It was not just Lyell's geology or Darwin's evolutionary theory of the origin of species that made necessary a new look at Genesis, but the results of literary analysis of the biblical texts themselves (Wellhausen) and then the data of Near Eastern archaeology and epigraphy. A new look at Exodus was made necessary not only by Newtonian physics but also by the discovery of the Code of Hammurabi and other Assyro-Babylonian law codes and epic poems.

A Roman juridical principle is: *audiatur et altera pars*, let the other side be heard, *que le juge ecoute les deus cotes* (cf. Acts 25:16). This legal principle is present in a radicalized form in the biblical exhortation to impartiality in judgment. But it is also present *implicitly* in the care with which the Bible presents multiple, *parallel* versions of the same events: two versions of the creation story, two versions of the flood, multiple versions of some episodes in the Exodus and Sinai cycles (two versions of the Decalogue, and of the water from the rock episode, for example), three versions of the conquest of the promised land, two complete versions of the Israelite monarchy: the Deuteronomistic (1–2 Samuel, 1–2 Kings) and the Priestly (1 and 2 Chronicles); two views of the Israelite monarchy, one hostile (1 Sam 8:11–18; 10:17–24; 12; Hos 7:3–7; 13:9–11; Ezek 34:1–10), one favorable (1 Sam 9:1—10:16), to present it a little too simply; multiple prophetic and hymnic traditions which can be studied as parallels; two different versions of the Esther story and of Susanne and the elders; four (!) different gospels, which cry out for comparative analysis (a process begun by Eusebius' canons (cf. Nestle-Aland, *Novum Testamentum Graece*, 27th ed., 84–89), and carried on more intensely since Griesbach's pioneer Gospel synopsis of 1775) as they present the life story of Jesus from partly different viewpoints; different versions of Paul's conversion, mission and thought as found in his own letters and in Luke's *Acts*, besides the partly critical evaluations of Paul found in Jas 2:14–16 and in 2 Pet 3:15–16. The Bible itself presents all of this material for comparative analysis. Scholars have not (only) imported extraneous problems, questions and methods to the Bible. The Bible itself poses these problems and questions and invites us to study them. The Bible also provides some juridical principles to help answer them. To be sure, the Bible is primarily given to the church for the nourishment of the life of faith, hope and love in Christ. But secondarily, the Bible invites those who have the time, money, and interest to study it comparatively in detail, for intellectual delight and spiritual profit. "She is a tree of life to those who lay hold of her; those who hold her fast are called happy" (Prov 3:18). "Turn it and turn it, for everything is therein" (*m. Abot* 5:22). In short, historical-critical questions are not foreign to the Bible but are present within the Bible itself and some of the principles for their resolution are also present in the Bible.

Another passage which gives rules for judges in Israel is found in Deut 16:18–20: "You shall appoint judges and officials throughout your tribes in all your towns that the LORD your God is giving you, and they shall render just decisions for the people. You must not distort justice; you must not show partiality; and you must not accept bribes, for a bribe blinds the eyes of the wise and subverts the cause of those who are in the right. Justice, and only justice, you shall pursue." We can easily transform this text into a rule for historical scholars: truth, truth, shalt thou pursue! Or, more technically: objectivity, objectivity shalt thou pursue! Put this way, the principle immediately provokes the objection that objectivity is unattainable in this life; it is an illusion, an impossibility, worse still, a male pretension. In that case all we are left with is our own subjectivity, our prejudices, party allegiances and nominalism. That is an extreme position, a counsel of despair, but one which is widespread in the post-modernist intellectual climate. Let him accept it who will.

To be sure, absolute objectivity is unattainable in this life. But we may move toward it if we will, and approach this goal little by little, asymptotically, as two lines in mathematical asymptotes. And it makes an enormous difference whether one tries or not. This striving for objectivity is what characterizes the great historians from Thusydides to Tacitus, from von Ranke and Mandell Creighton to Lortz, from Sarpi to C. V. Wedgwood and Jedin. The key tests here are whether the historian of a controversial matter is willing to admit some fault on the side he is defending, in other words, some embarrassment to his own cause, whether he is willing to make some concessions to the opposition. (Of course this is where he comes into conflict with the politicians, the power brokers on his team, and their publicists and spin-masters. This is also why some have thought atheism or agnosticism the only honest or neutral or objective position in matters of religious controversy.)

Another source of the corruption of the search for truth for its own sake stems from the social pressure exerted by a social mass. But Scripture teaches: "You shall not follow a multitude [the majority] to do evil" (Exod 23:2).

The hammerblows of the Enlightenment fall most directly on the miracle stories of the Exodus and the Gospels. Here the conflict between science and religion, between reason and faith, seems most acute. The problem is a delicate one. The general principle for the Christian believer should be: I accept neither a blanket denial of the possibility of all miracles (that would be unscientific) nor the total affirmation of every event which is claimed to be a miracle (that would be credulous and uncritical). Rather the believer should follow a middle path of understanding miracles as "signs" of the divine presence and revelation that are to be received and interpreted by a discerning faith. The Scriptures themselves recognize that miracles are intrinsically ambiguous and require interpretation to be meaningful. Thus we must understand Jesus' walking on the water in terms of Ps 77:20(19): "Your way was through the sea, your path, through the mighty waters; *yet your footprints were unseen.*" God's actions remain invisible, imperceptible, uncanny.

In concluding this section, we should mention that the historical-critical method is a general term that in the course of the last two centuries has come to refer to a series of specialized branches. Today the term embraces all these different techniques or operations: (1) textual or lower criticism, the comparison of manuscript variants of the same text; (2) source criticism, the identification of sources underlying the biblical final text, sometimes called higher criticism; (3) form criticism, the study of the characteristics of micro-genres such as apophthegms, parables, miracle stories; (4) redaction criticism, the study of the specific viewpoint of each biblical author in his editing of a common tradition, e.g., of the life of Jesus. Many other techniques could be added, such as the collection and analysis of biblical and extra-biblical parallels and analogies, or the study of the biblical authors' use of rhetorical techniques whether indigenous or classical.

THE TRANSFORMATION OF THE HISTORICAL-CRITICAL METHOD THROUGH THE LIFE OF THE CHURCH

As the historical-critical method becomes the normal and quasi-normative way of reading the Bible in the church, it must begin to bear some of the burden of the older, edifying approaches. It must thus sharpen the sight of the preacher so that he/she can preach better and more accurately, by respecting the redactional accents of the three gospel accounts of the baptism of Jesus, for example, or of his transfiguration. Such redactional attention enables the preacher to say something new and fresh each time he/she preaches these texts in the three year lectionary cycle.

So too catechetics must learn to use Scripture as more than a stone quarry; that is, it must learn to pay more attention to the context of biblical affirmations. The same holds true for the use of Scripture in dogmatic and moral theology. The Bible continues to serve as a basis for community and personal prayer. But the liturgy and private reader of the Bible have already for a long time now, consciously or unconsciously, benefited from the progress of biblical studies, especially from new translations of the Bible based on critical editions of the original texts. A striking example of how critical analysis contributes to liturgical practice is the case of the hymn to Christ in Phil 2:6–11. This was first identified as a hymn by Ernst Lohmeyer in an address to the Heidelberg academy of sciences in 1928. Yet now it is required that all priests of the Latin rite recite it at Vespers once a week. Most of these priests have never heard of Lohmeyer, heroic figure though he be.

A final word. It is true that the historical-critical method has philosophical presuppostitions, some of which are unacceptable to living faith. But it is not true that having a different, better philosophy would automatically solve all biblical problems. It would neither guarantee the correct interpretation of every pericope in the Bible, nor give us the correct date and author of every book, nor tell us the right use of the documents from Ninevah, Luxor, Ugarit, Nag Hammadi, or Ebla. Properly biblical-critical work must do that.

So to the question posed in my title "The Historical-Critical Method in Modern Biblical Studies: Yes or No?" I must conclude with an emphatic *yes*.

2

The Normativity of Scripture and Tradition in Recent Catholic Theology

> "Is not my word like fire, says the LORD,
> and like a hammer that breaks a rock in pieces?"
>
> (JEREMIAH 23:29)

Our topic is the normativity of Scripture and Tradition in recent Roman Catholic theology and official documents. We should realize at the outset that in discussing this topic we are committing a sin. We should rather be listening to and discussing a passage of Scripture itself. That is why I have begun with a passage from Jeremiah that asks whether God's word is not more powerful and interesting than any merely human word. But there is an undeniable interest in this topic, so I have agreed to address it.

That said, let me begin with my hero, M.-J. Lagrange (1855–1938), founder of the French biblical and archaeological school in Jerusalem (1890). After being the "fair-haired boy" of Pope Leo XIII for thirteen years, he fell into disfavor in 1903 and for the rest of his life. (He won posthumous victories in 1943 and 1965.) What had he said to upset church authorities? He began his new life in the Holy Land by walking around the Sinai desert, Bible in hand. He thus saw that the Exodus account could not be topographically sound in every detail. He was also confronted with the first publication of Hammurabi's Babylonian law code. He felt the need to analyze this code in comparison with the three law codes in the Pentateuch. Then there was the Gilgamesh flood narrative that needed to be studied with Genesis 6–10, Noah and the ark. Lagrange popularized his results in a little book, *The Old*

Testament and Historical Criticism (1903). In its last chapter he wrote that students of the Bible, especially the Old Testament, needed to pay attention to the different literary *genres* used by the biblical authors. They did not always intend to write history in the sense of nineteenth-century positivistic historiography. They also wrote what he called primeval history, not to mention poetry. (In the background of his concerns there also lay the issue of different sources of the Pentateuch, as synthesized by J. Wellhausen.)

In this fateful year (1903) Leo XIII died and Pius X was elected pope. Pius was guided in intellectual matters by several curial cardinals whose diplomatic goal was the restoration of the papal states to their full extent, in central Italy. This was no longer a realistic goal, but, in this pursuit, these cardinals (the best known are Rafael Merry del Val and Pietro Gasparri) felt that they must block all compromise with the modern world (the world created by the events of 1789). Because of his thesis on biblical literary genres, Lagrange became a suspected modernizer. His career in the church was stopped in its upward ascent. He barely escaped condemnation. He was saved by his own prudence, by his sense of loyalty to the church, and by a saintly protector, H. Cormier. Lagrange died in 1938, still under a cloud of official suspicion.

But by 1935 the curial cardinals who enforced the rules of this period of theological suppression were all dead. Catholic theology began to emerge from the cellar (Chenu, Congar, Mersch, Jungmann, Rahner, de Lubac, Daniélou, Bouyer). A group of French Catholic school teachers, led by Jean Guitton, petitioned the elderly pope, Pius XI, that the question of the genre of Genesis 1–3 be reopened. He said that it was a difficult matter. He would leave it for his successor to tackle. The successor, Pius XII, took up the challenge. In 1943, in the middle of the war, he commissioned a Dominican, Jacques Voste, who had studied with Lagrange, and a Jesuit, Augustin Bea, to draft an encyclical letter that conceded the point about literary genres. The letter was called *Divino Afflante Spiritu* (1943). It was a posthumous vindication of Lagrange. His little book of 1903 was now officially accepted, forty years after it appeared and five years after Lagrange himself was safely dead. The encyclical said:

> 35. What is the literal sense of a passage is not always as obvious in the speeches and writings of the ancient authors of the East, as it is in the works of our own time. For what they wished to express is not to be determined by the rules of grammar and philology alone, nor solely by the context; the interpreter must, as it were, go back wholly in spirit to those remote centuries of the East and with the aid of history, archaeology, ethnology, and other sciences, accurately determine what *modes of writing*, so

to speak, the authors of that ancient period would be likely to use, and in fact did use.

36. For the ancient peoples of the East, in order to express their ideas, did not always employ those *forms or kinds of speech* which we use today; but rather those used by the men of their times and countries. What those exactly were the commentator cannot determine as it were in advance, but only after a careful examination of the ancient literature of the East. The investigation, carried out, on this point, during the past forty or fifty years with greater care and diligence than ever before, has more clearly shown what *forms of expression* were used in those far off times, whether in poetic description or in the formulation of laws and rules of life or in recording the facts and events of history. The same inquiry has also shown the special preeminence of the people of Israel among all the other ancient nations of the East in their mode of compiling history, both by reason of its antiquity and by reasons of the faithful record of the events; qualities which may well be attributed to the gift of divine inspiration and to the peculiar religious purpose of biblical history.

37. Nevertheless no one, who has a correct idea of biblical inspiration, will be surprised to find, even in the Sacred Writers, as in other ancient authors, *certain fixed ways of expounding and narrating*, certain definite idioms, especially of a kind peculiar to the Semitic tongues, so-called approximations, and certain hyperbolical *modes of expression*, nay, at times, even paradoxical, which even help to impress the ideas more deeply on the mind. For of *the modes of expression* which, among ancient peoples, and especially those of the East, human language used to express its thought, none is excluded from the Sacred Books, provided the way of speaking adopted in no wise contradicts the holiness and truth of God, as, with his customary wisdom, the Angelic Doctor already observed in these words: "In Scripture divine things are presented to us in the manner which is in common use amongst men." For as the substantial Word of God became like to men in all things, "except sin," so the words of God, expressed in human language, are made like to human speech in every respect, except error. In this consists that "condescension" of the God of providence, which St. John Chrysostom extolled with the highest praise and repeatedly declared to be found in the Sacred Books.

38. Hence the Catholic commentator, in order to comply with the present needs of biblical studies, in explaining the Sacred Scripture and in demonstrating and proving its immunity from all error, should also make a prudent use of this means, determine, that is, to what extent *the manner of expression or the literary mode* adopted by the sacred writer may lead to a correct and genuine interpretation; and let him be convinced that this part of his office cannot be neglected without serious detriment to Catholic exegesis. Not infrequently—to mention only one instance—when some persons reproachfully charge the Sacred Writers with some historical error or inaccuracy in the recording of facts, on closer examination it turns out to be nothing else than those customary *modes of expression and narration* peculiar to the ancients, which used to be employed in the mutual dealings of social life and which in fact were sanctioned by common usage.

39. When then such *modes of expression* are met within the sacred text, which, being meant for men, is couched in human language, justice demands that they be no more taxed with error than when they occur in the ordinary intercourse of daily life. By this knowledge and exact appreciation of *the modes of speaking and writing* in use among the ancients can be solved many difficulties, which are raised against the veracity and historical value of the Divine Scriptures, and no less efficaciously does this study contribute to a fuller and more luminous understanding of the mind of the Sacred Writer.

The main point of this text is the nine-times repeated affirmation that the interpreter must pay attention to the "forms or kinds of speech," the "modes of expression," used by the ancient biblical writers. This is Lagrange's idea of literary genres. But there are also some subsidiary points. (1) Six times "the East" is mentioned, especially in the phrase "going back wholly in spirit." These themes echo the romantic idea of history-writing which goes back to J. G. Herder, F. Schlegel, and F. D. Schleiermacher: the *Einfühlung* or feeling oneself into the past. They also reflect what Edward Said was later to label Orientalism, the idea that the Near Eastern mind is substantially different from the Western European mind. (2) The passage also briefly mentions the genres of poetry, law, and history (see below). (3) It also says that the commentator cannot determine the genre *in advance*. This is written against the a priori, deductive approach of systematicians like Louis Billot who wanted to dispose of biblical criticism with a few Cartesian logical arguments. (4) At its close the passage alludes to the theological nerve point: the doctrine that the Bible must be inerrant in all matters, including scientific ones (see below, on Vatican II). This encyclical, for all its caution, was a great help to biblical scholars in the Roman Catholic Church. The issue of inerrancy would only be settled in 1965.

At this point let us pause to reflect for a moment on the fact of multiple genres in the Bible. For the Old Testament, it is clear that there are five main literary genres: (1) history and history-like narrative; (2) law; (3) prophecy; (4) wisdom; (5) praise. These genres are often present in the same books. The Pentateuch for example contains elements of all five: Moses's story is told; he is presented as prophet and law-giver (king), as a wise man or sage, who sings the praise of God. The danger is that we would privilege one of these genres to the exclusion of the others. Rather, ideally they should be maintained in a sane balance, in a mutually corrective dialectical dance. In reality, this is not so easy to bring off. Past experience has shown some of these errors. (1) In the nineteenth century, with its historicist positivistic obsessions, orthodox interpreters often felt that they had to defend the historicity of every detail, e.g., Moses wrote the account of his own death (Deuteronomy 34); Jonah stayed for days in the belly of the whale. The Bible was thus reduced to history and history only. (2) In reaction to Pauline Christianity, some forms of Judaism tended to concentrate on the detailed *law* of the Bible. (3) By concentrating on the phenomenon of prophecy, Thomas Aquinas gave the impression that the divine element in Scripture resided in the prophets (*Summa theol.* 2–2.171–78). (4) The Enlightenment reduced the Bible to rational wisdom, common sense and natural law; the Jesus seminar tends to see Jesus as a Cynic sage, without apocalyptic prophecy. (5) For the devout, the Bible is primarily a book of prayer, singing the praises of God in the Psalms. (For aesthetes, the Bible is of interest as a series of objets d'art, e.g., parables.) Such selectivity impoverishes us. It cordons off parts of the biblical tradition for special privilege or for special neglect, and so prevents readers from receiving the Bible in all its rich variety.

This selective one-sidedness was provoked by real problems. (1) Once the idea became fixed in place that, because the Bible was the inspired word of God, it must be free of error in every respect, the mind of the logician could push for wilder and wilder conclusions, further and further from the intention of the text. As the apologist labored to keep God free from the taint of evil, the hyper logician fought to keep God free from the taint of error. Among the knights of consistent inerrancy were Louis Billot and James Montgomery. They argued that the honor of God required verbal inerrancy. (2) How should we understand Genesis 1–11? As history, as science, as myth or as primordial history which includes elements of ancient science and myth? The last of these alternatives was Lagrange's response to

Hermann Gunkel's challenge laid down in his *Creation and Chaos in the Primeval Era and the Eschaton* of 1895. (3) Another big problem has been the right relation of Scripture and church tradition. In the wake of the Reformation criticism with its slogan "Scripture alone!," the Council of Trent responded with a both . . . and. Divine Revelation is to be found both in the Scriptures and in sacred Traditions. This issue became lively in the 1950s after Pope Pius XII made a dogma of the bodily assumption of Mary into heaven. Oscar Cullmann, the Alsatian Lutheran, weighed in with an important essay, to which Jean Daniélou responded. Above all, the publication of the debates behind Trent enabled J. R. Geiselmann to free the interpretation of Trent from a view consciously rejected by the council fathers. This view held that revelation was partly (*partim*) contained in scripture and partly (*partim*) contained in Tradition, with the implication that Scripture itself had been materially insufficient. That meant that there were doctrines to be believed that were necessary for salvation that were not contained in Scripture. Geiselmann could show that this view had been considered by Trent (the *partims* were in a draft) and freely set aside. That is, there are no *partims* in the final text of Trent and the view that Scripture is materially insufficient was not accepted as a dogma, although it was (and remains) a tolerated theological opinion. Geiselmann went on to offer his own proposal as to the right relationship between Scripture and Tradition. Here is an English translation of his conclusions:

> How is the relationship between the Holy Scriptures and the unwritten traditions to be determined? We have, by means of the proof from tradition that there is a material [i.e., content = *inhaltliche*] sufficiency of Holy Scripture as to what concerns faith, and that there is a material insufficiency as to what concerns *mores, consuetudines et leges* (morals, customs and laws) of the church; we have, I say, created the presupposition to be able to answer the question concerning the relationship between Scripture and tradition. As a result, it becomes apparent that this relationship cannot be determined unequivocally.
>
> With respect to faith, the Holy Scripture is materially sufficient [as to its contents]. But, thereby the Sola-Scriptura principle is not yet expressed. For the Holy Scripture is, with respect to the canon of the Scriptures, dependent upon tradition and upon the decision of the Church. For it was the Council of Trent which first definitively settled the canon of Holy Scripture. And with respect to the understanding of Holy Scriptures, it needs the clarifying tradition of the Fathers in matters of faith and morals. Tradition in these cases exercises the function of

traditio interpretativa. Besides, the Holy Scripture is dependent upon the *sensus* which the church maintains and has always maintained, for the explanation of its contents which concern faith and morals.

Here thus holds true with respect to faith the principle: *totum in sacra scriptura et iterum totum in traditione*, completely in Scripture and completely in tradition.

The situation is otherwise with respect to the *mores et consuetudines* of the church. Here Scripture is insufficient and needs tradition for its completion in content. In these cases, tradition is *traditio constitutiva*.

Here holds true with respect to the *mores et consuetudines* the principle: *partim in sacra scriptura, partim in sine scripto traditionibus*, partly in the Holy Scriptures, partly in tradition.

So for Geiselmann Scripture is sufficient in what is necessary for salvation, while Tradition plays an important role in interpretation. This view has been supported by the thorough study of Yves Congar and was not condemned at Vatican II, as some had expected. Thus it remains a permitted view within the Roman Catholic Church. It is not however embraced by all theologians, including some important ones.

Other aspects of this issue of the relation of Scripture to interpretative tradition include that the Bible is not a good book of rubrics; it does not say how exactly one should celebrate the Lord's supper, or whether one could baptize with wine or beer. More troublesome, it does not treat expressly the morality of nuclear weapons or the use of computers. Already at Nicea, the council fathers felt that they must use a non-scriptural word, *homoousion* = of the same substance, to save the scriptural doctrine about Jesus Christ from the wily Arians. This is a significant test case, as is the question of who decides the limits of the biblical canon.

(4) This leads to fascinating and multi-faceted issues of canon criticism, reception history of the canon, the diversity of reading communities. Here I would only make a few remarks. First, regarding the deuterocanonical-apocryphal books of the Old Testament, that is, the longer canon of the Bible, I can only testify that to understand the New Testament I have found it helpful to have these additional books to fill in certain blanks, e.g., John's reference to the Feast of Dedication (10:22) presupposes Maccabees. Romans 1 presupposes Wisdom 13–15. James 1:13–15 presupposes Sirach 15. It we are serious about the Bible as a history of salvation, we need to know what happened between Malachi (ca. 400 BC) and Jesus. Even understanding Daniel requires the Maccabees. My second remark concerns the importance of the dialectical mutual correction and balancing provided by

different biblical books read in the same community of faith. For example, I find John ethically poorer than the synoptic gospels, because he leaves out the love of enemies. John is better for its teaching on the person of Jesus, the Holy Spirit, and the sacraments, Matthew is better for its ethics (Sermon on the Mount). A balanced church needs both these voices.

(5) We come now to the Dogmatic Constitution on Divine Revelation (*Dei Verbum*) of the Second Vatican Council, voted on and approved with virtual unanimity by around 2800 bishops and other delegates, 18 November 1965. This document is not long, yet it was one over which the council wrestled till the last minute. I will here try to offer the student a brief guide in six points, three major and three minor. The three key breakthrough paragraphs are 9, 11 and 19. The ninth paragraph treats of the relation of Scripture and Tradition.

> 9. Hence there exists a close connection and communication between sacred tradition and Sacred Scripture. For both of them, flowing from the same divine wellspring, in a certain way merge into a unity and tend toward the same end. For Sacred Scripture is the word of God inasmuch as it is consigned to writing under the inspiration of the divine Spirit, while sacred tradition takes the word of God entrusted by Christ the Lord and the Holy Spirit to the Apostles, and hands it on to their successors honestly, so that led by the light of the Spirit of truth, they may in proclaiming it preserve this word of God faithfully, explain it, and make it more widely known. Consequently it is not from Sacred Scripture alone that the Church draws her certainty about everything which has been revealed. Therefore both sacred tradition and Sacred Scripture are to be accepted and venerated with the same sense of loyalty and reverence.

We have already treated this matter and only need to point out that the council affirms the roles of both Scripture and Tradition. That is doing no more than stating a historical fact. The council does not try to explain their relationship. Thus various theories which do try to work out their relationship are given free run, including Geiselmann's. Further, the council teaches that Christian ministers have the duty to preach, explain and spread the scriptural Word of God. Finally, borrowing an elegant turn of phrase from Trent, the council says that both Scripture and Tradition are to be received with a like feeling (*affectu*) of piety. Reliable interpreters of Trent say that this phrase is only a rhetorical flourish, not to be pressed too closely, as though the council intended to say that Scripture and Tradition were absolutely equal in value in every respect. A sympathetic interpreter can easily understand that the devout believer should normally revere both Scripture and the saintly heroes who suffered for the faith like Athanasius or Chrysostom, Justin or Irenaeus. But this does not mean that Athanasius never had a weak moment (he did). Nor does this phrase mean that we should not try to sift the abundance of church traditions for what is truer or more helpful in a given situation. Nor does it exclude further distinctions of tradition, for example, that Christ is the Tradition with a capital T (based on Matt 11:27 and parallels), and that there are other traditions of varying weights. As a teacher of Scripture I can attest that when interpreters past and present differ on a significant matter such as the sense of the Bread of Life in John 6, I find it helpful to know that the weight of tradition understands John 6:51–58 as referring to the eucharist.

The real breakthrough at the council came in paragraph eleven which limits the inerrancy of Scripture to matters regarding our salvation. That is, Scripture can err in all other matters. As a line attributed to Galileo has it, the Bible teaches us how to go to heaven, not how the heavens go.

> 11. Those divinely revealed realities which are contained and presented in Sacred Scripture have been committed to writing under the inspiration of the Holy Spirit. For holy mother Church, relying on the belief of the Apostles (see John 20:31; 2 Tim. 3:16; 2 Peter 1:19–20, 3:15–16), holds that the books of both the Old and New Testaments in their entirety, with all their parts, are sacred and canonical because written under the inspiration of the Holy Spirit, they have God as their author and have been handed on as such to the Church herself. In composing the sacred books, God chose men and while employed by Him they made use of their powers and abilities, so that with Him acting in them and through them, they, as true authors, consigned to writing everything and only those things which He wanted.
>
> Therefore, since everything asserted by the inspired authors or sacred writers must be held to be asserted by the Holy Spirit, it follows that the books of Scripture must be acknowledged as teaching solidly, faithfully and without error that truth which God wanted put into sacred writings *for the sake of our salvation*. Therefore "all Scripture is divinely inspired and has its use for teaching the truth and refuting error, for reformation of manners and discipline in right living, so that everyone who belongs to God may be efficient and equipped for good work of every kind" (2 Tim. 3:16–17, Greek text).

It took a century to arrive at the crucial phrase "truth . . . for the sake of our salvation." Cardinal Newman had taught that Scripture sometimes made *obiter dicta*, incidental remarks, without intending to affirm them with full authority. At the time this solution was rejected by the Pope. In making its restriction the council returned to the teaching of Augustine and Thomas. After the council, some die-hards tried to play with the Latin word *causa*, which can mean either the noun *cause* or the preposition *for the sake of*. This maneuver had to be put down and it was. This teaching on a qualified inerrancy is important, but it remains on a very general level of truth. It does not address the issue of conflicting teachings on salvation within the Bible, e.g., Matt 5:17-20 versus Galatians 2-3. It is this particular conflict which gave us the Lutheran Reformation. Nor does it address the issue that faces the exegete every day, viz., how to interpret the variants in parallel versions of the same incident in the Pentateuch or the gospels, or successive rereadings or rewritings of the same tradition within the Bible.

The third major teaching of the council here concerns the specially qualified character of the history contained in the four canonical gospels. It amounts to a cautious reception of the form criticism of the 1920s: K. L. Schmidt, Martin Dibelius, and Rudolf Bultmann. Paragraph 19 reads:

> 19. Holy Mother Church has firmly and with absolute constancy held, and continues to hold, that the four Gospels just named, whose historical character the Church unhesitatingly asserts, faithfully hand on what Jesus Christ, while living among men, really did and taught for their eternal salvation until the day He was taken up into heaven (see Acts 1:1). Indeed, after the Ascension of the Lord the Apostles handed on to their hearers what He had said and done. This they did with that clearer understanding which they enjoyed after they had been instructed by the glorious events of Christ's life and taught by the light of the Spirit of truth. The sacred authors wrote the four Gospels, selecting some things from the many which had been handed on by word of mouth or in writing, reducing some of them to a synthesis, explaining some things in view of the situation of their churches and preserving the form of proclamation but always in such fashion that they told us the honest truth about Jesus. For their intention in writing was that either from their own memory and recollections, or from the witness of those who "themselves from the beginning were eyewitnesses and ministers of the Word" we might know "the truth" concerning those matters about which we have been instructed (see Luke 1:2-4).

The main points to grasp are that for the council the four gospels contain the *tradition* about Jesus. The sacred writers wrote with the deeper understanding they received *after Easter*, a particular emphasis (or admission) in John's gospel (14:26; 16:13); so John is not just a videocassette recording of the historical Jesus, without theological reflection. The evangelists shaped their material through selection, condensation and the style proper to preaching. (This point is the key concession to form criticism.) Finally, the council shares an apologetic concern to emphasize that the gospel writers strove for honesty and truth (and did not intend to deceive.) This paragraph builds on a key document of the Biblical Commission published only the year before (1964). We will treat this document a little later.

Three further contributions of the council can now be listed. The first concerns the issue of the canon within the canon. That is, granted the 27 books that make up the New Testament, are some more important than others? Does the reader prefer one or two and tend to neglect the others? Does a believing community do something similar? Among Bible knowers, it is easy to position someone ideologically by what texts the other person quotes (and, by implication, neglects). Marcion wanted only an expurgated Luke and Paul in his canon. Luther cordoned off Hebrews, James, Jude and Revelation as a ghetto of the unsound in his Bible. The Tübingen school of F. C. Baur had emphasized the conflicts within the New Testament canon (James versus Paul, with Luke-Acts and then John as harmonizers and reconcilers). Ernst Käsemann revived this model and led to its widespread discussion. The council's paragraph 18 teaches that the four gospels enjoy pride of place because of their special witness to Jesus. After the gospels come the letters and other writings of the New Testament (paragraph 20), and the whole Old Testament (14–16). This prioritizing is visible in the liturgy. The order of reading is: Old Testament, epistle, Gospel. The Gospel enjoys the climatic final position. Worshippers sit for the first two readings and stand for the Gospel, which may be accompanied by candles and incense. The reading of the Gospel is normally reserved for deacons and priests. It should be noted that the council does not address the issue of the relative merit of each gospel in relation to the other three, e.g., the relative ethical poverty of John or its spiritual superiority.

The council also concedes an important point to Karl Barth in its paragraph 10. There we read that the teaching authority of the church (the *magisterium*) *is not above the word of God* but at its service. I interpret this so: the church, pope, bishops, clergy, devout lay readers of Scripture are not simply to sit in judgment on Scripture; they must not dictate to the Bible what it should or should not say. Rather, they should humbly submit to the purifying lash of Scripture, as the great saints and reformers tried to realize (St. Francis of Assisi, St. Catherine of Siena, more quietly St. Benedict, less successfully Savonarola and many others). The Scriptures, especially the prophets and Jesus, rather sit in judgment on the church (and synagogue). The council adds that the church should listen to the Word carefully and lovingly, preserve the Bible (by handwritten copies or printed editions of the original texts, by memorization, and by interpretative study), expound it and derive its message from it. And here there emerges an implicit, dangerous, yet inevitable qualification. No one can prepare a sermon without in some sense sitting in judgment on the biblical text, at least to select what to emphasize, to decide what it means for this audience at this time. Thus in reality there in a never-ending dialectic between text and interpreter, no matter how reverently it is done.

The third lesser point that has emerged in the reception of the conciliar text is a phrase that occurs in paragraph 12: "Sacred Scripture should be read and interpreted in the same spirit in which it was written." This apparently harmless phrase, derived from St. Jerome, has become a major arm in the war chest of the conservative backlash in the church. It is used as a club with which to beat the historical critics. It is taken to exclude any reading of the text which is not immediately devotional and edifying. It implies that the whole Bible must be taken as "spiritual reading," as if the whole Bible should read like the long prayer which is the letter to the Ephesians or some of the best loved Psalms, e.g., Psalm 23. But even the pearl of the Psalter, 139, contains cursing and hatred (vv. 19–22, often omitted in modern usage), as does 137 (v. 9). To the extent that this view prevails, it means the end of all critical scholarship within the church. Only the enemies of the faith would enjoy critical freedom. The church would be left defenseless and uninformed. This is a poisoned cup. The church is better served by intelligent scholarship, which presupposes a reasonable academic freedom.

(6) In our attempt to understand the normativity of Scripture and Tradition in recent Catholic theology we turn now to a less solemn organ of Catholic thought on Scripture, the Pontifical Biblical Commission. Since its reform in the sixties, this commission consists of twenty members, named by bishops conferences and the pope. The members are from different regions of the world and meet annually during Easter. They work on a document over five years, on a problem proposed by the pope.

Let us mention three of their documents plus one from the Commission for Dialogue with the Jews. The first dates from 1964. It concerns the nature of the historical truth of the Gospels. The "Instruction" helped prepare for the reception of form criticism at Vatican II, which we have already treated (*Dei Verbum*, 19). Here it is only necessary to mention its reception of the form critical method's idea of the three *Sitze im Leben* (life settings) of the gospel tradition. The instruction refers to these as three *tempora traditionis*, times or stages of the tradition: the time of Jesus, the time of the apostles and the oral transmission in the earliest church, and then the time of the writing down of the Jesus story in the four gospels by the four evangelists. This was a helpful developmental clarification.

In 1983 the Commission for Dialogue with the Jews put out an outstanding document on how to present the New Testament picture of the Jews, especially the Pharisees, in preaching and catechetics, without historical injustice, without contempt or hatred, without supersessionism. This latter term refers to the idea that the revelation in the New Testament has simply replaced (superseded) the revelation in the Old, that the church simply replaces the synagogue, that the Jews of today have no right to a continuing separate existence, that Jesus renders Moses superfluous. The document explains that polemics at the time of writing led Matthew and John to a harsher view of the Pharisees than was historically justified or than we find appropriate today.

Starting around 1970 there occurred a methodological explosion in biblical studies. There was for example a narrative-aesthetic, ahistorical, reader-response literary method that became very popular in state universities. No Greek or Hebrew or ancient history were needed to apply it. Structuralist approaches came in from France, purely formal. The social sciences entered the field with an emphasis on the anthropology of honor and shame, not to mention liberation theology from Latin America. An analysis with the principles of ancient rhetoric was advocated. Feminists, psychologists, and fundamentalists joined in. (This list is not exhaustive.) This explosive manifold of methods led to student confusion. Professors who had invested in one option, e.g., rhetorical analysis, felt frustrated that their choice was prevented from achieving a complete triumph due to the competition. Rhetoric got lost in the shuffle. (Besides, rhetoric had already acquired a bad reputation in Plato's day. He rejected it as sophistry and style. Aristotle's *Rhetoric* took a calmer approach. Students still regard it with reserve.)

Into this lively, confusing debate the Biblical Commission entered in 1993 with a much appreciated document (130pp) called *The Interpretation of the Bible in the Church*. We cannot enter into much detail here. We must select a few points. First, in reading the text it is important to have an edition which provides the address of Pope John Paul II welcoming the document. There he makes a crucial statement: "Catholic exegesis does not have its own exclusive method of interpretation, but, starting with the historico-critical basis (freed from its philosophical presuppositions or those contrary to the truth of our faith), it makes the most of all the current methods by seeking in each of them the 'seeds of the Word.'" This sentence makes three points. (1) The historical-critical method is the basic, normal method. Other methods are grafted on to it or otherwise assimilated to it. (It has been assimilating new methods since the eighteenth century: text, source, form, redaction criticisms.) (2) The church is open to new approaches and tests them for what is true and good in them (1 Thess 5:21). (3) Methods come with philosophies or theologies. We may not share these; e.g., an exclusion a priori of the possibility of miracles; or, the view that Scripture can never teach anything other than justification by faith alone.

The document itself then goes on to list, describe, and evaluate methods old and new, making a distinction between rigorous methods and mere "approaches." This may be too subtle or unfair. A planned section on materialist (Marxist) exegesis was dropped after the fall of Communism in Eastern Europe. Feminists are warned not to grab for power, but why should they differ from other groups who do the same? Conservatives felt the treatment of fundamentalist exegesis was not well informed. Nevertheless, this first half of the document can be recommended to the student as a useful guide and survey.

When the document passes to larger hermeneutical issues: the role of philosophy, the different senses of Scripture, the relations between the two Testaments and between the different branches of theology, inculturation, the roles of patristic and rabbinic exegesis, the uses of the Bible in the Church, the reader feels that the text is less successful. Nothing is false. It is simply that the issues are too complex to be soluble in such a brief treatment. It is already a service to raise the issues. But they require further work.

The Biblical Commission fully realized that more work needed to be done. Their next document was entitled *The Jewish People and their Sacred Scriptures in the Christian Bible* (Vatican 2002). In it the relation between the two testaments is illustrated by examining nine themes that link them: creation, anthropology, the saving God, election, covenant, law, prayer, judgment, the promises to Abraham about a people and a land. Under this last theme are included the themes of the kingdom of God and the Messiah. So this document contains a pocket biblical theology. Besides this, the document powerfully resists all tendencies to a Marcionite rejection of the Hebrew Scriptures. It also addresses the problem of some apparently anti-Semitic texts within the New Testament (e.g., Matt 23:13–36; 27:25; John 8:44; 1 Thess 2:14–16). Jewish leaders were pleased by its affirmation that "the Jewish messianic wait is not in vain."

More important by far for the daily life of believers and worshippers is the new liturgical lectionary, the selection of biblical readings for Sundays and weekday. By designing a three-year Sunday lectionary the liturgists ensured that the people who attended service would be exposed to a wide range of Scripture, especially the Gospels. Year A focuses on Matthew, Year B on Mark, Year C on Luke. John is used at Christmas and Eastertide and to fill out Mark's year, since Mark is so short. Many of the great texts of the Old Testament and the Epistles are also read to the people. It is a true feast of the Word of God. It also has major ecumenical implications. Many other Christian denominations have adopted this Sunday lectionary system to their own use. This means that on most Sundays, Christians of different denominations hear the same gospel reading. This already contributes to a growing unity of Christian life. (The Church of England tried another system, emphasizing John, for ten years and then abandoned it.) This lectionary has been criticized by Christian anti-Semites for its abundant offering of the Hebrew Scriptures, but so far this has not had a great effect. but so far this has not had a great effect. Christian publishers are learning to market for the Year of Matthew, the Year of Mark, and so on. But that reflects the real objection to the lectionary: it is not easy to preach well each Sunday on such a rich variety of texts. It is hard work. That is the challenge in this blessing.

Let us conclude with a word of Scripture, delicious in its ambiguity. It is about the Logos, the word of God, today commonly understood to refer to the Bible but which the Fathers understood to refer to the Word Incarnate, Jesus Christ. Notice the shift in pronouns in the NRSV translation:

> Indeed, the word of God is living and active, sharper than any two-edged sword, piercing until it divides soul from spirit, joints from marrow; it is able to judge the thoughts and intentions of the heart. And before *him* no creature is hidden, but all are naked and laid bare to the eyes of the one to whom we must all render an account. (Heb 4:12–13)

3

Review of *The Future of Catholic Biblical Scholarship: A Constructive Conversation*

by Luke Timothy Johnson and William S. Kurz, S. J. Grand Rapids/Cambridge: Eerdmans, 2002. Pp. xii+299.

This is an unusual book, with an uncommon structure, on a subject of some significance. Though it seems to be addressed to Catholics only, its five "premises" are derived from a Jewish author (James Kugel), and its deepest concerns will touch all readers interested in relating the Bible to contemporary life and faith. The first five chapters are by L. T. Johnson, with a sixth chapter by W. S. Kurz in response. The second half of the book is by W. S. Kurz and is focused on the gospel according to John, particularly the Prologue, the Feeding of the 5000 and the Bread of Life Discourse (John 6), and the forgiveness of sins in John 20. This part concludes with a response by L. T. Johnson to W. S. Kurz. The book then finishes with a thirteenth chapter by both authors together and consists of ten questions to which each author gives a short answer.

Johnson's half of the book is the most provocative and debatable. It is an attack on a too one-sided acceptance of the historical-critical method by believers. This half of the book is governed by a major irony: the author's constitutional aversion to NT polemic makes him polemical. Yet his polemic enables him to unmask some prejudices and to see some limits to the method. In his opening chapter, he lists four limitations of the method: (1) the method is only interested in historical reconstruction; (2) the method is over-extended; it cannot fulfill all the hermeneutical needs of the faith community. (This book is the Catholic equivalent of Walter Wink's useful *The Bible in Human Transformation* (Philadelphia: Fortress, 1973) minus the Jungian therapeutics.) (3) The method is hegemonic, excluding other approaches to the Bible as uncritical or pre-critical or unscholarly. (4) It is not neutral but dominated by prejudices. He unmasks these prejudices. (1) The method as usually practiced has a preference for origins over development, for acorns over oaks. Chronology becomes value-laden: early is good, late is bad. Origins define essence. Development means decline. (2) To have a successful career in religious studies today the candidate must be antireligious. (3) The method neglects the biblical books as literary wholes. Johnson prefers a both-and to the either-or; he wants to reconnect with tradition, to see the organic growth of the Bible and tradition as positive, to find a place for the figurative and the imaginative, that is, for patristic and medieval interpretations. He is opposed to the Lutheran exclusive particles, especially to *sola scriptura,* and to historical Jesus research, which he regards as chimerical.

This opening chapter is crucial. It began as an attempt to answer the simple question: what is still Catholic about Catholic exegesis? When an earlier form of this chapter was presented at a meeting of the Catholic Biblical Association in Seattle in 1997, it provoked an astonishing, passionate reaction, partly perhaps because it seemed to say that the unmerited sufferings of scholarly heroes of the past (e.g., M.-J. Lagrange) had been in vain and useless (disrespect for the martyrs is offensive to Catholic sensibilities), partly because it seemed to imply that Catholics should not try hard to study the historical Jesus, thereby abandoning the field to less responsible scholars, encouraging sloth, and showing a lack of confidence that good money could drive out bad. Disrespect for the martyrs of the past has disappeared from the book form (but not disrespect for still living heroes, e.g., Schillebeeeckx, p. 127, n. 12). (On Schillebeeckx, see B. T. Viviano, *Trinity–Kingdom–Church* [NTOA 48; Fribourg: Fribourg University Press, 2001], pp. 75–88). Major issues are at stake.

The second chapter is also highly programmatic. It begins with a lament over the crisis in the discipline (and in the humanities in general), over the evils of over-specialization, over the lack of mastery of Latin and Greek by the young. It goes on with familiar, perennial, vague antitheses between: science and wisdom, mind and heart, church and academy, ancient and modern, communal and oral (implicitly warm and fuzzy) versus private and written (implicitly cold and prickly), a denunciation of dismissive, contemptuous attitudes toward pre-modern exegesis (while making the nearly fatal admission on p. 45 that the ancients wrote fewer verse-by-verse commentaries than they did homilies, hymns and antiphons). Who can deny that sometimes the most effective commentary is through music? Johnson seems deaf to the permanence and fruitfulness of certain dialectical polarities, e.g., Dominican versus Franciscan, or, in Judaism, Litvak misnagdim versus Galitnik hassidim, the academic and the devotional, the sober and the emotional. He seems also deaf to the reality that some people feel they must choose, while others prefer to fuse and synthesize the options, e.g., Belarussian yeshivot where, through the musar movement, both tendencies met and were held together. (This Jewish example shows that the issues are common to most religious communities.)

Johnson next settles down to presenting five premises of pre-modern interpretation, borrowed and adapted from James Kugel, *The Bible As It Was* (Cambridge: Harvard University Press, 1997), pp. 17–23. (1) Both testaments form a unity grounded in the one divine author. (2) Scripture speaks harmoniously. (3) The Bible, Word of God, is authoritative, and should be read docilely, on one's knees, as it were. (4) Scripture has more than the literal sense of (human) authorial intention, so that typology and allegory have their role. (5) Scriptural interpretation should be generous toward the text, rather than suspicious, and should build up charity rather than division in the faith community. The five premises are intended to work together and are deeply opposed to modern approaches. Modernity means (a) a single, objectively realizable meaning of the text, (b) a referential understanding of truth, (c) a claim to universal [public] reason. Post-modernity, which denies these claims, can become an ally of pre-modernity. The goals of Johnson's project are "to restore the soul of biblical scholarship as a scholarship" in the church, holiness for the individual, edification for the community.

Chapters Three and Four then try to show the value of reading Origen's and Augustine's scriptural works. On the whole these chapters are well informed and offer practical help to any student open to the subject matter. Johnson rightly singles out Origen's commentary on Numbers 33, a dry-as-dust catalogue of Israel's camp sites in the desert, as a good example of patristic exegesis making a silk purse out of a sow's ear: the camp sites become stages in the spiritual development of the believer. On the treatment of Augustine, two remarks may be pertinent. (1) It is regrettable that Johnson defends the link of the beatitudes with the seven gifts of the Spirit as "penetrating of the *text*." (2) Augustine's basic hermeneutical principle of charity as the guide to interpretation, admirable in itself, should be used primarily by those who have no chance to study the Bible in the original languages, to study exegesis or to use a library, as a short cut and as a hasty rule of thumb. It was not meant by Augustine to replace scholarship.

The fifth chapter engages modern science (Hawking and Sagan) and systematic theology. Here Johnson proposes four elements in recovering a scriptural imagination: concentrate on the risen Christ present (rather than the historical Jesus in the past); live in a community of practice (worship and works); engage in playful allegory or haggadah; connect the Bible with the life stories of people you know. Johnson praises the eighty homilies of Bernard of Clairvaux on the Song of Songs as a model. (The first of these homilies considers various kinds of spiritual kisses, for twenty pages. Tastes will differ on the worth of this.) Thomas Aquinas filled the need some have for a scientific sorting out and coherence after contradictory rhetorical excesses of which Bernard is an example.

In the response to Johnson, Kurz first tries to ground the proposals in a more sober Thomistic theology. He then tries to show links between the five premises of pre-modern interpretation with official church documents, like the conciliar constitution on divine revelation (1965), and the *Catechism of the Catholic Church* (1994). Kurz's own chapters on John's gospel have already been listed. In them (and one other, on abortion), he tries to show the harmony between, for example, John's prologue and the Nicene Creed, John 20:22-23 and the *Catechism*.

The concluding chapter tackles ten questions, such as: why should one claim a distinctive Catholic identity within biblical scholarship? What should be the positive characteristics of such scholarship? How should it be critical? Of what value is historical study for it? The role of the magisterium; the relation to liturgy and preaching; the empowerment of the laity.

This book is a bit of a hodge-podge. Yet it is timely, it captures in print issues that are in the air, and that need to be addressed. It surveys the field after the battles over the Bible in the Church, which raged from 1907 to 1965, are over, and after the harvest of freedom from 1966 to 2000 has been gathered. Its fight for the right to a devotional reading of the Scripture alongside scholarly approaches is legitimate. Its defense of non-literal interpretations can also be accepted, if such are limited to the Pentateuch and the Song, following here the example of the Fathers (so de Lubac). Its opening critique of methods is thought-provoking and often persuasive.

Yet the reviewer is old enough to remember the stupidity and shackles of the past vividly, so that he thinks we need more biblical scholarship rather than less. He prefers to honor American heroes like R. E. Brown and J. A. Fitzmyer, than to side with this book. He laments the continuing weakness of American Catholic scholarship in Hebrew Bible studies, There is still no major Catholic commentary on any book of the Pentateuch, since Lagrange was not allowed to publish his work on Genesis. (Reading Congar's recently published diaries would give younger scholars a vivid sense of the struggle.)

The two authors miss the significance of the admission of non-historical genres in the Bible by *Divine Afflante*, and the breakthrough on inerrancy at Vatican II. On one thing at least we can agree. Students should be encouraged to learn their Greek irregular verbs.

4

The Renewal of Biblical Studies in France 1934–54 as an Element in Theological *Ressourcement*

BACKGROUND

French Catholics have had their work cut out for them. In France's Golden Age under Louis XIV (reigned 1643–1715) there were simultaneously two sorts of thinkers: Cartesian rationalists valuing clear and distinct ideas, and historical-critical philologists like Richard Simon (1638–1712). His pioneer biblical criticism was anything but clear and distinct. It was sunk in the mud of historical and literary particularity, not to mention the confusion of religious variety. Among his many titles to honor are his early struggles for the right of French Jews to respect and understanding. This muddy confusion opened him to the simplistic salvos of the great bishop Jacques-Bénigne Bossuet (1627–1704), learned in patristics. As a result of Simon's harassment, leadership in biblical studies passed out of the hands of Catholics for a long time. The debate between Simon and Bossuet foreshadowed the twentieth-century conflict between Daniélou-de Lubac and de Vaux. The suppression of the Jesuits (1773) did not help Catholic biblical studies.

We need make only one point about the mid-nineteenth century: when conservative scholars (Catholics, Protestants, Orthodox Christian, and Jewish) hesitated to embrace the newer critical theories about the Pentateuch, the Psalter, the Gospels, and the Epistles of Paul, they usually did so in good conscience and with sincerity. The theories were not yet sufficiently tested. This sincerity was not the case in the twentieth century.

With Pope Leo XIII (1878–1903), a new era began: the Holy See spoke with a new voice, of positive teaching and encouragement, instead of condemnations and lamentations. This voice expressed itself in a series of encyclical letters, the basic goal of which was a general revival of Catholic cultural and intellectual life. It began in 1879 with a letter on the renewal of Catholic philosophy and theology, especially, but not exclusively, through the study of Thomas Aquinas. It continued with the opening of the Vatican library to researchers of different denominations and with letters on the value of historical and biblical studies. It culminated in a famous encyclical on social questions (recognizing, for example, the right of workers to form unions and the right to a just wage), as well as an effort to persuade French Catholics to support the Third Republic (1870–1940). This meant giving up their sterile, doomed policy of trying to restore a Bourbon, legitimist, absolute monarchy. This nostalgic monarchism is well illustrated in Henry James' early novel *The American* (1877), as well as in the novels of Marcel Proust. Leo's well-intentioned shift in policy, expressed by Cardinal Lavigerie's 'toast' to the Republic in Algiers, was not accepted at the time by France's aristocratic Catholic elite. It was put on hold by the bitter disputes occasioned by the Dreyfus Affair, as well as by the rejectionist policies of the Action Française movement.

But before the dawn was seen to be in part false, a French Dominican named Marie-Joseph Lagrange (1855–1938) enjoyed a thirteen-year period of glory and success. His Christian name was Albert, and he had trained as a lawyer in Paris, a useful *métier* when he later found himself in trouble, and as an Orientalist in Vienna. Oriental studies helped him with the Bible as well as with the new discoveries from Mesopotamia (Iraq): the Code of Hammurabi, the Gilgamesh epic, and the creation account, Enuma Elish. These needed to be integrated into the study of biblical law and of the biblical accounts of the creation of the world and of the primeval flood.

Lagrange had been asked by his superiors to open a school of biblical studies in Jerusalem, on property the Dominican order had bought a few years earlier. He opened the school in 1890. Here he hoped to re-examine the Bible in the light of the new comparative material. He launched the quarterly *Revue biblique* in 1892, and a commentary series, *Etudes bibliques*, soon thereafter. The journal quickly earned respect in the learned world, due to its regular publication of newly discovered inscriptions, found in the fields of Ottoman Palestine and Jordan. Seminarians interested in ideas devoured the *Revue* as bringing in a fresh theological tone. Priests of various dioceses and religious orders were happy to collaborate, as were lay scholars. Best of all for a devout Religious who wanted to work for the good of the Church, for thirteen years Lagrange enjoyed the favour of Pope Leo XIII. As a 'fair haired boy', he was showered with signs of favor. His school church was elevated to the rank of a basilica. Such success to be sure evoked some measure of jealousy and hostility.

With the election of Pius X (1903–14) the ill winds blew stronger. Jesuits were ordered to halt all collaboration with Lagrange. A rival biblical institute was set up in Rome (1909) by Leopold Fonck, SJ. Lagrange's brilliant doctoral student, Rev. Joseph Bonsirven, was denied his doctorate in Rome. With the papal documents *Pascendi Dominici Gregis* and *Lamentabili*, biblical studies were frozen in place. A timid thaw began around 1935, for which the death of Fonck, along with the signing of the Lateran accords (1928–29) prepared the way. The deaths of Cardinals Pietro Gasparri and Rafael Merry del Val in 1935 removed further obstacles to progress.

THE RENEWAL: PHASE 1 (1935–43)

The rise of fascist and totalitarian regimes and their eventual defeat or disintegration can be understood as the last gasps of the Baroque absolutist model of government. The Baroque model is pre-modern, satisfying for the politically immature. During its Western twilight, glimmers of the next step could be seen in the French Church. In the midst of the Second World War, the important encyclical on biblical studies, *Divino Afflante Spiritu*, was released by Pius XII. In addition to its encouraging tone, a return to Leo XIII, it conceded the key point for which Lagrange had pleaded and on which he had published in 1903, 40 years earlier, namely, that there are many literary genres in the Bible, not just one. This seems banal, but the issue at stake was whether everything in the Bible was literally, historically true or not. Besides history, the other main genres in the Bible are law, prophecy, wisdom, and praise. Present in the Bible are also edifying fiction (e.g., part of Jonah) and the re-use in purified form of ancient Near Eastern myths (e.g., in Genesis 1, Daniel 7, Psalm 29, Revelation 12). The deeper point is that the Bible was not necessarily inerrant in matters (geography, astronomy, chemistry) not directly related to human salvation. That point was not conceded until 1965.

Another significant event of the war years was the publication in 1942 of the Louvain professor, Canon Lucien Cerfaux's *Theology of the Church according to St. Paul*. It was published in the Unam Sanctam series, started not long previously by Yves Congar, as the vanguard in the renewal of ecclesiology. His book balanced the then-current obsession of regarding the Church as the body of Christ, with other Pauline ecclesial models, notably the Church as the people of God and the Church in relation to the future Kingdom of God. In doing so he anticipated by a year the encyclical letter on the church as the body of Christ. *Mystici Corporis Christi*, in turn informed by the studies of Émile Mersch, who was killed in 1940, and by Sebastian Tromp. The letter represented an ecclesial step forward, but it did not give a full picture of the biblical data. Cerfaux was supported by the systematic theology of M. D. Koester; their studies would be integrated into the Vatican II Constitution on the Church, *Lumen Gentium*.

THE RENEWAL: PHASE 2 (1944-54)

Even hardened secular observers noticed that a revival of Catholic intellectual life took place in the period 1944-54. It involved a certain conjunction of Christ and culture, a new harmony of faith and reason. Fear of the worker-priest experimental collaboration with Communist trade unions led the CIA to support a work by the respected sociologist, Raymond Aron, *The Opium of the Intellectuals*, which denounced this alliance. The curtain came down on this brief honeymoon period with a papal condemnation of the worker-priest movement and its theologians in 1954. The synthesis had fallen victim to the Cold War. People thought the drama was over. And then came the death of Pius XII, the election of John XXIII, and the convocation of the Second Vatican Council. The working of the Holy Spirit in the Church could be and often is resisted, yet it continues underground and has occasional eruptions that are visible and palpable.

With regard to biblical studies, too, the pace quickens in this period. First, a new series in biblical theology was launched: *Lectio Divina*, accompanied by two other series: *Cahiers Sioniens* and the first fascicles of the *Bible de Jerusalem*. The first and third of these projects are still going strong today. The second, the *Cahiers*, rendered great service in its day by showing the complementary lights shed on the Bible by the Christian, Jewish, and Islamic traditions of interpretation. This took place especially in a series of collective volumes on some of the great biblical personalities: Abraham, Moses, and Elijah.

Second, a magisterial development occurred. Catholic school teachers and intellectuals had for a long time been troubled by how to present the origins of the world and of humankind in a way which took into account both the biblical narratives of Genesis 1-3 and the views of modern science (the evolution of the species, the great antiquity of the planet, the descent of man from lower primates). The Jesuit palaeontologist, Pierre Teilhard de Chardin (1881-1955), was pushing from behind the scenes for the freedom to publish his hypotheses on the phenomenon of man and on the goal of the universe (the Omega point), but met with consistently firm opposition from Rome. His allies, Jean Guitton and Mgr. Bruno de Solages, tried their best. Other scholars wanted to publish on Genesis. The encyclical *Divino Afflante Spiritu* was insufficient as support for an imprimatur. On 16 January 1948 a letter was released by the secretary of the Biblical Commission, Jacob Voste, OP, who had been a student of Lagrange. The letter was addressed to the Cardinal Archbishop of Paris, Emmanuel Suhard. It assured him and concerned scholars that Genesis 1–3 should now be addressed with all the resources of modern science and critical scholarship.

There then appeared in quick succession a commentary on Genesis by Joseph Chaine (Lyon); a study of the first sin as the presumption of moral autonomy by Canon Joseph Coppens (Louvain); and a study of Genesis and modern science by Canon Charles Hauret (Strasbourg). As for poor Teilhard, his work could only be published after his death in 1955. In America, books on Genesis in this spirit were published by Bruce Vawter and John L. McKenzie.

On the whole, these works did not affect the general public as other events and publications did, such as the revelation, in 1945, of the full horror of the Nazi genocide (the Shoah), symbolized by Auschwitz. This, combined with the establishment of the State of Israel in 1948, led Christians of all denominations to gradually reassess their thinking, teaching, and prayers about Jews and Judaism. At the same time, two events of major significance for biblical theology did impinge on the public imagination.

The first was the discovery of the Dead Sea Scrolls at caves on the sides of Wadi Qumran by an Arab shepherd boy. Thanks to the sensationalist evaluation of the find by the archaeologist W. F. Albright, and the literary presentation by the critic Edmund Wilson (initially in the *New Yorker* magazine), the discoveries unleashed a firestorm of excitement and interest, drawing in academics, churches, synagogues, mosques, and governments. It increased interest in the Hebrew Bible, the inter-Testamental period, the origins of Christianity and monasticism (Jewish monks had become barely conceivable after Freud's pan-sexualism, although the record was already there in Philo and Josephus). The discovery increased confidence in the reliability of the Hebrew manuscript tradition, since it included two complete leather scrolls of the longest of the writing prophets, Isaiah, which strongly supported the medieval manuscript tradition. To be sure, fragments of other passages from the Hebrew Bible, e.g., Jeremiah and 1 Samuel, showed greater variety and at times greater proximity to the Septuagint or Old Greek translation.

Such a discovery needs to be crystallized around a person, and in this case, that person was the French Dominican and director of the French archaeological school in Jerusalem, Roland de Vaux. He looked the part: wiry and bearded, he combined active on-site digging with published scholarship, spirituality with humour, faith with reason, ability in both Arabic and Hebrew, Gallic flair with accented English. The media made him a star and the University of Harvard gave him a visiting professorship in 1963.

This is not the place to tell the whole long and complex story of the Scrolls. But one clarification might be helpful in the present context. There is a distinction to be made between the *site* of the discovery of the Scrolls (involving archaeological exploration) and the publication of the *texts* of the Scrolls, involving paleography, Semitic philology, and all the elements of interpretation: literary analysis, structure, history and theology. Fr de Vaux was involved in both aspects. As far as archaeology is concerned, once Israel's war of independence was over, the sites of both Qumran and the École biblique were in Jordanian or West Bank Palestine. It was quickly agreed that the excavation should be a joint project of the British and French archaeological schools in Jerusalem. But the director of the British school had suddenly become the head of the Jordanian antiquities authority based in Amman, and, as he was not free to share the work, leadership fell by default to Fr. de Vaux, although he had not sought this responsibility.

So it was too with the publication of the texts. Given the complexity and size of the task, and the worldwide interest it had acquired, it was decided early on that the responsibility for the editing should lie with an international, interdenominational team. Unfortunately, due to the sensibilities of the Jordanian authorities, Jewish scholars could not then be included. At the time, this was not considered a problem, since the Israelis had just acquired the main body of intact scrolls and had enough to do editing them. Things changed again after 1967, when the West Bank was overrun by Israel. Fr. de Vaux was appointed editor-in-chief of the fragmentary texts (mostly from Caves 4 and 11) and head of the team for Oxford University Press. This arrangement worked for a while, but personality problems within the team and de Vaux's untimely death in 1971 slowed the pace of publication down. Only recently have all the fragments been published in careful editions. But in those first heady years, in the late 1940s and 1950s, the Scrolls gave a powerful impetus to the biblical *ressourcement*.

De Vaux was clearly riding too many horses at the same time, as he became the key figure in the second major event of biblical significance that affected the general public. This was the publication of the *Bible de Jérusalem* in one volume in 1955. This project had begun ten years earlier with a series of fascicles covering the entire Bible, and with extensive introductions and notes, as well as a fresh translation from the original Hebrew and Greek, a translation that could at times benefit from the new readings provided by the Qumran manuscripts. This Bible and its notes were soon translated into the main Western languages. The English version was published in 1966 as the *Jerusalem Bible*.

This Bible was reaping the harvest of sixty-five years of scholarship in Jerusalem, at the École biblique, and elsewhere in the French Catholic world. It represented a collaborative effort by the many different streams of Catholic clergy: Dominicans and Jesuits in the lead, followed by members of many other religious orders and diocesan priests. This in itself represents an 'internal ecumenical' breakthrough, astonishing when one considers the animosities of the past. Many distinguished laymen contributed to the literary quality of the work, such as Étienne Gilson and Henri-Irénée Marrou.

The *Bible de Jerusalem*, with its fresh approach and its elegant production, was a best-seller from the start. It provided the Catholic renewal with an up-to-date Bible. The notes included a mild version of the documentary hypothesis concerning the sources of the Pentateuch (Julius Wellhausen and Hermann Gunkel, among others), stated in a calm, serene tone that did not frighten readers. (Lagrange had already tried to promote the documentary hypothesis in 1898.) However, the *Bible de Jerusalem* was less successful in its introduction to the synoptic Gospels, because it failed to present clearly the commonly accepted two-source solution to the synoptic problem, the relationship of the Gospels to one another and to their sources. Through a collaboration between a Dominican scholar (Raymond-Jacques Tournay), a Jesuit musician (Joseph Gelineau) and a Jewish poet (Raymond Schwab), its Psalter was soon being sung around the world. Recordings of this collaborative Psalter won phonograph prizes. An English reviewer declared the *Jerusalem Bible* to be the best Bible in the world at the time.

This translation also had an impact on Protestant editions of the Bible. Liberal French Protestants had produced an intelligent, annotated version in the first part of the century, the *Bible du Centenaire*, in three large, expensive and impractical volumes, thus selling few copies. The editors wanted it to be reproduced in a cheap, compact version by the Bible Society. This however could not be done because the rules of the society did not allow notes. The Catholics had no such rules. When Oxford University Press learned of the plans to translate the *Bible de Jerusalem* into English, they rushed into print their own annotated Bible (1965) to preserve their share of the market. Oxford University Press was not bound by the rules of the Bible Society. But the *Centenaire* had been the forgotten pioneer.

Although the Jerusalem Bible is often used in worship, it is important to understand that it is in no way an official Bible. It is a private initiative, undertaken by a publisher, Éditions du Cerf, and a school, the École biblique. School and publisher, both Dominican institutions, had always operated within the Church; the Bible has always carried the imprimatur.

Winning the discreet but real support of the Vatican had been a triumph for de Vaux's diplomatic charm. The effect on individual spiritual lives is beyond calculation.

We may add a few additional remarks on the contribution of the French scriptural *ressourcement* to Vatican II. First, the studies on the inspiration of scripture by Pierre Benoît, OP, themselves nourished by Thomas Aquinas and Lagrange, made a sharp distinction between inspiration and revelation. Thus all Scripture is inspired by God, but only parts contain divine revelation, in the sense of religious truths that are unattainable by reason alone. This distinction supported the distinction made at the Second Vatican Council between inspiration and inerrancy. That is: all Scripture is inspired, but only those truths revealed for the sake of our salvation are necessarily inerrant, free from error. Other statements, e.g., of geography, history, or astronomy, can be erroneous (*Dei Verbum*, no. 11). Second, Benoît also contributed biblical support for the declaration on religious freedom (*Dignitatis Humanae*), mainly through the parable of the wheat and the weeds (Matt 13:24–30). Finally, Albert Gelin provided a valuable gift to Christian spirituality with his little book on the poor and the afflicted (*anawim, aniyyim*) in the Bible.

SCRIPTURE AND PATRISTICS

Among the masters of the *ressourcement*, alongside Chenu and Congar, Louis Bouyer and Albert Gelin, were the Jesuits Henri de Lubac and Jean Daniélou, both of whom were known for their great knowledge of the Church Fathers. But at times their relationship to professional biblical scholarship was troubled, precisely because of their love of the Fathers. This requires a word of explanation.

First of all, it goes without saying that all Catholic exegetes accept and presuppose the whole long tradition of Christian interpretation of Scripture that begins with the Fathers. On this point there is no dispute. The debate turns rather on developments that have occurred since the Fathers, especially since 1450 or since 1800. Must these developments be rejected out of hand because they are not all found in the Fathers? Again, is it legitimate to have a direct access to Scripture, to analyse and to discuss it, without always passing through the views of the Fathers? In their enthusiasm for the Fathers, de Lubac and Daniélou at times give the impression that the answers to these two questions are yes and no, respectively. These answers have provoked disagreement.

In trying to understand these issues, it is important to have some chronology clearly in mind. For example, de Lubac's best known work, *Catholicism: The Social Aspects of Dogma*, was first published in 1938, when the author was 42. The whole aim of the book is to try to correct an unhealthy Christian individualism, an individualistic turn taken by St. Augustine. This is a praiseworthy goal. The book made a contribution to the Vatican II Constitution on the Liturgy, especially on the Eucharist. (The footnotes were at times taken over in their entirety.) But in chapter six, on the interpretation of Scripture, the book manifests a romantic enthusiasm for some of the more far-fetched, fanciful, and forced patristic interpretations, which goes beyond prudent limits. There is much of beauty and virtue in this chapter, especially on the harmony of the two Testaments and on the firm rejection of Marcionism. There is also an awareness that patristic exegesis can be excessive and abusive. Yet de Lubac manifests an impatience with the literal sense that could easily violate sound exegetical method. Why is this?

Allow me to offer some explanations. First, the chronology shows that the book was written before *Divino Afflante Spiritu* and Voste's letter. De Lubac and Daniélou were both formed and began writing in the era when *Pascendi* and *Lamentabili* reigned as the official line. As Jesuits with the fourth vow of special obedience to the Holy See, they both felt bound in conscience to keep to this line. They were victims, one could say, of their *sentire cum ecclesia*—thinking with the Church—understood as the Holy See. They did not yet benefit from the encyclical's openness to different genres, and its goal, for exegetes, of recovering the original human author's intention. To escape from a childish historicization of everything, they took refuge in patristic allegory and typology. Second, they did not expect that the Holy See would change its course. Père Lagrange may have died in 1938 in the same despair, after his article on the Old Testament patriarchs was turned down by the censors for the fifth time. Third, de Lubac and Daniélou had not yet clearly broken with the sterile politics of Bourbon restoration (Action Française); this break occurred after France's defeat by Germany, when the Vichy government of Marshal Henri Philippe Pétain (1856–1951) began to collaborate in the deportation of Jews to the extermination camps. Fourth, they felt it was sufficiently bold at the time to break with the Maurrasian Thomism that prevailed in some Roman universities and French seminaries, in favor of a renewal through the Fathers. That was risky enough. Fifth, any academic field of specialization tends to think that it is the most important one. Once the two had made the choice for patristics, it was natural that they should try to promote it. There had been a strong French tradition (at the Sorbonne and elsewhere) of patristic scholarship at least since the Maurist Benedictines of the seventeenth century, with their access to the royal Greek type-fonts to print their editions of the Fathers. Interest in patristic study increased and there were many dissertations on the Fathers. Moreover, it was repugnant to French national pride simply to copy the conclusions of German research. Besides, they were involved in an ecumenical collaboration with the Russian Orthodox theologians centered at the Institut Saint-Serge in Paris. The Fathers represented common ground. So for these five reasons, I suggest that de Lubac and Daniélou were not quite at home with modern exegesis.

At their most extreme, de Lubac and Daniélou adopted a somewhat antagonistic tone. For example, they both defended an allegorical interpretation of the Good Samaritan (Luke 10:25-37) as the originally intended, authentic meaning. Not content with this, Daniélou insinuated that, since this interpretation was so deeply rooted in the tradition of the Church, this interpretation was the true meaning of the parable, going back to Jesus himself, or at least to the 'elders' cited by Origen. There was no freedom not to accept it. The Jesuit Scripture scholar, Joseph A. Fitzmyer, in his fine commentary on Luke, brushes this interpretation aside as fanciful and remote from the text in context. In his history of pre-modern exegesis, de Lubac also adopts a rather aggressive tone. The allegorical interpretation of the Old Testament is a necessary and obligatory part of the tradition and cannot be ignored, on pain of loss of communion with the tradition.

My comments on this view will be based on my own experience of living in Jerusalem for twelve years, trying to understand the Hebrew Bible as a Christian, and observing how the rabbis present that Bible to their own people. The first thing I learned is that the Pentateuch is more important in classical Jewish liturgy and life than is the rest of the Hebrew canon. If you cannot make sense out of it, the door is closed to the Jewish faith and to the nourishment of our own Christian faith. Second, I came to understand that the Pentateuch is not history in the same sense that the succession narrative is history (2 Samuel 9-20; 1 Kings 1-2). It is something else: a mixture of history, myth, legend, poetry, and law. It is about the birth of a nation. It contains a constitution of a state. And it is a great book of religious revelation. Only a complex reading approach will do justice to its complexity. Third, when one reads the Sabbath sermons of modern orthodox rabbis like Pinchas Peli, one realizes that they are desperate to find meaning anywhere. Historical criticism, the rabbinical and Christian traditions, philosophy, psychology, science, literature—all are placed at the service of the great and difficult task of making the Torah meaningful to people today, especially to people of good will.

Given this experience, one is more disposed to give de Lubac a favorable hearing, despite his excesses. This is especially true because of two points he makes. The Fathers used allegory not for all the books of the Old Testament but only or primarily for the Pentateuch and the Song of Songs. This is good and appropriate news, because, even if every word of Wellhausen were divinely inspired, his words would not suffice for a full, rounded, intellectually, aesthetically, and spiritually satisfying understanding of the Pentateuch. It suffices to read him to be convinced of that fact. He simply did not write commentaries on the Torah (although he did on the minor prophets and the Gospels). So here de Lubac's defence of allegory is appropriate. Second, de Lubac argues that if we do not accept non-literal, 'spiritual' senses of Scripture, much of the Old Testament, and particularly the Pentateuch, becomes spiritually unavailable to the faithful. This seems true to me. A small example may suffice. In Exod 15:27 (cf. Num 33:9) we read: "Then they came to Elim, where there were twelve springs of water and seventy palm trees, and they encamped there by the water." Even if this is literally, historically true, it does not say much, by itself, to the modern reader. It comes as no surprise, then, that the Fathers interpret the twelve springs as the preaching of the twelve apostles, and the seventy palm trees as the seventy pagan nations of the world to whom they are sent to preach (or the seventy elders of Luke 10:1, 17). It is no wonder that Philo and the rabbis said something similar about the twelve tribes and the seventy nations, since some meaning is better than none.

Nevertheless, reading the Fathers on Scripture will not solve all of our exegetical problems. Roland de Vaux said this tersely, politely, firmly in his review of Daniélou's book on Origen. To be sure, Origen was a genius. He was often better than some of the childish, apologetic literal-mindedness of the nineteenth century. But we must still have the courage to bite the historical-critical (often German Protestant) bullet before we can have a credible word of our own to say.

In our own day, a spirit of discontent with modern exegetical methods is noticeable among both younger Jewish and Christian scholars. The French *ressourcement* theologians can, then, still be of service. Our weakness as Catholics remains the fact that we are still deficient in good full-scale commentaries on the Old Testament, especially on the Pentateuch. Perhaps the long delayed publication of Père Lagrange's commentary on Genesis will help to open up the dam. Christoph Dohmen's commentary on Exodus may be a sign of better things to come.

5

American Catholic New Testament Scholarship

THE FIRST SPRING

Passing over the period before the American Civil War (1861–1865), we can begin our story with the founding of Catholic University of America in Washington DC in 1889, under the progressive papacy of Leo XIII. To help them launch the biblical department on a high academic level, the founders invited a French priest named Henri Hyvernat who quickly established himself in early Christian languages, especially Syriac and Coptic. This was the time of the discovery of heaps of papyri in Egypt. The grand financier J. Pierpont Morgan bought up large quantities for his splendid library in Manhattan. The Greek papyri could be read by the Protestant scholars available in New York City. But for the Coptic he called in Fr. Hyvernat who did the catalogue of the collection. Because of the relative safety of linguistic study in the following period of Catholic church history, Morgan helped pay for a department of Semitic languages at CU, but not of biblical studies. That would have been too dangerous.

At this point I would like to say a word about Hyvernat's youth and his French allies. In the major seminary outside Paris, Hyvernat befriended two classmates, Pierre Batiffol and Albert Lagrange. All three were dismayed by the weakness of French biblical and patristic scholarship in comparison with the German enemies of France. The three lads pooled their francs and together were able to purchase the best critical edition of the Greek New Testament, Tischendorff's *octava critica maior*, with a vast collection of manuscript variant readings in the apparatus criticus. This was intended as the first step in their project to redeem the honor of French biblical scholarship. Metaphorically, it was their blood oath as a band of brothers. Batiffol went on to become the rector of the Catholic university of Toulouse. Lagrange became a Dominican and founded the first permanent school of biblical and archaeological studies in modern Jerusalem. Hyvernat tried to invite Lagrange to America, but the superiors feared the danger of increased attention and said no. But Lagrange's essays were translated and published in new journals in New York and Washington.

Meanwhile another center of progressive Catholic thought was taking shape in New York. The archdiocesan seminary at nearby Dunwoodie was directed by a gifted Msgr. Ford. He founded the *New York Review*, which published biblical scholarship, including Lagrange's articles. After the antimodernist decrees were published in 1907, the archbishop felt he had to remove him from the seminary. But he also knew he needed a competent representative as pastor of the Roman Catholic parish nearest to Columbia University. Ford was pastor of Corpus Christi for many decades. The educational philosopher John Dewey reigned supreme at the University across the street. Ford had a progressive grade school staffed by the Dominican sisters of Sinsinawa. They were not allowed to study at the university in those days, so Ford invited Dewey to lecture the sisters in the convent. Those sisters taught the recently deceased comedian George Carlin. This story is typical of the way Catholics stayed in contact with intellectual currents while maintaining the appearance of being unsullied by the real world. I know. I grew up in it. I knew some of the sisters.

Another aspect of this early period concerned the aftermath of the Spanish-American War. The Spanish defeat of 1898 was a great humiliation for the Spanish crown and culture. Spanish curial cardinals in Rome combined with French monarchist reactionaries, Bourbon legitimists, to demand a consolation prize from the aging and weakening Pope. So in 1899 Leo XIII published an encyclical condemning the heresy of Americanism. Although the contents were bland, namely that some American Catholics favored the active virtues over the contemplative ones, the more serious issue was American parliamentary democracy and the separation of church and state, both of which were being proposed as models by Catholics in France and elsewhere. The American bishops were being crushed between two millstones, the need to appear patriotic and the need to appear submissive to Rome. They made light of the charges, claiming that no American Catholic held these views. They called it the phantom heresy. But in fact the leading bishops, especially John Lancaster Spalding, the driving force behind the founding of Catholic University, were ardent exponents of the American model of church-state relations, and of romantic idealist theology.

Catholic University, and with it American Catholic intellectual life in general, almost died from the one-two punch of the two encyclicals, the one against Americanism, the other against Modernism. Americanism we have just mentioned. Modernism in this context was a label attached to movements in various countries whose goal was to narrow the gap between the church and the modern world. These movements were condemned in two papal documents from the time of Pope Pius X: the encyclical *Pascendi* of 8 September 1907, concerned with modern philosophy and apologetics; and a decree of the Holy Office called *Lamentabili*, concerned with issues of biblical exegesis and the history of dogma. It touched on the matter of biblical inerrancy, on the divinity of Christ, on the origin of the sacraments and of the church. The latter decree especially had a chilling effect on biblical studies. A hunger for intelligent theology was so great, however, that the young shoot did not die of asphyxiation, even though it was a blighted spring. The spirit of resilience was manifested in a story told about the *Catholic Encyclopedia* of 1914. To be a success, it required the approval of the American bishops of the first volume, which covered the letter A. After several drafts of the article on Americanism had been rejected by the editorial board as too dangerous, the whole project was in jeopardy. Suddenly the general editor, Msgr. Pine, a professor of philosophy at CU, cried out: "What's the name of that encyclical? *Testem, testem benevolentiae*! We will put under Americanism the words "See *Testem benevolentiae*." That article will appear in the final volume. By then the project will have been successful." And so it was.

In the meantime some of the major religious orders decided to build their houses of study around the university, beginning with the Dominicans in 1905 (they had first considered Yale). When the U.S. church ceased to be considered as a mission territory by the Vatican in 1908, the Americans responded by creating their own missionary order, Maryknoll (men 1911, women 1912). Each of the older orders gave them a gift, whether chalices, vestments, art works, or books. All agreed that the Dominicans gave the best gift of all, two professors of Scripture, C. J. Callan and J. A. McHugh. These two educated the first two generations of Maryknoll missionaries and are buried there, the only two non-Maryknollers in the cemetery. They wrote the first American Catholic commentaries on many biblical books, e.g., the Psalms (last edition 1949). These works were very timid, but they were a start. A better work was a translation of the New Testament from the Greek by Francis Aloysius Spencer, OP, who had been educated as an Episcopalian priest. It had to wait until after his death and after the publication of another encyclical to be published as he wrote it.

THE SECOND SPRING

By 1936 the old crocodile cardinals in Rome who had tried to enforce the anti-Modernist measures had themselves all died out. A theological comeback began. In 1937, in St. Louis, the Catholic Biblical Association of America was founded. The next year the *Catholic Biblical Quarterly* began its publication. Within ten years the Association had published a new translation of the New Testament. It was met by leading British Catholic scholars with condescension and disdain, doubtless deserved, but again, it was a beginning. The translation was followed by a commentary. But even sooner, once the breach had been made, the Dominicans founded *The Thomist* in 1939, the Jesuits founded *Theological Studies* in 1940. You see the pattern. Once the biblical people had shown the way, the rest could follow.

You might think that the war would put a halt to such studies. But this did not happen. In 1943 Pope Pius XII published an encyclical on biblical studies (*Divino Afflante Spiritu*) that admitted that there were other literary genres in the Bible besides history. This was an enormous help.

Meanwhile in the United States something else was happening, though no one spoke of it in public. Before the war American academics often had an inferiority complex in regard to Europe. The brightest Lutheran boys were sent to Erlangen to receive the stamp of German Lutheran orthodoxy and authenticity. Bright Presbyterian boys went to Edinburgh. Bright Jewish boys went to Berlin. Bright Catholic boys were sent to Rome or Jerusalem or Munich. But once the war broke out in Europe, even before the U.S. was involved, American students could no longer go to Europe. What to do? Without any coordinated plan the various religious leaders decided that one man and one place were right. They could safely entrust their brightest students interested in Scripture to the care of Professor William Foxwell Albright of Johns Hopkins University, Baltimore. And so these American students sat around the same seminar table, Jews, Lutherans, Presbyterians, Roman Catholics, and became friends and colleagues, long before it was permissible for them to study theology at schools that did not belong to their denomination. Why? How did this happen?

It all had to do with Albright. A son of Methodist missionaries, he was born in Chile. He remained an (unhappy) Methodist till the day he died. But first of all he claimed not to be an exegete, not a biblical scholar, but an Orientalist. That term has since taken on a colonialist, racist connotation, but at the time it suggested a kind of neutral, objective, rigorously scientific discipline comparable to physics and chemistry, a discipline that had nothing to do with faith, theology, or confession. This academic stance took in professors from other fields, journalists, the general public, and above all church leaders. His learned opponents, C.C. Torrey of Yale and Morton Smith of Columbia, suspected him, not without reason, of being a closet fundamentalist. But elsewhere he inspired trust and that was the main thing. The Presbyterians loved his love of the Old Testament. Catholics knew that his Episcopalian wife had become a Roman Catholic under the influence of the professors at the Ecole Biblique, that Albright built the new campus of the American School a stone's throw from the Ecole library, that his sons were raised Catholic and named after professors at the Ecole. The Jews knew he was a friend of Zion and spoke a sort of Hebrew. His discovery of biblical sites helped their cause. In the American spirit of optimism, the can-do spirit, he radiated the cheerful confidence that the very next decipherment of the inscription on a potsherd from a Palestine refuse pile would prove the Bible true in minute detail and refute two centuries of critical scholarship. Albright was also gifted at handling the press. He worked hand in glove with the Baltimore *Sun*, as would become clearer after the war in regard to the discovery at Qumran of the Dead Sea Scrolls. Among the Catholic priests who studied with him were Raymond E. Brown the Sulpician and the Jesuits Joseph A. Fitzmyer, William Moran, and Mitchell Dahood. Msgr. Patrick Skehan, professor of Semitic languages at nearby Catholic U., frequently collaborated in seminars. An underground alliance had been formed. (In the interests of chronological accuracy, it is necessary to point out that J. A. Fitzmyer began his studies with Albright only in 1953; Brown began in 1954.)

Once the war was over, the next big step was the discovery of the Dead Sea Scrolls. In the confused circumstances of the time, the British, then the Jordanian, department of antiquities felt the jobs of excavation and publication were too large for them alone. So the British School asked Roland de Vaux of the Ecole to excavate the site of Qumran. And an international, interconfessional team of scholars was gathered to edit and publish the fragments. Among these were the American Catholic scholars Brown, Fitzmyer, and Skehan. They thus gained national recognition for the first time. (Later on John Strugnell, a Qumran pioneer, became a Catholic. Eugene Ulrich and James VanderKam [Reformed] continued Qumran research at the University of Notre Dame.)

In the fifties other important events were the articles by the pioneer woman, Kathryn Sullivan, RSCJ, in *Worship* magazine, on the role of each book of the Old Testament in the liturgy and in great art. This was a peculiarly Catholic contribution and had a great influence on many, even adolescents. She died recently at over a hundred. For the first decades after its founding she was the only woman member of the CBA.

The first American Catholic theology of the Old Testament was published in 1956 by John L. McKenzie, SJ (Milwaukee, WI: Bruce). It was called *The Two-Edged Sword*. It was heavily dependent upon the three volume work by Walter Eichrodt, which had not yet been translated. It helped my generation to develop an interest in the Hebrew Bible. He later (1974) expanded it into *A Theology of the Old Testament* (Garden City, NY: Doubleday). He was the first Catholic president of the Society of Biblical Literature, a major breakthrough at the time. He was a tall, powerful, angry man, preoccupied with problems of authority, but he broke open many doors and was a light in his day. (More recently, Frank Matera has published a theology of the New Testament, gathered around five themes: anthropology, Christology, ecclesiology, ethics, and eschatology.)

In the waning days of the pontificate of Pius XII, the editor of the *Catholic Biblical Quarterly*, Fr. Edward Siegman, CPPS, was forced to resign under pressure from Rome because of his use of form criticism in the study of the gospels. The Association stood by him with gestures of sympathy and support.

From the point of view of the American Roman Catholic Church, the Second Vatican Council had two main effects. First, it limited biblical inerrancy to the area of salvation. Secondly, it introduced new lectionaries for Sunday and weekday liturgies. These were designed on the basis of redaction criticism, a triumph for recent biblical scholarship. The lectionaries also opened up much greater riches of the Scriptures for the nourishment of the faithful. It was a challenge for preachers to be able to preach on so many texts. Scholars were called on to provide helps to homilists. Alert publishers commissioned not only commentaries on the selections in the lectionaries but also books on the redactional theologies of each evangelist.

After the council, two major events occurred in the same year, 1970. In that year American Catholics celebrated a complete new Bible translation from the original texts, a translation that was their very own. Its Old Testament had a few flaws due to episcopal interference, some tactless notes and overly drastic textual choices, but it generally rendered good service for over thirty years. The New Testament was done more hastily and suffered from an overly chatty style. It was carefully and well revised in 1986. The 1970 Bible came just in time for use in the new lectionaries. In the same year members of the CBAA produced a one-volume commentary on the whole Bible, *The Jerome Biblical Commentary* (Englewood Cliffs, NJ: Prentice-Hall). It was translated into several languages. It had many flaws, especially a timidity in questions of introduction to the different books. It was characterized by the fact that all authors were Catholic, most of the men were priests, the women nuns, few had doctorates, but especially, most had pontifical licences. This was considered the minimal stamp of Catholic authenticity. Today it provides a snapshot of the state of biblical studies in the American Church of the time.

The seventies witnessed two major phenomena in this regard. The first was the publication of two major commentaries, one on John by R. E. Brown, the other on Luke by J. A. Fitzmyer, in the series founded by Albright to offer an interfaith forum for his graduate students to publish works in his spirit and in the spirit of post-Vatican II collaboration, The Anchor Bible. These two works were of such high quality that they set a standard for the other contributors. The works were widely adopted as textbooks in many schools regardless of confessional allegiance. They mark a new maturity in the American Catholic contribution to biblical studies. The major works of Brown were regularly reviewed in the *New York Times Book Magazine*, a rare exception to the general practice of the *Times*. At the same time it must be said that Catholic works of similar quality are rarely found on the books of the Old Testament. This remains a deficit, despite the honorable exceptions of J. J. Collins on Daniel, di Lella on Sirach and some shorter works by R.J. Clifford on the Pentateuch. On the other hand U.S. Catholics have been very active in the production of popular and middle level commentaries of all sorts, and also in summer workshops and institutes to help people with the lectionary or the Bible in general. The lay publisher Michael Glazier rendered a great service, providing an opportunity for younger scholars to publish monographic works and popular commentaries.

The other major phenomenon of the seventies was the widespread practice of Catholic doctoral students in the old centers of biblical studies in America, Harvard, Yale, Duke, Chicago. The transformation which this diverse formation wrought was easy to see in *The New Jerome Biblical Commentary* (Englewood Cliffs NJ: Prentice-Hall, 1990). Here the contributors for the most part had doctorates, and many had them from historically Protestant universities, even if they also had pontifical licences. In this edition the introductory matter to each book was much more frank about authorship and date. The two-source theory of synoptic gospel relationships was favored.

By the mid-nineties three Catholics took important professorships at Yale Divinity School (Harold W. Attridge, John J. Collins, and Adela Yarbro Collins). This caused dismay to many traditional Protestants. On the other hand, such Protestants were consoled by the soft-focus approach to the historical Jesus offered by the former priest-monk professor at Emory University, Luke Timothy Johnson. Johnson and John P. Meier almost came to blows at a meeting of the Catholic Biblical Association, when Johnson, in an address entitled "What Is Catholic in Catholic Biblical Exegesis?" said that the suffering of Pere Marie-Joseph (Albert) Lagrange was in vain and unnecessary because the precritical exegesis defended by those who persecuted him was right after all. Biblical criticism served no useful purpose. There was screaming and outrage. To my knowledge there had never been screaming and yelling at the CBA before. Catholics are taught to venerate the martyrs. We do not like to hear that their suffering was in vain.

Perhaps we may add a few more remarks about the evolution of the Catholic Biblical Association of America over the last 65 years. There is a photograph of an annual meeting in the early fifties, about 70 participants, all male except for Kathryn Sullivan, all clerical and many in habit or soutane. Nowadays it would be hard to tell who is who, because almost all of the 300 participants are in informal summer dress. Not only are there laypeople, sisters, and other Catholic women, but also many Protestants, especially members of the Churches of Christ, a few Jews, and an occasional Eastern Orthodox. In the first decades, the majority who attended were uncreative seminary hacks who came to listen to and pick up a tip or two from a handful of stars. In the seventies the program had to be redesigned so that the many young and ambitious scholars who had recently joined could have a chance to be heard. Imitating the poverty of Christ, we still meet in university student housing, celebrate daily mass or prayer, try to meet with the local ordinary, have a nightly social hour where young and old can meet on a footing of equality. Because of the royalties received from the biblical translations, we have become one of the wealthiest of the learned societies in the humanities in the U.S. So we sponsor scholarships and research grants and digs. We try to invest the money in ways that do not violate a Christian conscience.

Many CBA members are also members of the Society of Biblical Literature, which is larger and less intimate, less fraternal and prayerful, and meets in hotels. Several CBA members have become presidents of the SBL. Besides McKenzie, also Brown, Fitzmyer, and Roland Murphy, as well as Philip King, received this honor.

On the bolder edge of biblical studies we may mention Mark S. Smith's *The Early History of God* (several editions and revisions), John A. Miles' *God: A Biography* (a literary, aesthetic approach to the Old Testament, translated into several languages), and his *The Christ* (mainly on Jesus as a literary character in John). John Dominic Crossan became one of the best known members of the California-based Jesus Seminar, with his work *The Historical Jesus: The Life of a Mediterranean Peasant*. In this work Mark no longer enjoys pride of place as the earliest narrative source. John S. Kloppenborg's *Excavating Q* is another major work emanating from a member of the seminar. John P. Meier's four-volume *Jesus: A Marginal Jew* represents the main work on Jesus by an active member of the CBA.

Two Anglican scholars wrote books before the Council telling Anglicans why they should not become Roman Catholics. I am thinking of Charles Gore and Reginald H. Fuller. Both gave as a main reason the lack of freedom to do honest biblical scholarship in the church of Rome. It may be that that was a good reason back then. But one would not give that as a main reason today, whatever else might be side on the matter of dissuasives to Rome.

I would like to conclude with two final illustrations of progress in U.S. Catholic biblical studies.

Biblical studies progress by the discovery of new comparative material (e.g., the Dead Sea Scrolls, Nag Hammadi, Targum Neofiti, Ebla, Ugarit, Tell El Amarna, inscriptions, papyri) and by the development of new methods of literary analysis: text, source, form, redaction and narrative criticism. American Catholics have participated in all these projects. But sometimes the breakthrough contribution consists in seeing for the first time the historical, literary, and theological connections within a set of facts that has been known for a long time.

There is such a case in the Johannine literature. Every manual will tell you that the gospel according to John has two endings, 20:30–31 and 21:24–25, and that chap. 21 has the air of a later addition. Every manual will also tell you that there are three letters of John that seem close in style to the gospel but with some differences. But no one was sure how the three pieces of the puzzle fit together, chap. 1–20, chap. 21, 1-2-3 John. Then came R. E. Brown. He had written the commentary on the gospel. Now he was working on the epistles. He also took part in important ecumenical dialogues with the Lutherans and taught at a Protestant seminary (Union Theological Seminary near Columbia University). Suddenly he had a flash of insight. Chaps. 1–20 were written by an anonymous, spirit-filled genius who did not believe in canon law, church order, or apostolic authority. Then came a major schism in his community, as many drifted off to join a Gnostic heresy. The community's dismay and anger is visible in the First Letter, wherein the Johannines beat their gums in toothless frustration because they lack the canonical means of discipline, apostolic authority whose clout they even fear. After working through their grief and loss, they emerge from their depression and open negotiations with the apostolic churches in their area. They are now ready to submit to the apostolic staff provided they are allowed to keep their peculiar gospel, dearer to them than life itself. The apostolicals accept this condition but insist that the Johannines add a chapter in which Jesus gives pastoral authority to Peter, symbol of the apostles. This they do.

And so we now understand the right order of the documents: John 1–20, then 1-2-3 John, then John chapter 21.

When Brown presented this historical, theological, and literary hypothesis to the Society of Biblical Literature in San Francisco in December 1977, the three thousand auditors, mostly Protestant professors, gave him a standing ovation that lasted ten minutes. He had given them a biblical precedent for kissing the papal foot. The results were then published, first in the *JBL* 1978, then in the little book *The Community of the Beloved Disciple* (New York: Paulist, 1979). I believe that this is the most original and brilliant hypothesis in biblical studies developed by an American Catholic to this date.

The second illustration of our relative progress is contained in the review article by Scotland's recently departed glory, James Barr, wherein he compares the two complete translations of the Bible that had been published in 1970, viz., the New English Bible and the New American Bible. In the *Heythrop Journal*, Barr severely criticized the British production because of some of its arbitrary and even ridiculous translations. With this he contrasted the sober, sound method of the Americans who submitted their work to their colleagues; a consensus was eventually reached and then it was respected. The publishers of the NEB were furious with Barr. An American Catholic would be a fool to be duped by Barr's praise. He did not really care about the NAB, its virtues or it failings. His article was a cry of sour grapes against the editor of the NEB, Sir Geoffrey Rolles Driver, for his changing and overruling the decisions of the committee in which Barr had worked. It was an inner-Protestant polemic. The American product was stylistically flatfooted in comparison with the British, to mention no other flaws. Barr's valid point was one of method. One man should not be allowed to impose eccentric translations against the decisions of the committee. After Driver's death the British could go back to work and produce the Revised English Bible. And the Americans could continue to revise and improve their own work. Biblical studies are never done, but in this case, on the surface, the American Catholics appeared to have scored a goal. On another occasion, Barr said that Protestants should now avoid biblical theology, whereas it could still do some good for Catholics.

This last remark by Barr echoes a tradition of contempt or disdain or belittlement of Catholic efforts to appropriate the treasures of Scripture as the Word of God to disoriented, suffering, sick and often sinful humanity. The story we have tried to recount as tersely as possible suggests that such disdain is no longer appropriate, so long as one does not exclude the legitimacy of reading the Bible in a community of faith. In such a community the Bible is read to nourish reflection, ethics, prayer and praise, but also hope for the future. Such a reading is compatible with and requires both a minimum of creedal orthodoxy and a creative, interesting use of all the resources of historical and critical scholarship.

FOR FURTHER READING

Fogarty, G. F. *American Catholic Biblical Scholarship: A History from the Early Republic to Vatican II*. San Francisco: Harper & Row, 1989.

Harrington, D. J. "American Catholic Biblical Scholarship and Its Contributions to Today's Research," *Chicago Studies* (forthcoming).

Fitzmyer, J. A. *The Interpretation of Scripture: In Defense of the Historical Critical Method* New York: Paulist, 2008.

Johnson, L. T., and W. S. Kurz. *The Future of Catholic Biblical Scholarship*. Grand Rapids: Eerdmans, 2002). Online review by B. T. Viviano, *RBL* 2003. *Nova et Vetera* 4.1 (2002)

Montagnes, Bernard. *The Life of Father Lagrange*. Translated by B. T. Viviano. New York: Paulist, 2007.

Witherup, R. D. "Raymond Brown and the Question of Catholic Exegesis: The Contribution of a Legacy." Paper read at CBA meeting, 2008.

6

The Dictatorship of Relativism and the Right to a Non-Oppressive Public Religious Culture

Ner Adoni nishmat adam. "The spirit of man is the candle of the Lord" (Prov 20:27 AV). Text beloved of the Cambridge Platonists.

"Trust in the Lord with all thine heart; and lean not unto thine own understanding. In all thy ways acknowledge him, and he shall direct thy paths" (Prov 3:5–6 AV). Text beloved of Christian Evangelicals. Dialectical relationship with Prov 20:27. Cp. Luke 12:57; 1 Cor 6:5.

I

In the spring of 2005 a film was released about the Crusades bearing the significant title, *The Kingdom of Heaven*. The idea of such a film project is surprising because, in the present interfaith context, with such violence in Iraq, Afghanistan, and Palestine, and with wise religious leaders doing everything possible to reduce the tensions between the three Western religions, the subject of the Crusades is too sensitive to be treated as it has been in the past. It is politically incorrect because it opens old wounds instead of healing them. The script had to be laundered and scrubbed until all offensive content was removed. The film was a critical failure because it was not historical enough. But what could remain once the self-censorship and self-castration of the script writers had done their work? Oddly enough, what was left were the ethics of Immanuel Kant (1788). In the words sung by Jimminey Cricket in Walt Disney's version of Collodi's *Pinocchio*, "Let your conscience be your guide." That is, the autonomous self legislates for itself, isolated from God, history, community and divine revelation. By the end of the Crusades film, Jerusalem is reduced to a purely mystical, interior concept; it is in our heart, not in the world.

Our topic today is the dictatorship of relativism and the right to a non-oppressive public religious culture. This topic comes from several recent publications and lectures by Joseph Cardinal Ratzinger, who has since been elected Pope Benedict XVI. The Kantian reductionism presented in the film *Kingdom of Heaven* is echoed in these recent statements. In a Eurocentric way, the cardinal accepts the Kantian way of posing the question as a starting point to describe the present crisis of culture, while criticizing its inadequacy and recognizing its inapplicability elsewhere, i.e., outside of Europe. Already here there are difficulties, since some would say that the problem is not primarily relativism; rather it is nihilism, associated with Nietzsche and Heidegger, since this, combined with social Darwinism, the pseudo-sciences of eugenics, and anthropometrics founded by Sir Francis Galton, is what let to Nazi genocide, biological racism, and the despairing embrace of a twilight of the gods. That is why the new star in the theological firmament, David Bentley Hart, in his mini-Summa, *The Beauty of the Infinite* (2003), fights so hard against nihilism. Others would argue that the cardinal needs a great appreciation of the specifically Anglo-Saxon form of gentle, non-violent liberalism, in the form of John Stuart Mill's *Essay on Liberty* (1859), primarily the right to be eccentric.

In addressing the question of dictatorship of any sort, we should begin with antiquity and acknowledge the pre-Christian quest for freedom, the Greek quest for fearless freedom of thought and for freedom from domination by Asiatic Persia. We recall the struggles of the partly democratic Greek city-states against Persian tyranny, with its servile style of prostration (*proskynesis*) to the king; we also recall the battles of the Greeks at Marathon, Salamis, Thermopylae, and Plataea. We can see a partial analogy in exiled Israel's longing to return to its homeland, led by Ezra and Nehemiah, amazingly, with Persian permission (see Neh 2:1–10). Then came Alexander the Great with his dream of *homonoia*, a cultural concord or harmony, which respected local religions (at first) while integrating them into a common language (Greek) and superior culture. This vision carried him to Egypt, Iran, southern Russian, Pakistan, Afghanistan, and to the very gates of India. Biblically Alexander is memorialized in 1 Macc 1:1–8. Three cultures were able to resist in some measure, but they had to integrate the best of Greek culture in order to do so: the Romans, the Persians, and the Jews. The Jews revolted when their religion was no longer respected by one of the successors of Alexander's generals, Antiochus IV Epiphanes. The Maccabees won a brief respite of independence before they were overrun by the Romans.

The translation of the Hebrew Bible into Greek, the Septuagint, over time, represents a crucial adaptation of the prophetic faith to a broader world.

Already earlier there were interactions between Greek and biblical cultures, as wisdom literature moved alongside biblical prophecy. This only intensified with Philo in Alexandria and the whole New Testament. Nietzsche was right to see Plato received and popularized in the gospel according to John. Aristotle began to be received in the book of Wisdom, both the list of four virtues (8:7) and the analogical knowledge of God through creation (13:5). Zeno, the founder of the Stoic school, was from Cyprus, where the Greeks met Semitic, eastern, ethical wisdom and adapted it to their own culture. Their developments were then discriminatingly received by Matthew, Paul, and the church fathers. This ethical turn led to an understanding of philosophy as a way of life, as a school of holiness and spirituality, and not just a study of nature.

This synthesis between Hellenism and biblical, especially historical, revelation also gave rise to what can be called philosophical or metaphysical theology, and this enabled the three great religions of the Western world to adjust to the crises arising from new scientific developments. I am thinking of authors like Maimonides, Averroes, and Thomas Aquinas. To be sure, in each of the three traditions, there are those who resist this effort at integration. But it is a precious blessing, and where it has been banished, the religion suffers. I am thinking especially of the case of al-Ghazzali. If I am rightly informed, his rejection of Islamic philosophy and his flight to a predominantly mystical approach brought the glories of Islamic civilization to an end, despite his good intentions. He prepared the way, so to speak, for the Ottomans later rejection of the printing press.

Cardinal Ratzinger reminds us that early Christianity, as the religion of the Logos, that is, the divine reason and word in things, aligned itself with the best of ancient pagan philosophy against pagan religions. This is true up to a point, but this solution is a little quick and easy. First, it suggests that early Christianity was identical with the Johannine voice, but this is not the case; Matthew and apocalyptic also have a place. Second, it leaves out much of the Old Testament, the exception being wisdom literature. Third, it omits how both John and Clement of Alexandria tried to integrate the legitimate religious aspirations of classical *pagan religiosity* (not just pagan philosophy), giving their due to both Apollo and Dionysus, to both the mysteries and the Hermetica, and presenting Christianity as the true Gnosis.

Like any responsible theologian today, Cardinal Ratzinger was trying to face the challenge presented by Enlightenment rationalism in its most aggressively relativistic, postmodern form. This is, or should be, a task for thinkers of all three Western religions. It is a big and complex hydra and comes in many forms. We can distinguish political, scientific, and historical aspects of Enlightenment rationalism.

The Political Form of Enlightenment Rationalism

Here I base myself on Hannah Arendt's *On Revolution*, Henry May's *The Enlightenment in America*, and David McCullough's *John Adams*. It is obvious that the political form of the Enlightenment expressed itself in three great revolutions, the American, the French, and the Russian. For Arendt, of these three, only the first was successful and it was so because the leaders respected the results of the decisions taken in the local popular assemblies, where everyone who wanted had a chance to express himself. The other two failed because a single party quickly seized all power and imposed a *dictatorship of that party, the Jacobins in France, the Bolsheviks in Russia*. The damage done then is still in the process of being undone. In the American revolution, the role of the Congregationalist form of religious governance which prevailed in New England is not to be underestimated. Here the Enlightenment was not hostile to religious belief, but rather the fuller expression of some of its purest ideal. When one criticizes the Enlightenment, one must not forget this positive side of it.

The Scientific Form of Enlightenment Rationalism

If one looks up the word rationalism in the *Encyclopedia Britannica* with which I grew up, it will soon be clear that what is meant is the mathematically based physics of Newton, Descartes, Spinoza (a geometrical model of understanding), Leibniz, Wolff. This quantity-based approach to reality ("Whenever possible, count," Galton) is absolutely essential, indispensable and thus legitimate in the areas of engineering and computer science. We want our planes to land safely, our bridges to hold, our emails to be sent. But to understand human beings, as individuals and as social groups, we need something more than mathematics. We need history.

The Historical Form of Enlightenment Rationalism

Historical understanding, learning how human institutions arose through a study of their origins and development, is as legitimate a way of understanding parts of reality as the mathematical. Lessing rejected it as illegitimate; for him the "dirty ditch" between historical particularity and the truths of scientific reason was unbridgeable, because he took as his starting point that all scientifically valid truths must participate in the three qualities of being eternally, necessarily, and universally valid, like propositions of mathematics. This dogmatism blocks all understanding not only of biological evolution of species but of human beings today. That is why there arose, in the providence of God, a so-called Counter-Enlightenment, but which it might be better to call the historical form of Enlightenment reason. Its heroes are Hegel and Schlegel, its forerunners are Vico and Herder and Hamann. Inspired in part by biblical salvation history, but also by Tacitus and Augustine's *City of God*, these thinkers tried to understand the laws and the meaning of the human historical process. Their successors have been Spengler, Toynbee, Fukuyama, and Huntington, among many others. We can learn much from these authors too, but we must also discriminate. For example, Hegel says that *das Wahre ist das Ganze*, the true is the whole, that is, the only thing which enjoys full existence is the totality of social relationships. And that includes the end of the story, the end of history. Yet no one knows that end except God. For humans to talk or act as though they know that end is Promethean pretension. God's total grasp of the whole can be twisted in human hands into totalitarian systems of police control. Until God reveals the final page, human societies must be open societies (Karl Popper), prepared to be surprised. Another example: The Pentagon saw that Fukuyama's triumph would lead to drastic cuts in its budget, so Huntington had to be encouraged to publish *The Clash of Civilizations* to save the budget. This in turn has given us the present unstable situation in Iraq.

So we see that there are three types of Enlightenment rationalism, the political, the mathematical-scientific, and the historical. It is important to maintain an awareness of this diversity, precisely because there is a tendency to reduce the Enlightenment to its mathematical-scientific expression alone. To be sure, scientific Enlightenment has been the most successful, has arrived at the most indisputable results. Yet it does not suffice to understand human historical and political life. We need to continue to wrestle to understand our life together, even if the pessimistic conclusions of some of its representative figures gives it a bad reputation. I am thinking of Edward Gibbon's *The Decline and Fall of the Roman Empire* (1776–1788), and Spengler's *Decline of the West* (1918). People do not like to hear about decline. But this is not the only historical option.

In the last part of the eighteenth century Immanual Kant tried to master the Enlightenment crisis in his three Critiques. In the Preface to the second edition of his *Critique of Pure Reason,* Kant writes the famous sentence: "I have found it necessary to deny *knowledge* in order to make room for *faith*." In some respects, this is one of the un-wisest statements ever made.

Even if one grants that human reason is capable of great and good things (and who does not?), reason is still limited and even in some areas weak and inadequate. We need all the reason and knowledge we can get. This good reason does not eliminate the need for divine help, for divine revelation, and thus the need for human faith in this revelation. This implies no disrespect for reason, only an awareness of its limits, because reason alone does not solve all problems; it often arrives at ambivalent or inconclusive results. So there remain real problems for reason, such as the unceasing need to distinguish between real science and pseudo-science, the need to distinguish between sober and exaggerated claims (e.g., for medical cures). Note the recent Nobel Prize for medicine, which rewarded two Australians for giving a bacteriological explanation and cure for stomach ulcers, after sixty years of mythological misdiagnosis, from which my own grandfather suffered. Reason must continually struggle to distinguish between healthy theories and sick, destructive, hate-filled theories or systems of thought, e.g., certain theories about race, or the glorification of war and violence. Real problems exist for reason also in the realm of religious faith, e.g., conflicting claims about revelation, the Bible, or the Qur'an.

Kant's statement is as wrongheaded as saying that if some plan of life will probably make you happy, e.g., becoming a Dominican, it cannot be God's will for you; you must choose something that will likely make you unhappy, e.g., becoming a Carthusian monk. This way of thinking is wrongheaded because, although we must indeed be prepared to carry our cross in life, even if need be, daily (Matt 16:24; Mark 8:34; Luke 9:23), we do not need to go looking for it or to create it artificially ourselves. Our cross will come to us unbidden, and it will find us. Our task is rather to bear it well when it does come.

In Kant's *Critique of Pure Reason* (1782), the most famous part is where he treats the three antinomies of reason (Smith trans., pp. 369–421). Here he provides an agnostic conclusion to the question whether human reason can attain to certain rational knowledge about the three great issues: the existence of God, the immortality of the soul, and moral freedom of the will. To be sure, these questions are not all on the same level of clarity. In the view of classic, ancient philosophy one was certain of the existence of God (though not about God's nature) and of a certain degree of moral responsibility and thus freedom, whereas the immortality of the soul was less certain. In these matters Kant tried to position himself as a sober moderate. In reality, however, both in his own day and in recent research, Kant was, in metaphysics, probably a pure skeptic, and thus not without reason was known as the German Hume, the *Allzermalmer*. What Kant took away on the level of pure reason, understood as mathematical reason, he gave back as necessary postulates of practical reason. So there was to be no more metaphysics, but an ethics of the categorical imperative, purely formal and individual. This solution was weak on the objective, social, political, ecclesial, specific side of things; it was especially weak on nature, including human nature's need for the truth on the most important issues concerning the meaning and framework of human life. Its ethics for example left itself open to the charge of empty formalism, a charge laid by Max Scheler who so influenced Pope John Paul II. For an Aristotelian Thomist with Hegelian supplement, as is the present writer, the Kantian solution is a form of suspended animation, a constipation of the mind, a perpetual kissing of your sister, and it is in the long run unsustainable. People need a minimum of metaphysics concerning the truth about God and their real but limited moral responsibility. Because Thomas Aquinas was sound on these points, he was embraced by a school of medieval Jewish Thomists who regarded Thomas as the Maimonides of their dreams.

To be sure, there is another side to the Kantian antinomies. A benign interpretation of their role would argue that Kant put them in his *Critique* to protect the human freedom of faith, freedom to be contrary, to say no, to be different. He put them there above all to prevent wars of religion and religious persecutions. On this view, the antinomies are legitimately motivated by bitter experiences like the Thirty Years War (1618–1648), the Revocation of the Edict of Nantes (1685), the Huguenots coming to Kant's Prussia, and the expulsion of the Protestants from Salzburg when Kant was a boy, in 1731. On this view, the antinomies are not to be taken as real descriptions of the state of reason or of the non-knowability of the existence of God. They are rather to be understood as tactics for tolerance, as pleas for religious peace and for non-coercion in religion. In this sense their deeper intention can be gratefully received.

Kant's philosophy is an almost pure expression of the time and thought of Frederick II of Prussia: skeptical, cold, rationalist in a mechanical sense, unhappily celibate, anti-Pietist. It can serve as an Immodium of the mind, as an anti-diarrhetic, as a lesson in humility and finitude, an essay in restraint for those given to too wild speculation, to free association taken as real science. But it is not an adequate description of the real capacities of the human mind. Paul Tillich once said that Kant built a prison for the human mind. Those who took him seriously but wanted to break out of the prison appealed to his third Critique, of Judgment, as opening windows in the prison. Tillich said that this was not true, but that Kant only painted pictures of windows on the walls of the airless prison. The dictatorship of relativism begins in the metaphysical prison.

So then, one should be a "rationalist" in matters of mathematics, physics, and especially engineering, but not in other matters, especially not in human affairs, or in matters of historical interpretation. Biology, music, and ethics are curious mixtures of mathematics and other elements, whether evolution, or feeling, or historicity. Rationalism, in the classical sense of a mathematical-physical approach to the world, has a narrower range than human *reason*, which can also be applied to other areas of life, but not mathematically applied. A hundred years ago one could still appeal to "incontrovertible historical facts" and distinguish these facts from historical interpretation. For example, one thought it was a *fact* that Napoleon was defeated at the battle of Waterloo. But advanced thinkers no longer feel that there is any context-independent history. At Harvard, H. V. White has defended the radical view that history is a narrative construct, a verbal artifact and thus hardly distinct from fiction. Without a dose of common sense, we really are in the coils of relativism.

At this point it may be helpful to distinguish different concepts of reason. We can begin with Paul Tillich's fourfold analysis of reason into universal, critical, intuitive, and technical. Universal reason is the *logos* of early Greek philosophy and the prologue of St. John's gospel. The Greeks asked the question: how is the human mind able to grasp nature? Their answer was that the *logos*, the universal form and principle of everything created, is both in nature as a whole and in the human mind. The word is meaningful when we use it because it can grasp nature or reality. The opposite is also true. Nature/reality grasps the human mind, so that we can speak to and about nature. This logos concept of reason appears in Christian theology as a first principle. It is a principle of order and structure in all realities. As John says, "All things were made through him (i. e., the Logos), and without him was not anything made that was made" (John 1:3 RSV). The Logos is the principle through which God created the world. This is a fundamental insight of classical theology. Reality and mind both have a logos structure. As a structure of reality and mind, logos includes our power of knowledge, our ethical awareness or conscience, and our aesthetic intuition. These are all expressions of the logos in us. Reason or logos is thus in the tree, as well as in the person who names the tree and perceives the essence of treeness which reappears in every individual tree. This is possible because there is a structure in the tree which we are able to grasp with our minds, and since this is mutual, our minds are grasped by the structure.

Universal Reason

The universe has been created by an intelligent power, the divine ground, and since the world has been intelligently built, intelligence can grasp it. The world has a structure. This is equally valid in philosophy as well as in theology. This logos structure helps the church to hold together the doctrines of creation and redemption, and to avoid the Gnostic heresy of Marcion who opposed the Gods of the two Testaments, and doubted the fundamental goodness of creation, despite the ravages of sin. This remains a permanent temptation, under different guises.

Critical Reason

In its name the French revolution suppressed the free expression of religious life and beheaded the king and queen and even the best scientist of France, Antoine Lavoisier. Here was a revolutionary reason that was getting out of hand, very passionate to the point of unreason in its fight against the social control of the hereditary nobility and their brothers, the bench of bishops. Yet the leaders of the revolution and its chief beneficiaries were the upper middle class, the men of wealth and business. They applied to their affairs the calculating reason of the bookkeeper, the bottom line pioneered by Pierre de la Ramee (1515–1572), Ramus.

Intuitive Reason

We can relate this first to the Platonic perception of the essences in things, as well as the higher essences or values, the Good, the True, the One, Beings, and for some, the Beautiful. In the twentieth century this approach is associated with Husserl's phenomenology. One begins with as precise a description as possible of the object of study, whether Agassiz's fish or a passage from the gospels (J. Murphy-O'Connor). Eventually one sees the universal in the particular, and sees the novelist's truth, expressed by Hegel thus: Neither the universal is worth anything nor the particular, but only the concrete universal. The study of examples leads to broader concepts and to common meanings.

Technical Reason

The predominant meaning of reason today is technical. It analyzes reality into its smallest elements, and then construes out of them other, larger things. In this process of construction it uses precise mathematical measurements and calculations based on them. The result is the manufacture of tools. The success of technology, especially in the last decade or two, of information technology, is so great that it runs the risk of overwhelming all other forms of reason, not to mention the elimination of emotion and of religious authority. We all want good science and we rejoice in its progress, especially in medicine, communications and the ease of travel, while we worry about the long-term ecological effects of nuclear power and arms. We are fascinated by the bacteriological solutions to stomach ulcers and the chemical solutions to psychological problems like depression, while we worry about the reduction of everything to chemistry (Peter Kramer on depression; the 2005 Nobel Prize in Medicine). In our quandaries, we can be inspired by the religious piety and reverence of such great men of science as Newton, Priestly, Faraday, Pasteur, and Einstein. They were often motivated by the desire to understand the plan of God.

Tillich's list of four senses of reason is loosely structured in a chronological order. If we ignore that dimension we can reduce his list to two: 1. Universal-intuitive or Logos-historical reason, and 2. Critical-technical or mathematical-physical reason. So long as we accept that both senses really belong to human reason, there is no necessary conflict between religious faith and reason, no necessary dictatorship of relativism. An example to the contrary is the movement from reason to thinking to a form of prayer or meditation, present in all religions. John Macquarrie has well written that prayer as thinking should be characterized by four qualities: it should be *passionate* thinking, which integrates emotions with reason and searches for values and ideals beyond the bare facts. It should be *compassionate* thinking, which makes us sensitive to the needs and sufferings of others. It should be *responsible* thinking in which we are willing to answer to God for our actions. Finally prayer should be *thankful* thinking, "the lifting up of our hearts in thanksgiving for whatever is good in the creation and for whatever promises of something still better are held out to us."

The Kantian fear of religiously motivated violence and wars of religion has led many modern societies to remove religious expression as far as possible from public life and visibility. This leads to what Richard J. Neuhaus has called *the Naked Public Square*. The prohibition of the kipa or Sikh turban or Muslim veil (hijab) or monastic habit or showy cross is a trivial matter in comparison with the hesitation to acknowledge religious foundations and values in constitutions and legislation. This is the deeper source of anguish of Neuhaus and the Pope.

Concluding this first part, I would like to make just two points. The first is that we should try to see an analogy between religious conflicts and ethnic or nationalist conflicts. Many modern wars are due to over-heated, hate-filled appeals to national distinctiveness. Yet ethnic teasing has been a part of human nature since the dawn of time. I regard it as something as natural as children whining against their parents. No law could or should try to forbid it so long as it takes a gentle or humorous form, e.g., what the Greeks and Romans said against one another in antiquity, or the Swedes and the Finns today, or the French and the Belgians. But the teasing must not turn violent. So too it is normal for each religion to think itself as best or truest, and this is fine, so long as these claims to superiority do not turn violent.

My second point is that we can learn a lot from the difference between an abstract universal rationalism which seeks to impose itself by revolutionary force, and the biblical way of arriving at a universal perspective, message, and impact that begins with an individual (Adam), a clan chief (Abraham), a people (Moses), a nation (David and Solomon), a little kingdom of Israel; then with the prophets Deutero-Isaiah and Daniel in vision, and Jesus and Paul in mission, this universal perspective moves towards the kingdom *of God*, which embraces all peoples, nations, and languages on planet earth and in heaven. The biblical pattern respects organic development through the education of the human race (Lessing) by means of salvation history.

II

Now a few words on the toughest nut of the three great Western religions to crack and to digest, Islam. The first major Western thinker to face the challenge of Islam was St. John Damascene. He thought of the Muslims as Ishmaelites, descendents of Ishmael, and their religion was for him a Christian heresy. Voltaire, in his play *Mahomet,* had another view: Islam was the primordial religion, a return to prehistoric simplicity. It was what all religions had in common, only more so. Thus Islam can strike some as arid and rationalist. A third view, to which I subscribe, is held by Adolf von Harnack, Adolf Schlatter, Hans Joachim Schoeps, Claus Schedl, and Hans Küng. Schoeps thinks that Mohammed received a form of Christianity that was heavily influenced by Jewish Christianity. This is so on the points of the True Prophet, of strict monotheism (though Jesus is the Messiah born of the virgin Mary), of certain practices: ritual washings, circumcision, prayer in a certain direction, food laws. Schoeps says: "Though it may not be possible to establish exact proof of the connection, the indirect dependence of Mohammed on sectarian Jewish Christianity is beyond any doubt. This leaves us with a paradox of truly world-historical dimensions: the fact that while Jewish Christianity in the Church came to grief, it was preserved in Islam and, with regard to some of it driving impulses at least, it has lasted till our own time." To this I would add that, if this be true, the Muslims are our long lost brothers, who represent the other side of the New Testament, Matthew and James. The struggle described in Galatians between the pro-circumcision and non-circumcision parties remains a living issue. Further, if we could come to terms with them, it would be indeed the squaring of the circle, the times of universal restoration, the *apokatasis panton*, mentioned in Acts 3:21.

We are far from that point. Islam's initial thrust into Western Europe was halted by Charles Martel at the battle of Tours/Poitiers in 732. Then it was the turn of the Franks to disturb the Muslims in that long episode known as the Crusades, 1096–1290. The Muslims were gradually pushed out of Europe in a series of struggles, marked by the expulsion from Spain completed in 1492, the naval battle of Lepanto 1571, the lifting of the sieges of Vienna in 1531 and 1683, and the great push down the Balkans begun by Prince Eugene of Savoy in 1697, the battle of Zenta. This long history has left lingering reserves in the populations of Europe, particularly in Croatia and Austria, about the eventual admission of Turkey into the European Union, and about the possibilities of a deeper reconciliation. In my own limited experience it is difficult to engage in dialogue with traditional Muslims because there is so little sense of the historicity of truth in the Qur'an or in the subsequent theological development. The Qur'an is dominated by non-narrative literary genres, sapiential poetry, law, prophecy of a sort, and praise, but not history. There are timid starting points of historical criticism of the Qur'an, but these remain marginal to the main leaders and to the people. In addition, there are the four difficult traditions of Islam. 1. Dhimmitude. In a Muslim land non-Muslims are tolerated as second class citizens; *dhimmi* means "tolerated guest." They must pay a special headtax and wear identifying insignia. 2. The idea of the West as the *dar el-harb*, the land of war, the Westerner as the *harbi*, the enemy alien. 3. The theme of *jihad*, which is traditionally interpreted as holy war, but is now being interpreted in the Sufi spirit as spiritual training and ascetical exercises. Scoffers say, this only shows you can do anything with exegesis. But exegesis plays a valuable role in each of our traditions. 4. *Waqf.* This is a feature of Islamic law which regulates endowments, pious bequests, and charitable foundations. Thus a devout Muslim could leave a piece of property to the mosque at his death.

Once bequeathed, these properties are inalienably dedicated. These *evkaf* (Turkish) or *wakovia* (Greek) involved substantial revenues. They financed some of the masterpieces of Muslim architecture. But the property was often badly managed by the *ulema* (religious authorities). *Waqf* estates covered about a fifth of the arable land of the Ottoman empire. The temporal sovereigns coveted this land. Sultan Mahmud II, the Reformer, brought the *waqf* land under state control in the 1820s. But when the Shah of Iran, Reza Pahlavi, tried to do the same in his country in the 1960s and '70s, it led to his overthrow. In Jerusalem, the esplanade in front of the Western Wall is *waqf* property, so its use for other purposes is an offence. These four themes of Islamic law deserve further study during this coming year. In connection with the idea of *waqf* is Osama bin Ladin's objection to the stationing of American troops on sacred Saudi soil. The Qur'an says: "Whoever kills a human being, except as punishment for murder or other villainy in the land, shall be regarded as having killed all mankind." This verse forbids violent aggression, but the exceptive clause is easily used by militants as a loophole.

Other difficulties include the situation of women, as well as a long history of Muslim refutations of Christian "heresy," especially the doctrine of the Trinity and the gospel according to John. This history of polemics does not help. Another problem is the small number of translations of modern books into Arabic. Beyond the image of an Islamic monolith, there are debates *within* Islam. And practice can vary from place to place. There are countries in West Africa which have developed a serene modus vivendi between Muslims and Christians. In Saudi Arabia the educated young people chaff under the restrictions imposed by the religious police and are said to be ripe for revolt, even though they have Dubai as a safety valve.

The failure of Christian mission to Islam over so many centuries tells me that this mission is not God's will. We should, I think, strive for a situation of "separate but equal" treatment before the civil law, for an end to proselytism on both sides, and for structures of mutual respect and confidence building: if there are mosques in Rome, there should be churches in Riyad and seminaries in Turkey (Khalki). Western aggression does not help, nor does Twin-Towers-style terrorism. John Hick's inclusivism is unlikely to prevail. Rather, the religions must be allowed to express themselves fully, in public, but without violence. This may seem merely a naïve and pious wish, but we should at least try to be clear about the kind of solution we are looking for: not proselytism, but witness.

III

On Judaism I have only one or two brief points to make. The main one is that it will be helpful if Christians get used to thinking of the post–AD 70 synagogue as the "little sister" of the Church. This idea was developed by Origen in his commentary on the Song of Songs, esp. chap. 8:8 "we have a little sister, and she has no breasts." This idea has been taken up in modern times by Erik Peterson and Arnold Ehrhardt. To be sure, there was a pre-Christian Judaism that dates back to the Persian period, the return of the exiles from Persia/Babylonia to Jerusalem under Ezra and Nehemiah, permitted by the good king Cyrus. To this extent, Pope John Paul II was right when he visited the synagogue of Rome and greeted the assembled Jews as the "elder brothers" of the Church. The truth in Ehrhardt's position is however this. After the burning of the Temple AD 70, Jews lost their institutional center and had to find another. The Jewish Christians found theirs around James in Caesarea Maritima and Pella, the Gentile Christians eventually in Ephesus and Rome and much later in Constantinople. The heirs of the Pharisees, the rabbis, found theirs in the study of the Law and in deeds of loving kindness, in Jamnia/Jabneh, Tiberias, and Usha, and in the Babylonian academies of Sura, Pumbeditha, and Nehardea. The man who made the difference was, on this view, Akiba. He shaped rabbinic Judaism in a consciously text-bound, Hebrew-studying, anti-Septuagintal way, as a construct that was essentially contrary to Christianity, and he did this before his death as a martyr in AD 135, that is, well after Christianity had been launched. In this sense and in this chronology, the Akiban synagogue is the little sister of the Church. And one does not beat up on or persecute one's little sister, even if one disagrees with her. Rather, one tries to protect her from bullies. This is the interfaith tactical advantage in the Ehrhardt view.

Today, in the view of the Jewish scholar Ernst Ludwig Ehrlich, the Roman Catholic church, since Vatican II, with its *Nostra Aetate* (1965) and subsequent documents, has said and done everything that Jewish religious leaders could reasonably ask to provide a good basis for dialogue and friendly relations. The remaining concerns are that these policies be made more widely known, so that they can trickle down to all relevant members of the Church and be put into practice. On the other hand, Jewish leaders are dismayed by the rise of new forms of anti-Semitism. They are particularly concerned by policies of the World Council of Churches (Geneva) and some Protestant denominations to disinvest in Jewish companies.

IV

Turning to Christianity, we can understand it as the divinely guided expansion of the one God of Israel to all the nations, announced by Deutero- and Trito-Isaiah, with the extension of the kingdom of David in a new way to the kingdom of God for all people, nations, and tongues (Dan 7:13–14). This was the center of Jesus' preaching and hope, and this hopeful message was then spread beyond the borders of historic Israel through Paul and his many collaborators. The mission was universal, for the Jesus of the four gospels and for Paul, open to all. But today I think we have learned that it is not part of God's plan that there should be a direct proselytizing of Jews or Muslims, a direct targeting of them, as in the *Judenmissionen* of the nineteenth century. The Jews and Muslims already share with us faith in the same God, and they venerate the same patriarch, Abraham. The religion of Christianity in its lawfree form, as found in the letter to the Galatians, is full of the leading of the Holy Spirit; it is light and airy, a refreshment to burdened consciences, open to the ever new and to changing circumstances. But there is a danger of a mere empty formalism in ethics. It is not true, I think, that all you need is love. At least males need more specifics, something like the Sermon on the Mount, which includes the Decalogue, the love commands and the Golden Rule. Liberal Christianity is often criticized by Evangelicals for it normlessness, its *Uferlosigkeit* (banklessness), a concern I share. We need a sense of structure, of balance and limits, an awareness that there are things/actions that are intrinsically evil. We also need to recover a sense of modesty, such as was well expressed by St. Gregory Nazianzen: "We shall share in the pasch, for the present certainly in what is still a figure, though a plainer one than the ancient pasch. (This pasch of the old law was, I venture to say, a more obscure figure, a figure of a figure.) In a short time, however, our sharing will be more perfect and less obscure, when the Word will drink the pasch with us new in the kingdom of his Father, revealing and teaching what he has now shown in a limited way. For what is now being made known is ever new."

V

Let me conclude with a few more tangled thoughts. The Bible and our traditions have long wrestled with the tensions of universalism and particularity. An example is the sweeping vision of a pilgrimage of all the nations to Zion, described in Isa 2:1–4; Mic 4:1–3; and the more chastened, resigned realism of Mic 4:5, "though all the peoples walk each in the names of its gods, we will walk in the name of the LORD our God forever and ever." Another set of tensions concerns what is the greatest sin. It is usually said that in Judaism, as in the Reformed tradition within Christianity, the greatest sin is idolatry. For most Christians it would consist in the lack of charity (Matt 25:31–46; 1 Pet 4:8, 1 Cor 13:1–13). But for Jesus the unforgivable sin is the sin against the Holy Spirit (Mark 3:29), traditionally interpreted as final despair or impenitence (St. Augustine, Sermon 72), but probably based on the Decalogue (Exod 20:7), "you shall not swear falsely by the name of the LORD your God; for the LORD will not pardon one who swears falsely by his name." So a certain truthfulness in relation to God, the highest principle of life and conscience, becomes the decisive matter. Yet in 2 Kgs 5:18–19, Naaman asks pardon of the prophet Elisha for bowing in the temple of the Syrian god Rimmon, and Elisha says to him mildly and tolerantly, "Go in peace."

So we are back with the central issue of relativism and the rights of truth and, I would add, the fear of history. On the one hand, I do not believe we can attain a truthful understanding of human reality without the study of history. On the other hand, we cannot live humanly and calmly if our religious rules and practices can be lightly changed from day to day. I find some consolation in the three-speed scheme of Edward Schillebeeckx. He tracks the speeds (as in phonograph records at the three speeds: 78 revolutions per minute, 45 revolutions, 33 1/3 revolutions). There is ephemeral history as we find it in newspapers and fashion magazines; there is conjunctural history which works over several centuries; lastly there is structural history which moves across millennia at a glacial pace. "Even after a successful political and social revolution, eighty percent of the old, rejected structures 'recur' in one way or another . . . basic structures survive even the most radical of revolutions."

The second part of my title runs: "the right to a non-oppressive *public* religious culture." This right is already acquired in most countries of the West, on the level of liturgical worship, religious holy days, even street processions. But this is not so clear in education. The United States of America began a process of public secularization in 1971 with the Supreme Court decision of Lemon *v.* Kurtzman which halted Bible reading and prayer in public schools. Religious parents have fought for tax vouchers, for their educational taxes to go to their own religious schools. The latest book on church-state relations in American, by Noah Feldman, is prepared to revise Lemon *v.* Kurtzman in many ways, but remains adamant against school vouchers, perhaps because of his family connections with public school teacher's unions. In France the injustice to religious schools remains great. With the European Union France, because of its tradition inherited from its deeply flawed revolution, remains the great obstacle to a public historical recognition of the role of religion in the European Constitution. This bad tradition goes back, I think, to King Francis I, who supported the Lutheran reformation in Germany to keep Germany weak and divided, while fiercely persecuting Protestants in France to keep France strong and united. He sowed the wind and France (and Europe with it) has reaped the whirlwind. Cf. Gal 6:7. In other parts of Europe there is a move to transform university faculties of theology into faculties of religious studies or of the history of religions.

I would like to end on a note of hope based on the only opera Beethoven ever wrote. He has become a kind of patron saint of Europe, providing, with Schiller, its Union hymn, "The Ode to Joy," originally the Ode to Freedom. A great friend of Jerusalem, the late Sir Peter Ustinov, wrote a play about him, *Beethoven's Tenth,* which presents Beethoven as a deeply religious, God-fearing, Christian man, whose spiritual guides were Johann Michael Sailer and Saint Clement Maria Hofbauer. In Beethoven's opera *Fidelio,* Leonore, just after finding her husband in chains in a dark dungeon and crying out against the tyrant *Abscheulicher!* Monster!, sings a beautiful aria, asking hope to come ("Komm, Hoffnung, komm") and then gives a ringing affirmation of the power of love to overcome injustice and cruelty.

Our hope as believers is that both the love of God for us, our love for God, and our love for one another and for all human beings, when supported by a metaphysical minimum of truth about God and our moral responsibility and by a notion of the good, can provide a sound basis for peace and justice.

7

The Dogma of the Prophetless Time in Judaism

Does Prophecy Cease with Christ for Christians? Some Explorations

It is an odd fact that both inside of and outside of the Jewish Bible around the time of Jesus there is a complaint that prophecy has ceased, and this occurs at a time when many claimed to be prophets. For example, Ps 74:9 complains: "We do not see our signs; there is no longer any prophet, and there is none among us who know how long." This complaint can take the even stronger form of saying that the Holy Spirit has left Israel at some point: "When Haggai, Zechariah and Malachi, the last prophets, had died, the Holy Spirit disappeared from Israel, yet they [the Israelites?] were allowed to hear the *Bath Qol* [literally, the daughter of a voice; it means, a faint whisper from God] (Tosefta *Sota* 13:2). The rabbinical passage adds: "Hillel deserved to be a prophet, but his generation was unworthy of this."

This problem could fittingly be addressed by a historian or by a systematic theologian (Jewish or Christian) or even by a canon lawyer, because the implications are extensive, and the debate occurs in both Jewish and Christian sources. Here it will be addressed by a professor of New Testament, fortunate to have been a colleague of the honoree, Adrian Schenker, for eleven years. This essay will, however, stray outside of the New Testament boundaries.

A new start on this old question was made by the late Ragnar Leivestad of Norway, in a helpful, short, dense essay of 1971. He distinguishes between a relatively late rabbinic "dogma" of the end of prophecy (as in Tosefta *Sota* 13:2, already quoted) and an earlier conviction that there was an interim period (*Zwischenzeit*, interregnum) without prophets. At this point we need to note that Mishnah *Sota* (9:9–15), in contrast to the Tosefta, is rather cautious. It contains what is often called a "rabbinic apocalypse." It reviews Jewish spiritual history from the viewpoint of decline. Yet it is careful *not* to say that there are no more prophets, no more presence of the Holy Spirit. And it ends on an upbeat note: the hope of a restoration through the Messiah.

The conviction that there is an interim period without prophets resolves itself, upon closer examination, into three distinct motifs. (1) The sense that there is a dearth of prophets, a famine of hearing the words of the Lord (Amos 8:11), through prophets. (2) There is a longing for an endtime prophet. (3) There is a polemic against bad or false prophets. These three motifs could have eventually contributed to the deeschatologized, more absolute or "dogmatic" Formulation found in the Tosefta, the more so when combined with unhappy historical experiences like the failed revolts of AD 66–74 and 132–135. These three motifs are all already found in the Hebrew Bible. (1) The lament at the lack of prophecy: besides Ps 74:9, also Lam 2:9; LXX Dan 3:38; 2 *Baruch* 85. (2) The expectations of a future prophet: Deut 18:15, 18 (and its echoes in Qumran literature); 1 Macc 9:27; 4:44–46; 14:41; cf. 2 Macc 2:1–8. (3) The negative image of prophecy: Zech 13:2–6, where it is in parallel with idols; Neh 6:12–14; 2 Kgs 9:11; Hos 2:17; Zeph 1:4; Amos 7:14; 1 Kgs 18:28; Jer 23:9–22. The absence of prophets was at times felt as an abandonment by God, as a sign of God's displeasure or wrath, as a misfortune. One has the sense that we are dealing with a set of literary-theological *topoi*, with a mood, not with sociological-historical exactitudes. This suspicion is increased by the variety of views on who was the last prophet. "Some rabbinic texts . . . allude to the loss of the holy spirit usually in connection with the Babylonian Exile. Its presence is . . . one of the distinctions between the first and second temples, a position consistent with the tradition that Jeremiah was the last of the prophets." For Josephus, the last prophet was Ezra; since then there have only been false prophets, swindlers (*Contra Apionem* 1:8; *Bellum Judaicum* 1:68; *Antiquitates* 13:299). For the Tosefta, as we have seen , the last three prophets were Haggai, Zechariah, Malachi. For the anti-Montanist Christian Filastrius, the last prophet was John the Baptist. For the modern Old Testament scholar Claus Westermann, "prophecy . . . belongs to a definite period of time and is bound to this period. It is the period of time from the formation of the state to the loss of statehood in Israel—thus, almost exactly the time of the kingdoms. Prophecy is to be defined as a transitional stage in which the speech of the messenger is the form designated for the indirect revelation of God. God speaks no longer to the king, no longer directly in signs, or from the lot-casting oracle, and no longer by passing sentence upon the whole nation; God sends messengers." This amounts to the view that prophecy ceased with Jeremiah. If Westermann is right the Tosefta is too generous. Not even Haggai, Zechariah or Malachi would qualify as prophets, not to mention Daniel.

Harnack was probably right to think of a paradox: there were two simultaneously existing parallel tracks. One track consisted of those who thought that prophecy had ceased at some point. The other track lived with the continuing experience of prophets in its midst.

Yet for some time now some scholars, e.g., the Bultmann school or experts in the pseudepigrapha, have chaffed at the limits of the canon. They plead for an equal treatment of early Christian writings like the letters of St. Ignatius of Antioch, or, more recently, Gnostic works like the *Gospel of Thomas*.

On the other hand, and apart from that question of the close of the canon, many theologians are reluctant to legislate for God, to set limits to what God can or cannot do. It makes no theological sense to say that the Holy Spirit has ceased to operate (although one could still think of *degrees* of activity of the Spirit, of more or less manifest, striking, signs of the Spirit's presence, of different senses or expressions of prophecy). Indeed, Christians, who profess that Christ "will come again in glory to judge the living and the dead" (Nicene Creed), cannot in principle exclude that, when Christ comes, he will say something. That "something" would then count as new biblical revelation. To be sure, managerial types, bureaucrats of synagogue, church, or theological faculties, want a tidy, limited, body of material on the basis of which to administer their respective institutions: a biblical canon, a code of canon law, Shulhan Arukh, a Book of Concord, a Manual of Discipline. Otherwise, the task of governance becomes unmanageable. But "the spirit blows where it will" (John 3:8). It is not easy to give orders to or to tame the Holy Spirit, the irrepressible. As Amos says: "My Lord GOD has spoken; who can but prophecy?" (Amos 3:8b; cf. Jer 20:9).

Up to this point we have been raising issues, pawing the ground, setting the stage, leaving the reader with the impression that the problems are insoluble. Up to a point, this may be so. The issues point to mysteries we must live with. But not everything is equally unclear. Some light may emerge. The remainder of this essay will first report on a recent debate between two Jewish scholars (2.), then present the question from the viewpoints and data available in the New Testament (3.), and draw some conclusions in the form of terse theses (4.).

Religious authors have been saying for millennia that prophecy has ceased, as other religious authors have been presupposing for millennia that prophets emerge and speak whenever God raises them up, and that this occurs from time to time. Among the rabbis and among professional students of the Hebrew Bible like Wellhausen and Westermann (already cited), the older consensus view was that prophecy had largely ceased soon after the return from exile. Since the Second World War another thesis has been proposed: prophecy continued among the Jews but was unloved by the rabbis who often regarded it as illegitimate. (We will take the 1989 article by F. E. Greenspahn as the sharpest recent expression of this viewpoint.) But in 1996 B. D. Sommer wrote a learned defense of the older view. For him the Jews in the Second Temple period viewed prophecy as having ceased. The old consensus holds, is right, and has not been dislodged.

As we enter the fray, let us first note that P. W. Barnett has isolated in Josephus what he calls six Jewish "sign" prophets for the period AD 36–70. Barnett suggests that the six were influenced by hopes of a prophet like Moses (Deut 18:15–19), and by hopes of a world ruler messiah (based on Balaam's prophecy in Num 24:17). Further, the six sign prophets were stimulated to rise up, not only by these biblical texts and by the worsening political circumstances, but also by the recent prior examples of John the Baptist and Jesus, with as a goal *forcing* God to bring in redemption and freedom. That means concretely the restoration of Jewish sovereignty in the Land of Israel, the end of Roman rule there, the coming of the messianic age, the kingdom of God on earth (Dan 7:13–14). (Barnett does not mention the Maccabean model.) Josephus regards the six sign prophets as charlatans, but Barnett judges them to have been sincere in their intentions. For our purposes, the point is that Josephus mentions six Jewish prophetic figures after Jesus and before the fall of Jerusalem, despite his stated view that prophecy became irregular or ceased with Ezra. That such figures would not be lovingly remembered by the rabbis after the troubles of 70 and of 135 is perfectly understandable, but not decisive in proving that all Jews were convinced that prophecy had ended after Ezra.

Greenspahn's conclusion is that Jews "living in the post biblical period considered prophecy ... as possible ... [T]he rabbinic teaching on this subject does not reflect a general consensus." Greenspahn offers a number of arguments for this view. He notes that long before the exile, in the days of Eli and Samuel (at least according to the Late Source), "the word of God was rare ... ; there was no frequent vision" (1 Sam 3:1). (To this we may add as a partial parallel: "For lack of vision a people lose restraint" [Prov 29:18].) In Nehemiah (6:7–14) there are claims and counterclaims about the hiring of prophets, an indication that they existed, even if they were not regarded as always upright. More important from a theological point of view is the description of the beneficial works of Wisdom: "in every generation she passes into holy souls and makes them friends of God, and prophets" (Wis 7:27b). This verse reflects a Hellenistic Jewish accent on eternal continuity in the divine activity. It is a more optimistic view than one that admits that there are periods without prophets, periods of famine (as punishment for sin, Amos 8:11; Mic 3:5–7; Lam 2:9). The optimistic and pessimistic views are not necessarily logically incompatible, since the prophetic manifestation could be real yet discreet in a given period, due to its non-reception by the powers, due to hardness of heart. But the accent is different.

First Maccabees furnishes support for both camps. Twice the book introduces clauses with *mechri* or *heis* (both mean *until*): "until there should come a prophet to tell them what to do with them" (1 Macc 4:42–46); "until a trustworthy prophet should arise" (1 Macc 14:41). This last verse could be read to imply that there were often *untrustworthy* prophets; trustworthy ones were rarer. Moreover, the preceding part of the verse stands in tension with this concluding part: they "decided that Simon should be their leader and high priest *for ever*." This tension is resolved as follows. The office was to be hereditary in Simon's family, but since this was an act of the nation rather than of God, a trustworthy prophet might annul or confirm the decision. It is a sort of eschatological proviso: "unless and until God disposes otherwise." On the other hand, another verse could be read to mean that prophecy had ceased altogether. "Thus there was great distress in Israel, such as had not been since the time that prophets did not appear (*aph' hes hemeras ouk ophthe prophetes*) to them" (1 Macc 9:27). Such a reading is probably but not necessary. The absence of prophets could also be understood as an aspect of their distress and punishment, to be followed by better times, times of mercy and a new outpouring of the prophetic spirit (e.g., Joel 3:1; Eng. 2:28). It is little wonder that the conflict between Greenspahn and Sommer becomes acute over this verse.

> As for Josephus, besides his view that prophecy became irregular after Artaxerxes, and his "sign prophets" treated by Barnett, he also held that John Hyrcanus had the power of prophecy. (*J.W.* 1.2.8 §68; *Ant.* 13.10 §300)

From a Christian theological perspective, Greenspahn's effort to correct his predecessor E. E. Urbach is of even greater interest. Urbach knew that two church fathers had used this issue polemically against the rabbis: you lost the Holy Spirit *because* you denied that Jesus was the Messiah. Justin Martyr argues that the Spirit ceased among Jews and was given to all Christian believers. Origen goes further. There are four signs that God has rejected non-Christian Jews: the losses of the Temple, of the divine presence (Shekhinah), of the land, of prophecy. (This list may be a borrowing from similar Jewish lists.) Urbach understands the rabbinic early dating of the cessation of prophecy as motivated by the search for a reply to the Christian polemicists. In effect, the reply would run: "We did not lose the Holy Spirit because we denied that Jesus was the Christ; we lost the Spirit centuries *before* Jesus came." Greenspahn understandably judges this motivation as improbable, because (a) it makes too great a concession to the the Christians; (b) the rabbis could have based themselves on pre-Christian traditions such as 1 Macc 9:27. They did not need the provocation of the Christians to arrive at their view. Greenspahn holds rather that the rabbis had a sense that the age of revelation had passed. But they still felt in touch with the divine through prayer, miracles, and Bath Qol. Many thought that prophecy was still available. But they claim that while it is still available, leadership was now with the sages. This is the sense of the rabbinic chain of tradition: "Moses received the Torah from Sinai, and he delivered it to Joshua, and Joshua to the elders (Josh 24:31; Judg 2:7), and the elders to the prophets, and the prophets delivered it to the men of the Great Synagogue" (*m. 'Abot* 1:1). The rabbis were the heirs of these men. The prophets were a stage, a link in the chain. Late prophets may exist, but their status is diminished. The rabbis disliked their competition. They preferred voting in the academy, a routinized charism. Prophets could be viewed as a threat to the social order and, to that extent, as illegitimate. This is analogous to the Great Church's rejection of Montanism, or to Mohammed's view of himself as the "seal of the prophets" (Qur'an 33:41).

B. D. Sommer fights fiercely to argue for a negative answer to the precise question: "Did Jews in the Second Temple period tend to accept the possibility that God still communicated with the Jewish people by speaking directly to certain individuals?"

He argues this first by invoking some of the same texts we have already discussed, e.g., 1 Macc 9:27; 2 *Apoc. Bar.* 85:1, 3, as well as *b. Sanh* 11a, repeated in *b. Yoma* 99b, *b. Sota* 48b, *y. Sota* 9:13; *t. Sota* 13:3 (quoted at the beginning of this article); *Cant. Rab.* 8:11; *S. 'Olam Rab.* 86b; the examples in Josephus.

Then Sommer analyzes the phenomenon of post-exilic prophecy with some care. His thesis is that there was a decline in prophecy, or a transformation, which amounts to the end of the earlier forms of divine communication. When exceptions to this thesis occur, they are not part of a *continuity* of prophecy, but revivals of the dormant; the examples are really non-prophetic. The belief of the Jews at the time was that prophecy was waning. Evidence of prophecy among the *rabbis* is not convincing.

Often Zechariah is not addressed by God but by an angelic intermediary or by dreams (e.g., Zech 2:1–14; 4:1; 3:5. This last verse is disputed.

In the Septuagint the angel, as a member of the divine council, orders a diadem; in the Hebrew text the prophet himself orders it ("I" versus "he"). The context here favors the Septuagint.

Sommer distinguishes between prophecy *continuing throughout* the Second Temple period (which he denies existed), and the expectation of a *return* of prophecy on the eve of the eschaton (which he grants existed). Thus there was prophecy in the past and there may be in the future, but there is none in the present. One rabbinic tradition held that the Holy Spirit *hid* himself for a time. It further held that the Messiah will be a prophet, and will be accompanied by the prophet Elijah *redivivus*. Josephus and the New Testament fit into this eschatological perspective. But there was no *unbroken chain* of prophets in this period. When in later times Jews thought of contemporary prophets (Sabbatai Zevi, the Lubavitcher Rebbe), they did so in messianic terms.

In the Second Temple period, God used attenuated forms of communication, for example, the bath qol, for predictions, but not for religious practice (*halacha*). Among very Orthodox Jews (*haredim*) today, the *da'at Torah* (knowledge of Torah) possessed by certain leading rabbis is regarded as a form of divine communication, not as prophecy, but as a lesser, genuine, substitute. (Problems of definition and semantics here become acute.)

For Sommer, post-exilic prophets are a different "sort" of prophecy. Its inspiration is not fully equal; it enjoys a secondary status, less close to God, often through angelic intermediaries, or dreams or visions. (Haggai and Malachi are here exceptions. The word of the Lord comes to them directly.) Another distinction can be made between ad hoc prophecy and real prophets. The Levites in the books of Chronicles possess an attenuated form of prophetic inspiration, but they are called messengers (*melachim*), not prophets. Daniel is another important case. He studies the prophets; he does not speak directly to the people, but to a coterie. He receives messages through angelic intermediaries.

There is a fading of divine communication, a greater distance between God and humans. New ways are tried, e.g., a turn to pseudepigraphy, or a studious reliance on older texts: Daniel 9 reinterprets Jeremiah. The rabbis do not claim to be inspired (despite *m. 'Abot* 1:1), for Sommer. For him this is shown by their debates with one another. This amounts to an admission of their fallibility. (Here Sommer may suffer from a failure of imagination. He does not see that the rabbis thought that their final halachic decisions were supported by God, or that they believed that their very debates, as recorded in the Talmuds, were sacred. The entire process is inspired. To this we may add the Christian example of church synods and ecumenical councils, where some decisions can attain the status of dogmatic authority, because the Holy Spirit is thought to be helping.)

Both Greenspahn and Sommer quote a text: *t. Pesah* 4:14. In it Hillel says of his fellow Jews: "The Holy Spirit is upon them; though they are not prophets, they are sons of the prophets." This text can be used to justify either scholar's position, depending upon whether you emphasize the first words or the last.

In his conclusion Sommer provides three reasons for the cessation of prophecy in Israel: (1) the loss of the monarchy, (2) the loss of the ideological and imaginative world in which prophecy functioned, (3) the destruction of the Temple. This section surprisingly uses loose terms like philosophical and metaphysical, makes a mystique of the Exile, and uses slippery formulations such as "prophecy began to wane, to decline, to go into eclipse," its status was "precarious." We witness a transformation from prophecy to interpretation and exegesis.

This conclusion seems to the present writer rather subjective. Sommer forces the complex data in one direction. Even if one disagrees with his thesis, it is clear that some Jews writing at that time felt that there was a difference, a decline, a diminishment. Is this a matter of mood, or more?

To be sure, there is often a distinction in ancient historiography made between the heroic founding age and later prosaic periods. Moses and David take on mythic traits in later tradition. But the biblical narrative describes no real golden age. Saul, David, Solomon (even Moses!) are all portrayed as flawed. There is a deuteronomistic viewpoint increasing royal sin to explain and to apologize for the fall of the kingship and the Exile. Is Sommer taken in by this viewpoint?

There are differences in the Jewish story after 587 BC, but that does not say much in itself. There are always changes. One major development in the post-exilic world was the rise of the Chetubim, the writings or sapiential books. Did this development inevitably doom prophecy? Did Israel's contact with Hellenistic reason and natural science spell the end of all biblical value, ethics, prophetic judgment? Many believers have not thought so.

Rather than speak of the end of prophecy, it would be preferable, we suggest, to speak of a progressive enrichment and complexification of biblical revelation. This took place through further contacts with ancient near eastern wisdom and religious expression, as well as with Greek philosophy. The results are evident in the Wisdom of Solomon and in Philo, in Jesus, in Paul and John, in Hillel and other rabbis, in the church fathers. Even before the exile, prophecy was always only one of several options. Alongside prophets were judges, priests, kings and scribes. Some of these categories overlapped. Paul Ricoeur sees five principal biblical genres: law, history, prophecy, praise, wisdom. After the exile the scene becomes more varied and complex. But it seems that there was always a place for the prophetic gift. That later writers quote earlier prophets does not in itself count against their own inspiration. One of the main points of von Rad's theology of the Old Testament is the use and reuse of earlier biblical traditions by later texts. Michael Fishbane has taught us about inner-biblical exegesis. Therefore it seems wiser to speak about the *evolution* of prophecy rather than of its end.

This conclusion is reinforced when one looks even cursorily at prophecy and prophets in the New Testament concordance. Paul's earliest letter concludes with the parallel imperatives: "Do not quench the Spirit. Do not despise prophetic utterances" (*propheteias*, 1 Thess 5:19-20). These two verses, which say the same thing, each in different words, imply that the Spirit is active, that the gift of prophecy is available, that some accept it and others do not.

There is obviously here no question of going through every reference to prophecy, prophesying and prophets in the New Testament. That would require a book-length study, of which several are available. But we can attempt a brief survey.

Many New Testament passages refer to the prophets of ancient Israel and Judah. The rest can be grouped into four clusters: John the Baptist as a prophet; Jesus as a prophet; prophets and prophecy among the early Christians (especially the extraordinary chapter fourteen of 1 Corinthians); and the prophetic book of Revelation.

The gospel according to John makes a special contribution to the theme because it concentrates, not on prophets in general (for those see John 4:19; 7:52; 8:52-53), but on *the* Prophet, that is, the prophet like Moses promised in Deuteronomy 18:15-19. This text could be interpreted as making Moses the model of all true prophets in the future, or as the first of a succession of prophets. But at the time of the Fourth Evangelist (if not earlier, as among the Samaritans), some believers understood it as speaking of a definitive, final, endtime, absolute prophet, *the* Prophet, not *a* prophet. This usage occurs several times in John (1:21; 6:14; 7:40). It is one of the pillars of Johannine Christology. If this line of thinking were pushed to its logical conclusion there would be no further use for prophets. God would have spoken his final word in Jesus Christ. But this was not the view of early Christians, John alone excepted (and even there see John 16:12-13).

There were prophets and prophecy among the early Christians. First of all, in Matthew's missionary discourse, Jesus speaks as though there were to be prophets among his followers: "Whoever receives a prophet because he is a prophet will receive a prophet's reward" (Matt 10:41), prophets as people who proclaim the gospel. Later in Matthew, at the end of the woes against the scribes and Pharisees, Jesus promises to send "prophets and wise men and scribes" (Matt 23:34).

This expectation is fulfilled in the narratives of Acts and in the letters of Paul. Acts is understandably called the gospel of the Holy Spirit. It begins with multiple promises of the gift of the Spirit (1: 2, 5, 8, 16). It continues with the story of Pentecost (2:1–13) and Peter's commentary on this event, which includes a citation of Joel 3:1–5, that in the last days Israel's sons and daughters would prophecy, see visions, dream dreams, and claims that this promise has been fulfilled (2:33) and will continue to be fulfilled (2:38). Again, in 3:25, Peter addresses Israelites as the children of the prophets. More concretely, Agabus, one of the group of prophets, predicts a famine (11:27; he reappears in 21:10). Philip the evangelist "had four virgin daughters gifted with prophecy" (21:9). A group of six prophets and teachers in the church at Antioch is listed in 13:1, among them Barnabas and Saul (Paul) who are ordained for further mission (13:3). The list is extended in 15:32 to include Judas and Silas. When Paul arrives in Ephesus, he lays hands on some disciples, "the holy Spirit came upon them, and they spoke in tongues and prophesied (19:6). This link between the gift of the Spirit, glossolaly and prophecy is the basis or echo of Paul's teaching on charisms or spiritual gifts in his letters.

Paul and his school have a number of lists of charisms: Rom 12:6–8; 1 Cor 12:10, 28–31; Eph 2:20; 3:5; 4:11. Prophets usually come in second place, right after the apostles. But Paul's most extensive and powerful treatment of this gift is found in 1 Corinthians 14. Here, having just sung the praises of *agape* (chap. 13), Paul distinguishes it from the spiritual gifts, and places prophecy in first place among them (*mallon de*, "above all," v. 1). He then begins a long argument that prophecy is better than speaking in tongues. He explains that prophecy serves three purposes, all for the good of the community, building up, encouragement and solace. This list contrasts at first glace sharply with the predictive, corrective and revelatory purposes of prophecy prominent in the Old Testament, but could, with some effort, be harmonized with them. After all, forms of prophecy evolved, so that from harsh judgment one comes to the almost unrelieved consolation of Isaiah 40-55. For our purposes, only two points need be retained. (1) For Paul, prophecy is the supreme gift here. (2) *Everyone* is encouraged to prophecy (1 Cor 14:24, 31). There is not the slightest suggestion that prophecy has ceased or will cease. (Yet in 1 Cor 13:8, he does say that prophecies will come to an end!)

What is surprising in this rapid, selective survey of the New Testament data is the naturalness with which this Testament assumes that prophecy is available, that prophets can appear at any minute. It is simply a living part of the biblical heritage. God's Spirit is alive and active. Alongside this "naturalness," one must acknowledge a constant transformation of how one understands prophecy. There is no single, fixed, precise, tight, narrow generic model. When the gift manifests itself, it is a noteworthy occasion. To that extent prophecy does not become ordinary. Yet it is understood as a normally abnormal part of the divine-human relationship.

CONCLUSION IN SEVEN THESES

1. Theologically it makes little sense to say that God's prophetic spirit has ceased. It can go into eclipse, but not die. In the tension between 1 Macc 9:27 (as usually overtranslated) and Wis 7:27, Wisdom wins: "*In every generation* she passes into holy souls and makes them friends of God and prophets." 1 Macc 9:27 speaks about a temporary absence of prophecy.

2. Manifestations of God's Spirit in the scriptural recond can be more or less evident, more or less felt, more or less intense. Church history has known periods of spiritual awakening, renewal, after periods of spiritual dryness or decline. Even during moments of external disaster, trials, purifications, God does not abandon his people. Hidden streams of God's spiritual power are at work, sustaining the saints, famous or forgotten, martyrs, confessors, doctors.

3. Prophecy is always present in the lists of charisms provided by Paul and his school.

4. The manifestations of prophecy evolves in style, depending upon different historical circumstances. Prophecy enters into new combinations with other genres and cultures. Sir Isaac Newton was both a great early Enlightenment mathematical physicist and a serious student of biblical prophecy. Hellenistic reason and natural science do not spell the end of biblical values, but increase the biblical appreciation of creation (Gen 1:1—2:4a; Psalms 8; 104; Sir 39:12–35). There is a progressive enrichment and complexification of biblical forms of revelation.

5. There is a series of closures of the biblical canon. For Christians the canon is sometimes said to have closed with the death of the last apostle. This slogan cannot be taken literally, because some books of the New Testament are now dated to around AD 150, long after the death of the last apostle. But the slogan gives expression to a truth. There are special, unique irreplaceable times of foundation, like the apostolic era, which possess a mythic grandeur, even though the apostles really

existed and are not myths in the sense of fiction. It is the dimension that is mythic, not the persons involved. A closed canon, like a doctrine of scripture *alone*, can lead to a sober, scriptural faith, and can protect believers from an arbitrary imposition of superfluous doctrines.

The danger of this kind of teaching, that prophecy has ceased, that the canon is closed, it that it can give the impression that the Spirit of God has ceased to operate altogether. That would imply a denial of Pentecost, a denial that Christ bestows the Spirit upon his followers as his parting gift (John 16:12–13; 20:22; Acts 1:8; 2:1–4; 1 Cor 12–14; Rom 8). Such denials would be contrary to Catholic tradition. (1) For that tradition the Spirit is present and manifest above all in the lives of the saints, as well as in holy communities and families, the communion of saints. Some of these saints are deemed to have been endowed with prophetic gifts, e.g., Catherine of Siena, Bridget of Sweden. (2) The Spirit is also present in the tradition of thinking, reflection, theological debate and discernment, interpretation of Scripture, synodical, conciliar and papal decisions. All this can be called contemplation, and teaching (magisterium, *didaskalia*, 21 times in the New Testament). (3) The Christian "imagination," myth, legend, edifying fiction, can be an expression of the work of the Spirit, e.g., some the New Testament apocrypha, the Christian midrashim of Anna Catherina Emmerich, Christian novelists like Charlotte, Yonge, Ursula LeGuin, the Oxford Inklings (C. S. Lewis, J. R. R. Tolkien, Dorothy Sayers, etc.).

Moreover, the New Testament doctrine of the second coming (Justin's formulation) or return of Christ (e.g., 1 Cor 15:20–28; John 14:3; Rev 20:1–10; Matt 24:3, 27, 37, 39; 1 Thess 4:13–19), if taken seriously, cannot exclude that Christ will speak when he returns for judgment and government of the kingdom. What he speaks would count as additional divine revelation.

6. Alongside prophets the Bible saw a need for sages and priest; in the same way the church has need of thinkers, historians, theologians (a professional magisterium), as well as an administrative or managerial magisterium, ideally working in collaboration. Examples include the constellation of Catherine of Siena—Raymond of Capua—Pope Gregory XI; Theresa of Calcutta and Pope Paul VI; Yves Congar and Pope John XXIII; Lech Walesa and Pope John Paul II; but also Karl Barth and Dietrich Bonhoeffer against *Kulturprotestantismus* and National Socialism.

7. Prophecy included in biblical times, and includes today, two different aspects: (1) a telling forth, that is, a word of protest, correction,

criticism; (2) a foretelling, that is, what today is the role of futurologists and pundits. Verification can only occur after the event. Even then, the interpretation of the meaning of the event can alter with time.

8

New Testament between Scylla and Charybidis

Matthew and Inter-religious Dialogue

THANKSGIVING

I would like to begin as is fitting with a list of thanks. First to the most High God whom I learned to love through the mediation of Jesus his messenger, and through the Holy Spirit, who is always present but whose face remains invisible to us except in the faces of the Saints. Then I would like to thank my dear parents who transmitted their faith to me, their love, their taste for good cuisine, music, good use of language and their love for travel. I also thank my parents for their taste for politeness and a certain rudeness. I think also of my grandparents and particularly my grandfather Vincent, to whom I owe the fact that I am an anti-clerical cleric in the school of Garibaldi. Also my sister Patty and to my aunt Orsoline, who have never ceased to sustain me through the years. Finally I would like to thank my oldest friends E.J. and Mimi Nusrala, and Richard Echele who died young, a saint of the first generation of rock and roll.

I would also like to thank my teachers, first the Brothers of the Christian Schools, in particular Brother Cyril McDonald who led me to discover the Bible, the Gospels, Jesus, and the letters of Paul, but who also told me about the achievements of the Ecole Biblique de Jerusalem and of its founder Father M.-J. Lagrange. It is after having heard my teachers speak to me of the unjust suffering of which he was a victim that I decided at sixteen to study in Jerusalem and—an inexhaustible task—to fight to prevent scholars from being persecuted and silenced within the church.

My Greek teacher was Father J. Kenneth Downing, student of Werner Jaeger at Berlin and Harvard. In the Dominican Order I had for teachers: first, Fathers J. A. Weisheipl, R. A. Powell, B. W. Ashley and Andre Viard, then, Fathers Pierre Benoit, Roland DeVaux, M.-Emile Boismard, Jerome Murphy-O'Connor, Bernard Montagnes and Thomas F. O'Meara. In the course of my year at Harvard I benefited from the courses of Krister Stendahl, Helmut Koester, and John Strugnell. And the next year in Rome from Roger LeDeaut, Ignace de La Potterie, Albert Vanhoye, and Norbert Lohfink. At Duke University I had the honor to be the assistant to W. D. Davies, who was the director of my dissertation. I would also like to mention Dwight Moody Smith.

In the American Catholic biblical movement I recall my heroes, models, and also later my co-workers Raymond E. Brown, Joseph A. Fitzmyer, and Roland Murphy. Among Jewish scholars who have marked me, I would like to mention Jacob Neusner, Pinchas Lapide, David Flusser, David Daube ,and Jacob Taubes. To end this list I would like to thank Switzerland, of which G. A. Craig said that "it was the capital of liberty in the nineteenth century." This was the country that welcomed the biblical scholar W. M. L. de Wette pursued by the Prussian police. Switzerland also welcomed Wagner, (Nietzsche, Lenin), Karl Barth, Oscar Cullmann, Karl Ludwig Schmidt, the Jewish Dominican Jean de Menasce, and Jews like Ernst Ludwig Ehrlich and Eli Borowski. I think also of the influence of Pastor Alexandre Vinet on Camillo Cavour, and the Dominicans my venerable predecessors here at Fribourg Fathers Bernard Allo, Francois-M. Braun, M.-E. Boismard, Ceslas Spicq, Yves Tremel, plus canon Gregoire Rouiller. I may be a weak link in this chain but a link nonetheless.

TENSIONS, POLARIZATIONS, PINCER MOVEMENTS, AND WARS ON TWO FRONTS

I learned from Claude Levi-Strauss that boys, including those big boys who are called men, think spontaneously in binary oppositions, oppositions which can easily lead to conflicts and to wars. I was misled, for a long time a prisoner of these schemes which were too simplistic if not downright dangerous. Slowly, with a certain wisdom that comes of age, I began to appreciate the multiple richness of human and supernatural nature.

The contribution of the feminist approach has taught me to prefer Sarah's inclusive circle to Jacob's ladder. Jesus son of David is the new Solomon, a king who is wise, peaceful, and gentle. By teaching us to love our enemies, he prepares the transformation of our aggressive tendencies into a metaphorical militarism which must preserve the age old military values of discipline, courage, heroism, teamwork, but without physical violence or warfare. We could imagine that what the Queen of Sheba brought to the new Solomon, beyond gold and incense, was this wisdom of women. In fact, the parallel between the description of her bringing gifts to Solomon, as recounted in 1 Kgs 10:1-13, and the gifts of the Magi, is so close that I think that Matthew thought that among the Magi was at least one woman. One does not become a peacemaker in the spirit of Jesus until one finds the deciphering of a page of Greek more interesting and a greater challenge than a cavalry charge in red pantaloons.

According to the Protestant Tübingen school in the nineteenth century we should read the New Testament according to the following dialectical grid. St. Paul, as a good German, fought a war on two fronts: he positioned himself between the Jewish Christians faithful to the Torah of Moses and its 613 commandments, represented in the New Testament Canon by the writing of James and Matthew on the one side and a libertine Gnosis whose echo we find in Paul's correspondence with the church in Corinth on the other side. Paul sought a middle path between these two extremes. Paul kept the ten ethical commandments (Rom 13:8-10), on the one hand and the great commandment of the love of neighbor (Galatians 5:14), on the other hand.

After the fall of the Temple of Jerusalem in AD 70 the evangelist Matthew sought to fill the void left by the disappearance of the Temple with a Gospel that affirmed the permanent validity of the Torah of Moses (Matt 5:17-20) but which rejected for the most part the additional rules formulated by the Pharisees (23:13-33). At the same time Matthew distanced himself from Pauline radicalism (5:19) and he recommended St. Peter as a reconciling center (16:17-19). He favored at least for a time the mission to the lost sheep of the house of Israel (10:5-6; 15:24). In his own way Matthew sought the correct middle path, but at the end his Gospel opens itself to all the nations (Matt 28:18-20).

With St. John things are a little different. The first twenty chapters of the Gospel which bears his name do not recognize a clearly defined apostolic authority. Everything is centered on the Christ, community love, the sacraments, and the action of the Holy Spirit. After some time the Johannine community was wounded by a schism of the Gnosticizers who rejected the permanent, necessary, and universal lordship of Christ (1 John). The

Johannine community, at least what remained of it, then opened negotiations with delegates from the apostolic churches. An agreement was found whereby the apostolic churches accepted the Gospel of John and the Johannine community accepted apostolic authority (John, chapter 21). This is the famous thesis of the Sulpician priest Raymond Brown wherein the Johannine community after a one sided start arrived at a balanced solution between the Religion of the Spirit and the Religion of Authority (August Sabatier). One of my first powerful experiences here in Fribourg was at a faculty meeting during which a young professor of dogmatic theology declared "Professor of New Testament? I'm a professor of New Testament!" This remark leads us to a further reflection: that a professor of dogma would interest himself in the Bible is in itself a praiseworthy thing, and a thousand times preferable to the alternative, a complete ignoring of the Bible. Should one, however, use the New Testament in 2008 quite as one did in the fourth and fifth centuries at the time of Nicea and Chalcedon, as if we had not learned anything since about the way to understand the New Testament? Probably not. It seems obvious to me that we should try to find a harmonious collaboration between these two departments which share the facilities of the house of theology. It is also clear that we are somewhat victims of tendencies or of specializations which developed in sealed jars, airtight rooms, enclosed fortresses, and enchanted gardens.

In the nineteenth century we find in this regard a different practice in the German Catholic university theology faculties that it is worthwhile to recall. In those days, a young professor well trained in classical philology or a distinguished Hellenist began by teaching the New Testament, then went on to teach patristics, and finally, as the crowning glory of his career, dogmatic theology. This was the academic journey of J. A. Moehler, J. E. von Kuhn and of Paul Schanz. *Finis coronat opus.* The theologian thus learned the source and the meaning of dogmas more exactly as he moved along from stage to stage. There is here perhaps a lesson to be learned, even if present university requirements do not encourage a literal return to this practice. But it is certain that the two fields should work together in concert as much as possible, and that their respective borders remain the subject of tension. Pope Benedict XVI recently published the first part of his own reconstruction of the life of Jesus, something no other Pope has dared do until now, unless you count Peter's influence on Mark. That is a sign of the problem. In October 2008 the Synod of Bishops treated the role of the word of God in the life and mission of the church, another sign of how alive the subject is.

At the same time the professor of New Testament is led to meet frequently with the professors of the Old Testament in the department of

Biblical Studies. The Old Testament is much longer and more varied than the New, it covers more centuries. Worse than that, most of the human authors of the New Testament quote the Old Testament in the Greek translation of the Hebrew original. It remains nevertheless true that it is a constant pleasure for the professor of New Testament to work closely with his colleagues who are specialized in the other testament. It is in Jerusalem that I began to understand to what extent the authors of the New were soaked in the Old. I learned this first by living in Israel where public life is marked and rhythmed by the Torah of Moses. Then the exegesis of Father Boismard showed me that the marginal references in the Nestle-Aland edition of the Greek New Testament did not exhaust the allusions of the New to the Old. The inter-textual relationships, on the micro-level, as well as the relationship between the different books of the canon on the macro-level, are an inexhaustible source for the explorations of biblical scholars. It is between these two quite different poles that the New Testament researcher must find his or her path.

For two thousand years biblical and theological research sought the truth and the goodness within the sacred texts in order to help us find the meaning and the goal of human life. Theology, including exegesis, has however busied itself far less, at least formally, with the third element of the platonic triad of transcendental values, namely beauty. Beauty resided first in the creation of the world, then in the re-creation of a fallen world by Christ, from the ugliness of his death on a cross, to the glory of his resurrection. Beauty is present in the biblical texts, in their narrative art and in their message of salvation. Beauty is also visible in the perfection of love in the life of the saints. Beauty is in the art—that is architecture, music, painting, sculpture, cinema—produced by artists in the service of the faith, of the Bible, of the saints, and of the heroes of charity. But the formal task of the theologian was not to look at this surrounding beauty explicitly, at least not until the revolution worked by the Lucerne theologian Hans Urs von Balthasar. This revolution was perhaps legitimate but it is also dangerous. To wager everything on the beauty of revealed data of faith can lead to putting in doubt their truthfulness or their moral obligation to live them. Beauty can be deceiving and mendacious. The uniforms of the SS were smarter than those of the allied soldiers, but the cause they defended was less just. The exegete ought once again to navigate between Scylla and Charybidis, to steer clear of the shoals of pure aestheticism and of moralism without doctrinal foundation. In order to succeed in this the exegete must always seek the truth in the inspired text. The vision of the star brought the Magi an extreme joy but it did not prevent the lie of King Herod, nor the massacre of the innocents. The exegete must recognize the life-giving beauty of the star while always placing the accent on its meaning, namely the presence of God and of the child Jesus and on the moral lesson which the star delivers: the easy abuse of power and the abuse of children which occurs in every period. (Cf. my article "The Adoration of the Magi: Matthew 2:1–23 and Theological Aesthetics," chap. 10 below.)

CHANGES I HAVE LIVED THROUGH

Since 1972 I have been a professor of New Testament and early Judaism. This field of studies has undergone many changes in the period 1972–2009.

Historically, after the Second World War that raged during my early childhood, I have lived through two great events that I followed closely, the Second Vatican Council (1962–1965) and the fall of the Soviet empire in Eastern Europe (1989–1991). We might add the fall of China to Mao and the end of the great colonial empires. I started to teach soon after the end of the first postconciliar euphoria. I was aware, as I began, that I was going to be teaching in the ruins of an era when it could be safely assumed that students in theology knew Latin and when they could be expected (at least theoretically) to learn Greek. We professors had to try to keep the ship of theology afloat after the torpedo attacks, the unrest of 1968, to get the train back on the rails. It helped that we could use the valuable encouragement given by the Council to pursue critical studies in responsible freedom, within the bounds of the Nicene Creed, without having to take the oath against Modernism or other such burdens of conscience. Oddly, the question of whether to take the Council seriously has become acute today. That is a pity. (See J. W. O'Malley, "Vatican II: Did Anything Happen?," *Theological Studies* 67 (2006) 3–33; he followed this with *What Happened at Vatican II* [Cambridge: Harvard University Press, 2008].)

Technologically, we have gone from the typewriter to the electronic typewriter, and then on to the computer. I still have a nostalgic affection for a good fountain pen. My difficulties with the computer are the basis for well-founded raillery on the part of my colleagues, assistants, and confreres. I do nonetheless think that I have acquired the indispensable minimum skills of word-processing and sending electronic mail.

Methodologically, we have gone rather quickly from a more or less successful reception of the historical-critical method in the church to an explosion of different methods and approaches to the text. Perhaps the main new approach is a narrative one, which is sometimes hostile to any historical questioning of the text. The explosion of new methods, all occurring about the same time, meant that no single method could impose itself so as to exclude all the others. First, there were rhetorical analyses of the biblical text. There were inspired by structuralist and semiotic fads present at the University of Paris, until it was realized that these new methods were inappropriate to analyze the scribal writing techniques of ancient biblical authors. Then the biblical scholars turned to the manuals of classical ancient rhetoric. The professors were enthusiastic about their rhetorical analyses, but the students often remained reserved, because in contemporary usage the word rhetoric connotes a discourse devoid of substance or truth, empty talk.

Another new method calls itself anthropological. It concentrates on the dynamics of honor and shame in Mediterranean societies. An example would be: Jesus Christ, of divine origin, emptied himself, took on the condition of a slave, before he received a divine state more glorious than ever (Phil 2:6–11). The movement is from a state of honor to shame to honor. I hesitated for a time to accept this approach because I knew the founder too well. But now I see that this pattern has left its trace on parts of the New Testament; to notice its impact helps us to grasp the sense of the whole.

The sociological approach poses excellent questions, but often alas lacks sufficient data from antiquity to answer them. As with all methods, the feminist approach may be used in ways which are more or less adequate to the text. Though I am not known as a feminist exegete, I have tried to do justice to the presence of feminine wisdom and sensitivities in the text. In Jerusalem and Fribourg I would count as a feminist exegete because there was not much competition and because I at least mention it and take it seriously and help students who are interested to pursue it.

In the U.S. in the '20s the right was able to replace Marxist with Freudian jargon. Woody Allen is the clearest example. Growing up in this psychoanalytic culture, it was easy for me to apply psychoanalytic insights to the sacred text, where appropriate. For example, Freud's distinction between the ego, superego, and id can be fruitfully applied to the three characters in the parable of the Prodigal Son and to the struggle between spirit and flesh in Romans 7.

The history of the different "receptions" of the parts of the Bible remains a vast field of research, from the Church Fathers and Mothers, the rabbis, the scholastics, to the Reformation and the Counter-Reformation. In the U.S., in my native Middle West, the second largest church is the Lutheran; in my courses on St. Paul I engaged in lively debate with Lutheran students and colleagues. In Switzerland, however, there are not many Lutherans. Such a debate not only seems useless but downright impolite.

The research assistants in the biblical department know well of my interest in the history of modern exegesis. But they have a hard time trying to distinguish between intellectual history and simple gossip, in the way I tell it. I am now sufficiently old to have been able to know personally many of the makers of twentieth-century exegesis. The assistants have encouraged me to put my leisure hours to use to write a history of modern exegesis.

Finally, I have lived through another change, connected with those already mentioned. I refer to the amazing reserve that some younger colleagues manifest in regard to the cumulative model of knowledge. Bernard of Chartres became famous because of his saying that if we see further than our predecessors, it is because we are standing on their shoulders (preserved by John of Salisbury, in his *Metalogicon*). From my youth, I have always felt a respect and even a veneration for our ancestors, especially for the pioneers of modern biblical studies. In this area every major church has its martyr heroes, its innocent victims, its villains. I think especially of Pere M.-J. Lagrange, OP. For me it goes without saying that, if you want to study the text professionally, you must use the resources provided by text criticism, source criticism, form criticism, redaction criticism, each method adding some refinement to the preceding. Today in contrast I have the impression that some younger scholars no longer regard these methods as something to be presupposed. They want rather to start from zero, without presuppositions, and to reinvent the wheel. I call them the young and the cranky. I see this tendency both among Evangelicals and Catholics, but especially among Evangelicals who have become Catholics. Some of them want to take control of the American Catholic biblical movement. This desire is humanly typical and understandable, but I hope it does not end up in a simple refusal to address critical questions posed by the texts and by the classical methods. We must, I think, continue to venerate the ancestors of biblical scholarship, to learn from them, even as we strive to go beyond them.

Before moving to my fourth and final section, I mention the recent trend we could call the Empire fashion: Jesus and Empire, Paul and Empire, Matthew and the Roman Empire, and so on. To be sure, any well-founded connection between the NT and its political, military and social context, including awareness of the massive presence of slaves and slavery, is to be welcomed. Such studies help us to understand why the early Christians longed for the second coming of Christ, bringing with him the kingdom of God to earth, a kingdom of justice, peace and joy in the Holy Spirit (Rom 14:17). But we must avoid fads based on little evidence in the texts.

When I began studies on the NT, the use of rabbinic literature to comprehend the gospels and Paul had become widespread (Strack-Billerbeck, Ricciotti, J. Jeremias, W. D. Davies). This began to change in the '70s and '80s, as Jacob Neusner turned from historical to anthropological studies of the rabbis. (This made for duller books.) Neusner, Peter Schaefer, and then

Catherine Hezser began to apply rigorous historical methods to rabbinic literature in a way that separated this literature ever more from the study of the New Testament. I am still convinced that a knowledge of the rabbis is helpful to understand Jesus and the evangelists, but it does not hurt to be more careful in our use of the sources and to take more account of the dating of the rabbinic and targumic literature, the ocean of Torah, and the traditions they contain. The Dead Sea Scrolls literature, privileged because of its dating, does not provide a sufficiently broad basis to understand the world of the Gospels.

MATTHEW AND INTERRELIGIOUS DIALOGUE: THE LOVE OF GOD AND NEIGHBOR

Matthew and Rabbinic Judaism: From the Birkat ha-minim to Dabru Emet

It is a well-known paradox to lovers of Matthew: the very same gospel that seems so close to classical Judaism (for example, the words of Jesus on the permanent validity of the Law and the Prophets, Matt 5:17–20), also contains some very hard words spoken by the crowd: "His blood be upon us and upon our children" (Matt 27:25). This passage (and chapter 23) seems to make of Matthew one of the two most anti-Jewish books in the New Testament, the other being the gospel according to John (cf. 8:44). It was an alumnus of Fribourg who first dared to say in print that there was a dose of anti-Judaism in the New Testament. I refer to Gregory Baum's book *The Jews and the Gospel* (Westminster, MD: Newman, 1961). Since then the Pontifical Biblical Commission has addressed the same problem (2001).

But why did Matthew, the most Jewish-Christian of the evangelists, write down these harsh words, which have left a sometimes quite somber heritage, the teaching of contempt? For a long time we did not have a very precise answer to this question. Then, in 1964, my beloved teacher, W. D. Davies, found the answer in the conflicts between early rabbinic Jews and the Jewish Christian members of Matthew's church. After the destruction of the Temple, the rabbis were gathered in their academy at Jamnia/Jabneh, not far from modern Tel Aviv, under the direction of Rabban Johanan ben Zakkai. The school of Matthew was located somewhere in the south of Roman Syria, perhaps at Caesarea Maritima, not more than 30 miles from Jamnia. Each of the two assemblies sought to save what could be saved from the religious heritage of Judaism after the taking of the Jerusalem by the Romans in AD 70. The burning of the Temple represented for both groups a painful loss, a real institutional, religious, academic, financial and national crisis for the Judean Jews of that era. Until then, the Jewish Christians had continued to worship in the Temple and the synagogues alongside other Jews. The identity policy pursued by the rabbis of Jamnia led some of them to add a nineteenth blessing (really a curse) to the liturgy of the Eighteen Benedictions. "For apostates let there be no hope, and the dominion of arrogance do Thou speedily root out in our days; and let heretics and Nazarenes perish as in a moment, let them be blotted out of the book of the living and let them not be written with the righteous. Blessed art Thou, O Lord, who humblest the arrogant" (taken from the Geniza version available in C. W. Dugmore, *The Influence of the Synagogue upon the Divine Office* [London: Faith Press, 1964], pp. 119-20. Cf. Joel Marcus, "*Birkat ha-Minim* Revisited," NTS 55 [2009] 523-51.) By introducing this prayer into their liturgy they intended to cause the Jewish Christians to leave. This curse was not addressed to all Christians, to be sure, but only to Jewish Christians (and it has long since been rewritten in a less polemical fashion). (The martyrdom of James the brother of the Lord had taken place in 62, and that had already contributed something to poisoning the atmosphere. This same James became the heroic saint of the Jewish Christians.) The seven woes in Matthew 23 in their present form are, according to Davies, the answer of the Jewish Christians to this exclusion. (There is a milder version of the seven in Luke 11:37-52, so the woes are from the Q source.) The same dynamic of expulsion from the synagogue and the bitter resentment that that provoked is still visible in John (8:44; 9:22, 28; 12:42; 16:2).

That is the gloomy side of the relation between Matthew and the early rabbis. Their dialogue was thus in part a polemical dialogue. But the sunny side, in Matthew, is found in Jesus' teaching on the love of enemies. "Love your enemies, and pray for those who persecute you, that you may be children of your heavenly Father, for he makes his sun rise on the bad and the good, and causes rain to fall on the just and the unjust" (Matt 5:44-45; parallel Luke 6:27-35 = Q). In this way Jesus codified the practice of his ancestor king David, who twice spared the life of king Saul, who was trying to kill him (1 Samuel 24 and 26). And later in the gospel, when a Pharisee asks Jesus what is the greatest commandment in the Law, Jesus answered him: "You shall love the Lord, your God, with all your heart, with all your soul, and with all your mind. This is the greatest and the first commandment. The second is like it. You shall love your neighbor as yourself" (Matt 22:34-40; parallels Mark 12:28-31; Luke 10:25-28; sources Deut 6:5; Josh 22:5; Lev 19:18, 34). Of these two great commandments the first forms part of the daily prayer of the synagogue. The combination of these two commandments, which both come from the Pentateuch, is not found before the decades of Jesus and Philo. From the same period is dated the principle of Hillel the Sage, a hero for the rabbis: "Be of the disciples of Aaron, seek peace and pursue it" (*m. 'Aboth* 1:12, quoting Ps 34:15).

Both the rabbis and Matthew ascribed a high religious value to the study of Torah, the divine instruction. In the little treatise *Pirqe 'Aboth*, the study of the Torah is the very essence of Jewish existence. In Matthew, Jesus invites his disciples to learn from him (Matt 11:29). You never graduate from this school. You are enrolled for life. Rabbi Hananiah ben Teradion said: "Where two are seated and there are between them words of Torah, there too rests the divine presence (the Shekinah)" (*m. 'Aboth* 3:2). The Jesus of Matthew rewrites this saying so that it says: "Where two or three are gathered together in my name, there am I in the midst of them" (Matt 18:20). You see that here Jesus identifies himself with both the Torah in person and with the divine presence on earth, once you read it against the rabbinic original. There can be no doubt that there was a close relationship between the ideas and values of the rabbis and of Matthew, but the rabbis did not single out a single master teacher the way Matthew did (23:8): "You have but one teacher, and you are all brothers (and sisters)." For Matthew, Jesus is the Christ Emmanuel, God with us (23:10; 1:23). There is then a relationship between the rabbinical schools and the Jewish Christian schools, but there is a difference, what we could call Matthew's Christological concentration.

In reality, Matthew and the early rabbis inherited many of the same cultural, biblical and post-biblical, intertestamental and Hellenistic traditions. For Matthew the principle of selection was the Christ and his Church, for the rabbis the observance of the Torah and the preservation of the Jewish people. Matthew and the rabbis shared however the great hope, their lively hope of the Kingdom of God, coming soon in its fullness to earth, brought by the Messiah.

This common inheritance was recalled and revived by the Second Vatican Council in its Declaration *Nostra Aetate* (paragraphs 4 and 5) of 1965. Since then a valuable document has appeared, put out by the Vatican Commission for Relations with Judaism, entitled "Notes for a Right Presentation of Jews and Judaism in the Catechesis of the Catholic Church" (24 June 1985). Such documents and other friendly gestures led the late professor Ernest Ludwig Ehrlich (1921–2007) to state that the Catholic Church has done practically everything it could to satisfy the legitimate demands of Jews in regard to the Church. What remains to do, he said, is to spread the knowledge of these declarations and teachings to the members of the Church and to the general public. The recent regrettable signs of regression should not lead us to doubt or to weaken these earlier commitments.

A recent chapter in this history of Christians and Jews drawing closer together is to be found in the declaration entitled in Hebrew *Dabru Emet*, dating from 10/12 September 2000, written by four North American Jewish professors, each coming from a different branch of Judaism. Since its publication, this declaration has been signed by hundreds of rabbis and other Jewish leaders. The declaration is short, three pages, and consists of eight statements: 1. Jews and Christians worship the same God. 2. Jews and Christians recognize the authority of the same basic book, the Hebrew Bible. 3. Jews and Christians can respect the Jewish claim to the land of Israel. 4. Jews and Christians accept the moral principles of the Torah, including the sanctity of the life of each human being, and that humanity is created in the image and likeness of God. 5. Nazi ideology was not a Christian phenomenon. Jews do not blame the Christians of today for the sins committed by their ancestors. 6. The difference between Jews and Christians cannot be solved before the eschaton. 7. A new and better relationship between Jews and Christians will not weaken the observance of Jewish practices. 8. Jews and Christians must work together for justice and peace.

This declaration has been severely criticized as naïve by important authors like Wolfhart Pannenberg and J. D. Levenson. We should note that this declaration had been published before the attacks of 11 September 2001. The atmosphere was calmer then. Among these eight principles, the common moral base (number 4 above) is decisive for me: even if the two commandments to love God and neighbor are not explicitly mentioned (for reasons proper to Judaism), they are there implicitly and that is a capital fact.

MATTHEW AND ISLAM

Islam is the only one of the great world religions which was founded after Christianity. From the beginning Christianity was tempted to view Islam as a Christian heresy. St. John Damascene understood Islam as the religion of the Ishmaelites. Harnack and Schlatter understood Islam as a deviant form of Jewish Christianity and not without good reason: Islam and Christianity have the same God, the same basis in the prophetic phenomenon, Jesus as prophetic Messiah, born of the Virgin Mary, frequent prayer, a revealed moral law and a last judgment. Nevertheless, Muslim-Christian relations have not always been peaceful, to say the least. There have been Muslim jihads (religious wars) and Christian crusades. I think especially in the twentieth century of the terrible war between France and Algeria which raged between 1954 and 1962, or the violence in Bosnia in 1992-95, or in Iraq and Afghanistan since 2003.

Only three years after the peace settlements of Evian-les-Bains between France and Algeria, the Second Vatican Council made a declaration recognizing the positive side of Islam, while expressing reservations in regard to the position of women in Islam, reservations brought forward by bishops working in Muslim countries, reservations moreover not fully integrated in the final document.

Since those happy days the world has not stopped evolving. The threat of Stalinist Communism has vanished from the West. Francis Fukuyama announced the end of all major wars. The secretaries of defence felt their budgets threatened by Fukuyama's thesis. They desperately sought an enemy to justify their big budgets. The court theologian, the late Samuael P. Huntingdon, discovered the needed enemies in the world of Orthodox Christianity, in China and especially in Islam.

Later on, Pope Benedict XVI, elected in 2005, gave a provocative lecture on Islam, in Regensburg. It was intentionally so, I am convinced. After hostile reactions and a few deaths due to rioting mobs, the Pope prayed quietly in a mosque in Istanbul. These two events, to which may be added the bad image which Islam already had in the West, moved 138 Muslim scholars to publish their own declaration on 13 October 2007. It contained an open letter addressed to the Pope and to the other leaders of the Christian churches. It deals with the areas where Christians and Muslims can find common ground. Entitled "A Common Word between Us and You," the declaration is structured in three parts: the love of God as the first and greatest commandment of the Bible and the Qur'an, then the love of neighbor, and then a conclusion which recognizes the differences, obstacles and difficulties that remain between us. Nevertheless, the final appeal exhorts us to live together in mutual respect and in a healthy rivalry in the areas of justice and good works. The eight pages of this declaration are filled with quotations from the Qur'an and classical interpretations of the Qur'an, but also of quotations from the Bible and from the commentaries of the early church. It goes without saying that the teaching of Jesus and of Matthew on the primacy of charity plays a key role among these quotations.

The Holy See reacted swiftly and positively to this declaration. In November 2008, the first meeting between Muslim and Christian scholars ever held in the Vatican occurred. Two women were members of the Christian delegation. One of them was Barbara Wielandt, professor of the University of Bamberg, and recent honorary doctor of the University of Fribourg.

Today there is hardly a day that goes by that does not bring news of new atrocities and acts of violence committed by Islamists (often against their own people), but also news of a new step to create better relations between Christians and Muslims. And now the Muslims are trying to do something similar in a dialogue with the Jews.

Let us take a little distance from all this recent news and go back in time to a faraway place and to a period which only lasted a relatively short time. I am thinking of Muslim Spain in the Middle Ages, and the period of the Abbasid caliphate in Cordoba. There, over a period that lasted about a century and a half, Christians, Muslims, and Jews lived together in peace, in prosperity, and above all in an atmosphere of cultural and spiritual creativity to a great extent: it was a mutual cross-fertilization. I only mention the translation school of Toledo, which helped to transmit Greek science to the Latin West and the translation of the Qur'an into Latin under the direction of Blessed Peter the Venerable, which was achieved due to translators trained in Spain, even if the final work was done in France. It is the period evoked by Professor Maria Rosa Menocal in her fine book, *Ornament of the World*, finished just two weeks before the attack on the Twin Towers. In Spanish this peaceful period bears the name of *la convivencia*. This sort of *convivencia* is often a reality in France today when Muslim parents prefer at times to send their children to Catholic schools rather than to state schools. They prefer that their children grow up with God rather than in a neutral zone which is often in practice mocking and hostile.

CONCLUSION

It is clear that the common basis of the three Abrahamic religions, the condition of their possible peaceful coexistence, their *convivencia*, is the love of God and the love of neighbor, and what is more, the love of enemies (Deut 6:5; Lev 19:18; Matt 22:34–40; 5:38–48).

The liberalism inherited from the Enlightenment created a framework in which can flourish life-giving and warm beliefs and virtues which stem from the great Abrahamic religions. Matthew has contributed greatly to this heritage. He forgets neither Jesus Emmanuel, nor baptism in the name of the Father, Son, and Holy Spirit. He does not forget the fuller morality of the Sermon on the Mount, nor the great hope of the soon to come to earth Kingdom of God in its fullness. Both this morality and this hope are centered on the love of God and of neighbor. "Amen, amen, I say to you, whatsoever you did to the least of these little ones, who are my brothers and sisters, you did it to me" (Matt 25:40). Nor did Matthew forget the cross, the resurrection, the last judgment. But there too it is not the will of our heavenly Father that "one of these little ones should be lost"(Matt 18:14).

It has been a privilege and a source of unquenchable joy to teach these dear old texts for more than thirty years. I thank God for this gift and you for your attention.

9

Eschatology and the Quest for the Historical Jesus

This chapter's title, "Eschatology and the Quest for the Historical Jesus," correctly points to the fact that this long-standing quest has been deeply marked by debates over the exact character of the eschatological hope preached by Jesus. It is not too much to say that, for many authors of the modern period (from around 1780 to the present), Jesus' eschatology is the key to his personhood and to his mission, message, and meaning. The question of Jesus' eschatology is well-fought-over terrain. In this chapter, we can only hope to outline the history of the debates, in the process discussing a few key texts. But first, a few terminological precisions are in order.

ESCHATOLOGY, APOCALYPTIC, AND KINGDOM

Of the two main terms used in the modern discussion, eschatology and apocalyptic, eschatology is the broader, umbrella-like term, apocalyptic the narrower, more controversial term (although every element in this field has been controverted). Eschatology (etymologically, the doctrine about the "last things") refers both to the final destiny of the individual and to the final destiny of all humanity (or large collectivities within humanity, e.g., the elect people of God, believers, the "just"). Eschatology treats such subjects as resurrection from the dead, the particular and general judgment, heaven, hell (Gehenna), the intermediate state, purgatory, eternal life (beatific vision), the immortality of the soul, the kingdom of God, and the return or (second) coming (Parousia) of Christ; in brief, final salvation or damnation. There have often been Christians who are unhappy with the finality of much biblical eschatology, e.g., as presented in Matt 25:31-46. These Christians have developed the theory of the final restoration of all things (*apokatastasis panton*; see Acts 3:21; cf. Matt 17:11, parallel to Mark 9:12; Col 1:20). Their pioneering hero is Origen. Eschatology thus covers a broad field. It is normally only treated to a full extent in theological textbooks and biblical dictionaries.

The term apocalyptic covers a narrower range of topics. Its viewpoint is generally concerned with visions of humanity's collective future, both in this world and in a heavenly eternity, often expressed in the formula "the kingdom [or reign or kingship] of God." It is a formula or phrase not found as such in the Hebrew Bible, except in the Book of Daniel, where it becomes the dominant theme, mentioned at the conclusion of every chapter or set of chapters. In Dan 7:13–14, it is combined with the mysterious figure of "one like a Son of Man" (NRSV: "like a human being"). Elsewhere in the Hebrew Bible, the idea of divine control over or intervention in history is expressed by verbal expressions like "God reigns" (especially found in the Psalms) or the Day of the Lord (found especially in the prophets, e.g., Amos 5:18–20; Isa 13:6, 9, 13 [Holy War traditions]). In the Septuagint, the phrase "kingdom of God" is found in Wis 10:10 in connection with the patriarch Jacob. Its meaning there is not self-evident but its parallel is "knowledge of holy things" (Gen 28:12, 17, 22). This passage in Wisdom did not influence the synoptic Gospels.

When one analyzes the phrase "kingdom of God," one notices that it involves the combination of a political term, kingdom, with a religious term, God. It means that the user wants his politics to have something to do with his religion and his religion to have something to do with his politics. This is often such a dangerous combination that governments go to great lengths to separate church and state. Their efforts are not without reason when one considers the harm caused by such utopian projects as the Soviet Union and the Third Reich (Reich means kingdom or empire). Nevertheless, in many premodern forms of the great world religions, such a separation was not desired and is not, even today. The tensions to which it leads, for example in Iran, Iraq, and Israel, should help us to understand both the abiding fascination as well as the danger inherent in this theme of the kingdom of God. We are advised to proceed with caution.

KEY THEOLOGICAL DEVELOPMENT

Let us return to Daniel. When the night vision of the kingdom given to the one like a Son of man enters the gospel tradition, it leads to a number of theological developments which can only be listed here. (It is important to see the implications of the theme.)

1. Christology. The heavenly scene in Daniel 7:13-14 involves a transfer of power from one divine figure (the Ancient of Days) to another (the one like a Son of man). The sense of this scene was more clearly understood after the decipherment of the royal library at Ugarit (Ras Shamra) beginning in 1929. But already in the Gospels the identification of Jesus with the Son of man (whether by himself or by his followers) quickly led to understandings of Jesus as more than a man. The road to the Christological doctrines of Nicaea (325) and Chalcedon (451), that Jesus was true God and true man, was opened.

2. Early Jewish and Christian reflection on the kingdom of God and on God's plan of salvation for his people led them to a rough periodization, or theology of history. This periodization can take the simple two-step form: this world and the world to come (e.g., Matt 12:32; Eph 1:21). It can take the fuller form of seven periods: e.g., from Adam to Noah, from Noah to Abraham, from Abraham to David (note how in this Christian scheme, Moses is passed over), from David to the exile, from the exile to Jesus, from Jesus to his return in glory. This scheme is based on the seven days of Genesis 1 combined with the thousand years of Ps 90:4, and results in the millennium of Rev 20:1-10 (cf. 2 Pet 3:8). We find an extract of it in the genealogy of Matt 1:1-18.

3. The term "to judge," as in the phrase "he will come again in glory to judge the living and the dead," when understood biblically, as in the book of Judges, is not restricted to hearing cases and rendering judicial decisions. It means everything involved in the term "to govern." In this sense, the future glorious Messiah is expected to govern the earth for a lengthy period of time, in conditions of justice and peace (see Matt 6:33 and Rom 14:17). In this way the kingdom of God involves the realization of human hopes for social justice, an ethic, what would later be called a utopia. Such a hopeful vision can fire the imagination and lead to resistance to what are considered unjust regimes, to revolution, to (wars of) liberation, to new regimes. To this extent, kingdom talk can be very dynamic and history making, whether for good or ill. Since in the Gospels the kingdom of God is presented as a divinely given free gift (a grace), given at an unexpected future date (Mark 13:32; 1 Thess 5:2; Acts 1:3-7), the wide range of theologies of grace applies here to the question: what can we do to hasten (2 Pet 3:12) its coming? The options range from the quietist "We should do nothing but wait" to the Pelagian "We should take matters into our own hands and start building the kingdom here and now." (This is the dangerous option, and it is not to be found in the New Testament.) A middle option may

be called the John the Baptist model: we do not claim to build the kingdom directly but we prepare the way of the Lord's coming (Matt 3:3; Luke 1:76; Isa 40:3).

4. Finally, a distinction needs to be clearly seen between the end of the present eon or age or period of salvation history, as announced for example in Matt 28:20 (in modern careful translations), and the end of the cosmos in the sense of a final conflagration (*ekpyrosis*) or destruction of the planet. Such an end is taught in Stoic philosophy, echoed in 2 Pet 3:10–11; compare Mark 13:31 and parallels; Matt 5:18. So when modern scholars hostile to an apocalyptic prophetic Jesus proclaim that there never was an "end of the world" Jesus, they are narrowly correct. But they miss or obfuscate the high probability that there was an "end of the era" Jesus. The revolutionary vision remains intact in his message, despite their best efforts to make it disappear.

Having mapped out the territory, let us now turn to the history of the quest for the historical Jesus and its relation to his eschatology.

THE PREHISTORY OF THE QUEST

Before such a peculiarly modern quest could begin, certain conditions had to be present. The first was that the four canonical gospels (Matthew, Mark, Luke, and John) had to be written and accepted by what is sometimes called the Great Church. The writing of them took place between AD 69 and 120, granted the existence of pre-canonical sources like Q and oral and written free-floating traditions. Alongside this process of the canonization of the four, there occurred the gradual exclusion of the many apocryphal gospels, of which the two most important are the *Proto-evangelium of James* and the *Gospel of Thomas*. The latter plays an important role in the current quest. Once the four canonical gospels were in place, the process of how to relate them to one another could begin. One approach was to try to edit them into a single gospel harmony or fusion. This was done by Tatian and, by trial and error, was abandoned after some time. Irenaeus was the first to attempt a complete theological synthesis of both testaments and of all four gospels. His attempt was successful, but only at a certain level of generalization. Although his work was well received, it did not solve all the problems. Clement of Alexandria saw that John was different from the three synoptic gospels; he called it the "spiritual gospel." Under pressure from pagan critics like Celsus, Origen tried to overcome the contradictions between the four. Augustine also wrote a work *On the Consensus of the Gospels*.

Here we must introduce another distinction. Once Christianity became a predominantly Gentile religion and entered the Greco-Roman cultural world, its dialogue partner at the theological level became Hellenistic philosophy. It began to lose its roots in Judaism and in Jewish apocalyptic thought, even though Daniel remained in the Christian biblical canon, and even though the first Christian biblical commentary was on Daniel (Hippolytus, in Rome). To live like a Jew became a reproach alrready in Gal 2:14, and this reproach intensified in Ignatius of Antioch (ca. AD 115). As the Roman empire became at least nominally Christian with Constantine (ca. AD 311), Christian leaders began to quarrel among themselves over elevated issues of Trinitology and Christology, heavily dominated by reference to John's gospel. The other gospels were, however, still read to the people and could still influence their moral values and practice beneficently. But the apocalyptic element gradually ceased to be understood. To be sure, not every aspect of apocalyptic was lost. The people were attached to the hope of a personal, bodily resurrection, and this could not be hellenized away by the Platonizing theologians. In addition, other key apocalyptic elements entered the Nicene Creed: the final judgment, the glorious return of Christ, of whose "kingdom there will be no end." This last phrase was derived from Dan 7:14 and Luke 1:33. In its original context it did not contradict a this-worldly realization of the kingdom. But at the time the creed received its final shape, in a cultural context dominated by exaggerated neo-Platonic spiritualism and eternalism, the phrase could easily be interpreted to refer exclusively to eternal life in heaven. All connection with a hope for this world, this planet, was abandoned. The imperial authorities could rest secure. The common people were left with the ethics of the gospels, but not with their promise for this world. Salvation was now of the individual, no longer of the community.

In the Middle Ages matters remained in this area as they had been, for the most part. But three innovations are worth mentioning. First, Joachim of Fiore revived the effort to conceive a theological periodization of history, this time a Trinitarian one: the age of the Father (the Old Testament), the age of the Son (the New Testament, the Church), the age of the Holy Spirit (the simplified church of the future). Crude though this schema was, it did contain the revolutionary potential inherent in the message that salvation history in this world was not over. God would intervene again. The status quo was relativized, its spell was broken. The second innovation was the invention of a new literary genre, the writing of a meditative life of Christ. The main achievement in this area was the voluminous life of Christ by Ludolf the Carthusian, of Saxony (ca. 1300–1378). This work, full of pious reflections on the events in the life of Jesus, was one of the most popular books of the late Middle Ages. But this new genre, though a forerunner of the quest, could not yet be called a quest of the *historical* Jesus, because it did not yet make a sharp distinction between a critically tested historical portrait of Jesus and a theological-devotional portrait. It remained within the framework of ancient historiography, where history is regarded as a branch of rhetoric, a storehouse of instructie or edifying examples. The third innovation was the insertion into the greatest theological synthesis of the Middle Ages, the *Summa of Theology* of Thomas Aquinas, of a lengthy analysis of the principal "mysteries" (i.e. events) of the life of Christ (*Summa theol.* III, qq. 39–54). This insertion broke through the rather arid Christological discussions of the hypostatic union and theories of redemption, to reconnect with the gospel story. In regard to eschatology, Thomas did not live to complete that portion of his final *Summa*. But, in his earlier *Summa Contra Gentiles*, that section is complete. It is clear there that he maintains a full doctrine of resurrection (as well as the natural immortality of the soul), and the judgment, both "particular" (of the individual, immediately at death, Luke 23:43) and general, collective, at the return of Christ. This delicate synthesis was maintained only the greatest difficulty in the later Middle Ages because theology had lost the apocalyptic perspective that gave it meaning and coherence.

The sixteenth-century Protestant reformation so concentrated on Paul that little progress was made in the study on the synoptic gospels. Those most interested, the Anabaptists, were so severely persecuted that they could produce hardly any academic theology. But in the seventeenth century, within the more liberal wing of the Reformed tradition, there took place a revival of Christian humanist erudition in the spirit of Erasmus represented first by Hugo Grotius and Johann Jakob Wettstein, who attempted a more historical, less ideological or polemical, understanding of the New Testament. The search was on for classical parallels. Then came what has been called Baroque philosemitism. In Italy, the Netherlands, and England scholars became interested in the Jewish, rabbinical context of the New Testament. Ugolini and Surenhusius translated many rabbinical texts into Latin, e.g., the Mishnah, with Maimonides' commentary. John Lightfoot wrote a four-volume commentary on the New Testament out of rabbinic materials, a work still in print.

At the same time, however, as a reaction to the European wars of religion culminating in the Thirty Years War (1618–1648), a new attitude to the Bible arose in advanced circles (e.g., Spinoza and Hobbes). This attitude was marked by deism and rationalism. The Bible was to be read as any other ancient book, stripped of its inspiration and supernatural, divine authority. Above all, no miracles were to be accepted at face value. At its worst (e.g.,

Voltaire) this hostility led to shallow mockery of the Old Testament and to anti-Jewish attitudes. For much of the Enlightenment, Jews were only to be tolerated on condition that they abandon their particular way of life. (Montesquieu here represents an honorable exception.)

At the same time this dogmatically free way of reading the Bible could lead, in more serious thinkers, to a recognition of the apocalyptic eschatology of Jesus that lay on the surface of the synoptic gospels (Reimarus, published in extracts by G. E. Lessing) for those who could open their eyes. Given, however, the prevailing Newtonian model of knowing, viz. that all truths had to be like mathematical truths, universal, timeless, necessary, Lessing ran up against the "ugly ditch" separating historical data from mathematical truths. This roadblock was soon removed by Herder's rediscovery of the poetry of the Bible and especially by Schleiermacher's romantic idealist method of historical *Einfühlen* (understanding through historical empathy and imagination, controlled and supported by data contemporary with the biblical text). This method was worked out just at the moment when the great era of archaeological discoveries had begun, first at Pompeii, then in Egypt, Babylonia, and later in Palestine and Syria. The deciphered texts provided a concrete context for the Bible read historically. The stage was set now for the specific object of this essay, eschatology and the quest for the historical Jesus.

THE FIRST QUEST

The modern quest for the historical Jesus, *the first quest* (1835–1906), began with the remarkable, extensive work by a young genius at Tübingen, David Friedrich Strauss, *The Life of Jesus* (1835–1836). It was translated into English twelve years later by another young genius, the future novelist George Eliot (Mary Anne Evans), and also into French. Its contributions to our subject are as follows.

1. With a passionate erudition that had mastered the previous relevant literature, Strauss examined the gospel traditions with a careful eye for any inconsistencies between them. Critics criticized him for the ice-cold way in which he cataloged tiny discrepancies in the Passion narratives, as Jesus is bleeding to death on the cross for our redemption.

2. He made a sharp distinction between strict history and what he called myth. This means that nonmiraculous, nonsupernatural elements like the ethical and parabolic teachings of Jesus were passed over quickly as historical and noncontroversial. (These would then become the unshakable basis for later liberal-ethical, neo-Kantian lives of Jesus.) In examining the

more mysterious narratives, like the transfiguration, he would note the Old Testament background: not just the theophanies in Exodus 24 and 1 Kings 19, but the shining face of Moses in Exod 34:29–34. This was a helpful contribution, though it does not by itself explain everything in the Gospel story, much less guarantee that the story was a pure fabrication, since later authors related their experiences in terms marked by earlier literary forms and expressions, without this meaning that nothing new ever happens. The term "myth" in this context is ambiguous. On the one hand, it can have a positive meaning. In this sense, a myth is a deeply true story in poetic form, often a story of national or civic origins. It is a form of hyperreality, larger than life. Legends tend to attach themselves to founding figures like Christopher Columbus, George Washington, King Alfred, even though they themselves were quite historical people. Other stories, such as the Fall of Adam and Eve or the swallowing of Jonah by the whale or Pyramus and Thisbe may not be narrowly historical, or at least not demonstrably so, but they contain deep moral and psychological insight, the kind of truth that can be found in great fiction. The walls between this kind of myth and history are not airtight. On the other hand, myth in popular usage often has a negative sense. It simply means an untrue story. This is the sense found in the Bible itself (1 Tim 1:4; 4:7; 2 Tim 4:4; Titus 1:14; 2 Pet 1:16). As a son of both the Enlightenment and of romantic idealism (whose philosopher Schelling strongly promoted the positive sense of myth), Strauss used the term in both senses, but especially in the negative sense. And this of course offended greatly his orthodox readers.

3. On one point, Strauss was a traditionalist. He accepted that Matthew (not Mark) was the oldest and thus the most historically reliable Gospel. So, when he found myth in Matthew, it meant that the reliability of the whole gospel tradition was called into question. He also held that John's Gospel was not, for the most part, an independent historical source. Although this is commonly accepted in critical circles today, at the time it saddened not only mystics and theologians but also romantic idealist philosophers, since John was their favorite Gospel. Strauss's powerful challenges in this area, the critical testing of the dating, origin, and historical reliability of the Gospels, provoked the New Testament scholars of the next generations to arrive at new conclusions: the earliest complete Gospel was Mark, and before and alongside Mark there had been an anonymous collection of Jesus' sayings (not miracles or parables or supernatural events or sufferings). This sayings source (in German, *Logien-Quelle* or Q for short) was preserved scattered in Matthew and Luke and could be reconstructed from them, in all about 200 verses. The hypothesis was also formed that Q represented the original Aramaic Matthew, now lost, which had been spoken of by church authors

beginning with Papias (second century). If so, it would be the work of an apostolic eyewitness. Then it was noticed that, although Mark does not quote Q directly, he echoes similar traditions in about thirty cases. When you have two early, independent witnesses to the same tradition, you have come as close as is humanly possible in the study of ancient history to bedrock, to historically reliable material. All this came out of Strauss's shock therapy.

4. Before we leave Strauss, we must mention his view of the eschatology of Jesus. Strauss saw with complete clarity that Jesus taught a future hope of a new divine intervention in history which would be the full realization of the kingdom of God on earth. In other words, Strauss saw that the historical Jesus held to an apocalyptic eschatology to be realized in the near future. Strauss never doubted this. But Strauss was also concerned, as a religious thinker, to present a living message to his readers. He thought that Jesus had simply been in error on this point, that this message was meaningless for modern people, theologically useless. Strauss then attempted to replace Jesus' message of the kingdom, not to mention the received Christological and soteriological teaching of the church, with a romantic idealistic religion of a liberated humanity. (In this sense, he made his contribution to the revolution of 1848.) For our purposes, it is important to see that, on this point of Jesus' eschatology, Strauss remained paradigmatic for most theologians up until Moltmann and Metz in the 1960s. That is, Jesus' message is simply not taken seriously. It is regarded as an embarrassment and is replaced with something else.

In discussing Strauss, we have already mentioned the technical breakthroughs of the next generations: the priority of Mark, the discovery and then the reconstruction of Q. The key names here are C. H. Weise, H. J. Holtzmann, and Adolf von Harnack. Closer to our central concern is what happened in the burgeoning production of liberal lives of Jesus. We have already seen that Jesus' specifically social apocalyptic eschatology was rapidly lost with the increasing Hellenization of Christian theology. The kingdom of God was not a theme of theology for over a millennium. It was rediscovered as of intellectual interest by the philosopher Immanuel Kant, in his *Religion within the Limits of Reason Alone* (1793). There he devotes the third of its four chapters to the kingdom, understood in an eighteenth-century agnostic way as the ethical commonwealth. The kingdom on this view was no longer a divine gift but a human project of collective social effort. We build the kingdom. (In this brief sketch, we cannot hope to do justice to such a subtle thinker as Kant. In fairness, however, it must be said that he was not a crude Pelagian; and, despite his evasions, he was deeply marked by Christian thought and the deep piety of his Bible-reading parents. It is perhaps due to their influence that he was able to rediscover and to "retrieve" this central gospel value.) Kant's chapter on the kingdom exercised a decisive influence on nineteenth-century theology after Strauss and especially after the collapse of romantic idealism due to the (temporary) failure of the revolutions of 1848. In the liberal lives of Jesus, the Galilean became a teacher of Kantian ethics. Kant had glorified the golden rule (Matt 7:12; Luke 6:31), in the form of the categorical imperative, as the supreme ethical wisdom. The kingdom of God was interpreted as the kingdom of these formal moral values. It was the era of cultural Protestantism. The advancing colonial empires were to be filled with the cultural content of these Kantian Christian values. Churches were built to look like theaters or lecture halls where the great writers of the day (e.g., Ralph Waldo Emerson) could hold forth. The symbiosis of Christ and culture was nearly perfect. The goal was to build the kingdom, now. (The phrase "to build the kingdom" is not found in the Bible.)

This tidy package was first unraveled by a little book published in 1892 by Johannes Weiss: *Jesus' Proclamation of the Kingdom of God*. It bluntly affirmed that Jesus' central message was that God was to bring his kingdom soon and suddenly. Jesus, picking up from the beheaded Baptist, was preparing the people for its coming. He was so aware of its nearness that he sometimes spoke of it as already present (Matt 12:28 and its parallel in Luke 11:20 = Q). But mostly he speaks of it as in the near future (Mark 1:15; Matt 6:10, 33; Mark 14:25). It is not a product of Darwinian evolution or direct human effort. The effect of the book was like that of a brick hurled at a plate-glass window. The book was so offensive because liberal theology had a bad conscience about its suppression of Jesus' eschatology. It was not ignorant of it. It simply hoped to keep it a dirty little secret. Thanks to Weiss, the liberal emperor was seen to have no clothes. Weiss's scholarly elders tried to reason with him. They knew he was a superbly trained, brilliant, promising (he was twenty-nine) exegete of the Göttingen History of Religions School, a hope of the future. Under pressure from the tremendous outcry provoked by the book, Weiss caved in: he granted that, even though his book told the historical truth, it was a hermeneutically, pastorally useless truth. For contemporary Christians, the liberal neo-Kantian line was the right message. This calmed things down for a time. But a theology that prided itself on its historical foundations could not long remain satisfied with such a compromise. As other members of the school (e.g., Wilhelm Bousset, Hermann Gunkel) were integrating newly deciphered data from Assyria (e.g., cosmic combat myths with Genesis and Revelation), the accuracy of Weiss's reading of the Gospels was only reinforced. Worse was still to come for the liberals. In 1906, a young Alsatian Lutheran pastor and many-sided genius (musician, theologian, philosopher, medical doctor, missionary in Africa, and eventually Nobel Peace Prize winner), Albert Schweitzer, published a book whose English title is *The Quest of the Historical Jesus*. It took the form of a research report. It surveyed the nineteenth-century lives of Jesus from Reimarus to Wrede, rightly giving pride of place to Strauss, but also covering, with due contempt, Ernest Renan and the Kantians (e.g., Albrecht Ritschl). Schweitzer used Weiss's little book as a razor with which to slit the throats of the authors he surveyed. That is to say, he exposed the inadequacy of their presentation of Jesus' eschatology. With Schweitzer's work (and the First World War), the first quest for the historical Jesus came to an end. Yet the triumph of the apocalyptic viewpoint was delayed for a time, one might say until 1964. And even till today, its victory is far from being universally acknowledged.

(Before we leave the Göttingen school, a word of clarification is in order. Modern evangelical theologians reproach Bousset for his denial of the dogma of the divinity of Christ. This is a serious charge, and it is not without some foundation. But before the Göttingen historians are condemned on this point, it should be pointed out in their defense that they were all raised on Harnack's *History of Dogma*. Now one of Harnack's most original theses, whether right or wrong, was that the concept of Christian dogma was a postbiblical, Hellenistic-Byzantine development of a particular cultural type. For Harnack, this culturally determined expression had come to an end with Luther. This did not mean that Luther denied the divinity of Christ. It did mean that he denied the necessity of this cultural form of theological expression. In this sense, then, the Göttingen scholars may have denied the dogmatic form of the doctrine, but this does not mean that they denied the doctrine itself.)

THE SECOND QUEST

The next stage in the story is the period from roughly 1919 to 1964. This is the period of the second quest, of dialectical theology, of form criticism, of existentialist lives of Jesus, of the Luther renaissance (Holl and Althaus). During the 1920s, our story does not advance very fast. The dialectical theologians, notably Karl Barth and Emil Brunner, said that they were not interested in history or historical exegesis or the historical Jesus. They were interested in Paul (read as direct divine revelation, sometimes called positivism of revelation), in theological exegesis, in church dogmatics, in the revitalization of the Reformation heritage, in prophetic preaching, and, to some extent, even in the church. The two best-known pioneers of form criticism, Rudolf Bultmann and Martin Dibelius, at first sympathetic to dialectical theology, each did write a short life of Jesus. The shock of Germany's defeat in 1918 made northern German Protestants confessionally defensive. Bultmann's case is instructive. On the one hand, he shared with Barth a concentration on justification by faith alone (not an explicit theme of the synoptic Gospels), an interest he supported with the help of his Marburg colleague Martin Heidegger's existential phenomenological decisionism (what is important is that your will has made a decision, not your intellect; the content of your decision is also not important). Both Barth and Bultmann rhetorically and verbally affirmed the centrality of eschatology, but they did so in such an existential way that its apocalyptic, social, and ethical content was hollowed out. (Barth, Bultmann, and Dibelius all returned to the ethics of Jesus in the late 1930s, but by then the damage was done, the horse was out of the barn, catastrophe could no longer be avoided.) Bultmann added a special twist. For him, the teaching of Jesus did not belong to Christian theology; it belonged to the history of Judaism. Jesus was primarily a rabbi. His historicity in its details is irrelevant for Christians; what counts, for Christians, is the fact of his crucifixion.

During the Second World War, an honorable exception is represented by Dietrich Bonhoeffer, who gave his life out of fidelity to the ethics of Jesus. But he too regarded the eschatology of Jesus as premodern.

After the war, some members of the Bultmann school rebelled against the master. The easy dismissal of the historical Jesus and his teaching was no longer acceptable to students or professors. Ernst Käsemann wrote essays on Jesus, Günther Bornkamm a widely read biography of Jesus, Hans Conzelmann an influential lexicon article on Jesus, Herbert Braun a selective sketch. For all of them, Jesus' emphasis on the love command was meaningful, but neither his eschatology nor its related Christology of the coming Son of man were. The accent remained individualistic and existentialist.

After the war but outside of the Bultmann school, things were more promising. Oscar Cullmann's *Christ and Time* took seriously the Second Coming of Christ, to the great dismay of Cullmann's colleagues. Forged in the crucible of the war, Cullmann's idea was motivated not only by the biblical data, but also by the awareness that Christians needed to affirm the active and intervening lordship of Christ, over against the many mad claimants to the throne of the Son of man. Cullmann's view was supported by Bultmann's successor at Marburg, W. G. Kümmel. Cullmann and Kümmel were not only impressed by future-oriented texts like Matt 6:10 and Mark 1:15; 13:26, and the future hopes expressed in Jewish pseudepigrapha, Daniel, and the War Scroll of Qumran. They also argued that Jesus' reticence about the exact timing of the future event (Mark 13:32; Matt 24:36) allowed some room in his own thinking for the delay of the coming of the Day of the Lord, even though Jesus did expect it to come soon (e.g., Mark 9:1). Joachim Jeremias filled in more and more of the Jewish background of Jesus' actions and teachings, especially his parables, but remained evasive on what he called Jesus' "self-realizing eschatology."

In Britain, the field of New Testament studies was dominated by Charles Harold Dodd. On the basis of the Oxford–Cambridge tradition of Platonism and Johannism in Anglican theology, Dodd tried to interpret the sayings of Jesus about the coming of the kingdom in the future so as to harmonize them with the sayings about the kingdom being already present (by sign, anticipation, foretaste, in germ) in the ministry of Jesus, and also to make them fit with the comparatively less apocalyptic Gospel according to John (but cf. John 14:3, 18, 28; 21:22). In this program of "realized eschatology," Dodd was supported by the Anglican J. A. T. Robinson and by his fellow Congregationalist G. B. Caird. This line would have a North American sequel. This second quest was petering out.

But first we should add a word about what the Roman Catholics were doing (and not doing) during the twentieth century. The pioneer of modern Roman Catholic biblical studies was M.-J. Lagrange. Alerted by the lively debate around Johannes Weiss's little book (whose second edition he reviewed), Lagrange wanted to write his own book on the subject. His censors blocked this and forced him to turn the manuscript into a book on messianism. But his teaching inspired one of his most productive disciples, Joseph Bonsirven, to produce a book on the kingdom once the coast was clear (1957). It was flawed, full of Bergsonian evolution, but it was a first step. (Several Catholics wrote learned lives of Christ at this period. One of the best was by Giuseppe Ricciotti. But they tended to be long on Near Eastern background, and short on critical judgment, due to the heavy censorship in the period 1907–1958.) When the clouds lifted, Rudolf Schnackenburg wrote a very thorough and careful book on the kingdom which some consider the best ever written. However that may be, it arrived in time to free the Second Vatican Council from a too-simple identification of the kingdom on earth with the church. The council cautiously took some first steps in the rediscovery of this theme, steps which have been developed by subsequent church documents.

The story so far has given the impression of brief periods of historical lucidity and honesty (Weiss and Schweitzer, Cullmann and Schnackenburg) followed by periods of theological evasion. This state of affairs is in part due to the weakness of exegesis, left to itself, to impose its discoveries on the broader theological-ecclesial community. Exegesis needs the heft, the sustained, repetitive, reflective, even incantatory, power of systematic theological thought to break through the resistance of the Platonic mind. All the furniture in the theological mind has to be rearranged. The breakthrough occurred in 1964, to simplify, with the publication of Jürgen Moltmann's *Theology of Hope* (in German; the English translation appeared in 1967). With this work, Jesus' apocalyptic eschatology was taken seriously by mainstream systematic theology for the first time since Irenaeus.

It did not happen by accident. Moltmann's mind was prepared by the biblical theology movement initiated by Karl Barth and continued by Cullmann, transmitted to Moltmann by his Heidelberg teacher Gerhard von Rad. Moltmann's experience as a prisoner of war had already deepened his character. The final mental push was provided by the thought of the Jewish, Marxist, atheist religious thinker Ernst Bloch, especially his major work, *The Principle Hope*. (Bloch was expelled from East Germany as too religious; he settled in Tübingen where he was found to be too Marxist.) It was the period of the Marxist-Christian dialogue. Moltmann saw, in his dialogue with Bloch, that the Bible and the church had resources of hope for humanity even in this world, resources that were not being used out of fear of disturbing the status quo. Hope for this planet had been handed over to the Marxists. This would not do. Moltmann discovered in the biblical messages of Exodus (the liberation from Egyptian slavery) the resurrection from the bonds of death and Jesus' promise of the coming of the kingdom to earth, the resources he needed to answer Bloch and the Marxists, to give new hope to Christians drooping under the depressing messages of death-of-God theology, demythologizing, the Cold War, and analytic philosophy. Moltmann's breakthrough concept was quickly taken up and carried forward by both Protestants (Wolfhart Pannenberg, Douglas Meeks) and Catholics (J. B. Metz) in Europe and North America. Latin America awoke from its centuries of mental slumber with its own brand of liberation theology (Gustavo Gutierrez, Leonardo Boff). Richard A. Horsley and Warren Carter continued their research on the kingdom announced by Jesus and its relation to world empires, ancient and modern. Weiss's insight had finally found a home in Christian systematic theology.

THE THIRD QUEST

But Moltmann's success was not complete. Beginning at the University of Chicago, the third quest for the historical Jesus began in the last two decades of the twentieth century. A professor of New Testament there, Norman Perrin, who had once been an excellent historian of interpretations of the kingdom of God, decided to turn against apocalyptic expectations. The kingdom for him became a poetic symbol of an ideal state of justice, no longer a religious hope. The parables were reduced to beautiful artifacts, for aesthetic appreciation. (Perrin turned against apocalyptic expectations because they seemed too fantastic, mythological, unmodern to him.) The prophetic fire was extinguished once again. His Chicago ally, John Dominic Crossan, after years of aesthetic, formal analyses of the parables and aphorisms, which were often outstanding, very successful, and devoid on his part of any claim to historicity, took the fateful step of claiming to write a book on the historical Jesus. He did not accept an apocalyptic Jesus; he did not want to repeat what others had done. His new move was to claim that the Gnostic-Coptic *Gospel of Thomas* (found intact in 1946 at Nag Hammadi in Egypt) was an early independent historical source for the teaching of Jesus. It was pointed out that the *Gospel of Thomas* as we have it (fragments in Greek were known before the 1946 Coptic find) shows knowledge of all four canonical Gospels, and therefore it must be later than they are. This objection was answered by an appeal to an (uncontrollable) earlier stratum of the *Gospel of Thomas*, which was prior to or at least independent of the four. Another strategy is to say that the historicity of each logion must be evaluated separately. Some may be early, some late. (The *Gospel of Thomas* consists of 114 separate logia, or sayings.) This has become the common opinion. Another objection is that the *Gospel of Thomas* as we have it clearly expresses a Gnostic soteriology. To this, two answers are made: (1) the Gnostic elements belong to a late stratum; (2) the Gnostic elements are early and show that Jesus himself was a Gnostic teacher. The canonical four have misrepresented him. Crossan does not count any of the canonical Gospels as primary, preferring to them the earliest stratum of *Thomas*, the Egerton fragment, the *Gospel of the Hebrews*, the logia source (i.e., Q), and a "Cross Gospel" reconstructed from the *Gospel of Peter*. What this list omits is Mark. In accepting Q, Crossan accepts the earliest stratum of Matthew and Luke. To be sure, the three synoptics reflect considerable theological elaboration. But a Jesus tradition without narratives about him is inherently improbable, hence the need for Mark. Both Q and Mark present a Jesus who is an apocalyptic prophet and exorcist. The efforts to de-eschatologize Q are not convincing (e.g., the work of John S. Kloppenborg). Out of these new moves, Marcus Borg has developed a portrait of Jesus as a holy man, as an ironical sage, as a man of prayer and gentleness who shows us the way to a loving God. Eschatology plays little role here. (Borg, as a product of Oxford, carries on the Dodd–Caird line.)

This portrait has been criticized as culturally too easily adapted to a West Coast interest in undemanding spiritualities, close in spirit to New Age esoterics and to American Buddhism. Obviously no service to historical truth (supposing there is such a thing) will be done by denying that Jesus was holy, a man of prayer, united with his heavenly Father, leading disciples on a nonviolent path to love of God, neighbor, and even enemies. These features have been part of the Jesus tradition from the earliest strata. The problem with the third quest arises rather from what is left out or played down, namely, the prophetic and apocalyptic elements. Often the very word "kingdom" is so loosely translated as to cover up any link with Daniel. Other examples are: (1) the denial by the Jesus Seminar in California, founded by Robert Funk, that Jesus pronounced the woes over the unrepentant cities (Matt 11:20–24 paralleled in Luke 10:13–15 = Q) (it has been suggested that their Jesus is too politically correct to do such a rude thing); and (2) their lowering the probability that Jesus taught the Lord's Prayer (Matt 6:9–13 paralleled in Luke 11:2–4 = Q). To be sure, this prayer, for the coming of the kingdom to earth (in the near future) as it (already) is in heaven, played a key role in Weiss's argument. Moreover, the Jewish parallel, the Kaddish, close as it is to the first half of the prayer, is not certainly datable till long after the Gospels. Already Marcion had to rewrite the prayer to suit his prejudices: "thy holy Spirit come to us and purify us." It must nevertheless be honestly conceded that, in the present cultural-religious climate, a purely sapiential, pietist Jesus has found a market niche. It fulfills a real spiritual need, however distorted or selective its historical foundation.

The Dodd–Caird line is also carried further by the Anglican bishop of Durham, Nicolas Thomas Wright. In his voluminous work, he tries to renew the third quest by holding five questions in tension. The five questions concern: (1) the Judaism of Jesus' day; (2) Jesus' aims; (3) the causes of his death; (4) the early church; (5) the writing of the Gospels and their nature. It will be clear at once that only questions 2 and 3 directly concern the historical Jesus. By trying to deal with too many issues, Wright may have spread himself too thin and lost focus, blurring the distinctions between historical research and theology, between history and journalism.

On the sore point of eschatology, Wright is aware that, if he remains with Caird, he will be accused of "abandoning eschatology" altogether. Granted that this accusation would be partly unfair (he strongly affirms the resurrection of Jesus, for example), it remains true that Wright has great difficulty with the idea of a new, future divine intervention in the historical process. We can sympathize with him when he rejects the idea that Jesus expected the end of the world, i.e., the end of the space–time universe. It is also a step in the right direction when he says that Jesus expected the end of the present world order, i.e., the end of the period when the Gentiles were lording it over the people of the true God, and the inauguration of the time when this God would take his power and reign and, in the process, restore the fortunes of his suffering people. But he misses the seven-ages (or five-empire) scheme in the background; he limits the fulfillment to Israel as the people of God (thereby missing the universal sweep of Dan 7:13–14 and of Jesus); and he claims Jesus' prophetic predictions were fulfilled adequately in the events of AD 70, so that there is no further future hope for believers on earth, no literal return of Christ for judgment. Pertinent to Wright's options is a discussion of literal versus metaphorical understandings of apocalyptic images of the end-time events, e.g., the sun will be darkened, the stars will fall (Mark 13:24–25). While most scholars would agree that end-time discourse in Daniel and the Gospels is full of symbols, and while some readers would dismiss the symbols as empty and meaningless, among theologically minded interpreters many perceive the intention of the texts to refer to a future divine intervention in human history, and they attempt to respect that intention. Wright prefers to avoid a this-worldly hope coming from God in Christ. The issue is not so much literal versus metaphorical. It is, rather, granted metaphors, what is behind them? Only the events of AD 70 (per Wright) or something more? In addition, some critics suspect Wright of an apologetic motive: he wants to spare Jesus from committing an error on the exact timing of the end-time events. This concern is unnecessary, primarily because of the theological doctrine of Jesus' self-emptying (Phil 2:7). For Jesus, in Mark 13:32, "vigilance, not calculation, is required." In other words, though we should always be prepared for his coming, we cannot know when it will occur.

Fortunately for historical scholarship, there remain in our day scholars who continue to affirm the truth which Weiss so boldly proclaimed, that Jesus was an apocalyptic prophet, who could be tough as well as tender, who not only offered the individual sufferer and sinner healing and forgiveness, but also promised a new divine intervention in history for suffering, oppressed, misled humanity, a hope for all seekers of justice, peace, and joy. In America, the multivolume biography of Jesus by John P. Meier represents a solid contribution, besides the pointed shorter work by D. C. Allison, which is enriched by many examples from the history of religious and social anthropology, and the work of E. P. Sanders. In the French-speaking world, there are the recent biographies by Daniel Marguerat and Jacques Schlosser, and in Germany the works by Gerd Theissen and Annette Merz and Joachim Gnilka.

CONCLUSION

As we come to the end of this all-too-rapid survey, a few red threads are visible. The rigorously historical investigation of Jesus had to wait till the late eighteenth century. Only then were all the historical data in place, plus the mental freedom to bracket all post-Easter Christological developments. The new idea was to look with concentration on the teaching and ministry of Jesus of Nazareth in the three years AD 28–30. What did he teach and preach? Once this strictly defined, narrow question was asked, the answer was not far to seek: he taught and preached, not exclusively but mainly, the soon-to-come kingdom of God, as spoken of in the Book of Daniel. Once this answer was given, as already by Reimarus and Strauss, one could decide that Jesus was mistaken, or accept it and try to make theological sense of it, in one way or another. Or one could try to interpret it away, so that Jesus said or meant something other than what it seemed on the surface. That is the story we have told.

In the version of historical reality here recounted, the heroes of historical truth are Weiss and Schweitzer, and the heroes of theological truth are Moltmann and Metz. All that deviates from them is misleading.

In the postmodern cultural context, however, the very idea that there could be such a thing as an objective historical truth is often regarded as naive, uncritical, unattainable. We could call this epistemological postmodernism. But this idea can also be regarded as politically suspect, even dangerous, as hegemonistic, imperialistic, reflecting the desire to impose a master narrative on the vagaries of history. We could call this literary postmodernism or the hermeneutics of suspicion. On this view, the different lives of Jesus are only time-bound social constructs, with little or no basis in historical reality. We could call this sociological postmodernism.

In the course of our survey, we have in fact made implicit use of every one of these three postmodern critical approaches, to expose and to set aside views we regard as unsound. So we did not end up in a dead end, an epistemological nihilism. To be sure, the attainment of historical truth in ancient history is very difficult. But it makes a difference whether one thinks it is at least possible to attain historical truth or not. If one thinks it is possible, one keeps trying, asymptotically, to come closer and closer to this goal. If one thinks it is not possible, then it is better to stop trying.

BIBLIOGRAPHY

Allison, Dale C. *Jesus of Nazareth*. Minneapolis: Fortress, 1998.
———. *A New Moses: A Matthean Typology*. Minneapolis: Fortress, 1993.
Althaus, Paul. *Die letzten Dinge*. Gütersloh: Mohn, 1970.
Berlin, Isaiah, Sir. *The Crooked Timber of Humanity*. Princeton: Princeton University Press, 1990.
Bloch, Ernst. *The Principle of Hope*. Cambridge: MIT Press, 1986.

Boff, Leonardo. *Jesus Christ, Liberator*. Maryknoll, NY: Orbis, 1980.
Bonhoeffer, Dietrich. *The Cost of Discipleship*. New York: Macmillan, 1959. German orig. 1937.
Bonsirven, Joseph. *Le Regne de Dieu*. Paris: Aubier, 1957.
Borg, Marcus J. *Conflict, Holiness and Politics in the Teachings of Jesus*. Lewiston, NY: Mellen, 1984.
———. "Jesus and the Kingdom of God," *Christian Century* (22 April 1987) 378-80.
Bornkamm, Günther. *Jesus of Nazareth*. New York: Harper, 1960. German orig. 1958.
Bousset, Wilhelm. *Die Offenbarung Johannis*. Göttingen: Vandenhoeck & Ruprecht, 1896.
Brown, Raymond E. *An Introduction to New Testament Christology*. New York: Paulist, 1994.
Bultmann, Rudolf. *Jesus and the Word*. New York: Scribner, 1958. German orig. 1926.
———. *Theology of the New Testament*. Translated by Kendrick Grobel. New York: Scribner, 1951.
Caird, G. B. *The Language and Imagery of the Bible*. Philadelphia: Westminster, 1980.
Carter, Warren. "Evoking Isaiah and Matthean Sociology." *JBL* 119 (2000) 503-20.
Collins, John J. *Daniel*. Hermeneia. Minneapolis: Fortress, 1993.
———, ed. *The Encyclopedia of Apocalypticism*. 3 vols. New York: Continuum, 1998.
Conzelmann, Hans. *Jesus*. J. Raymond Lord. 1959. Philadelphia: Fortress, 1973.
Crossan, John Dominic. *The Historical Jesus: The Life of a Mediterranean Jewish Peasant*. San Francisco: Harper, 1991.
Cullmann, Oscar. *Christ and Time*. Philadelphia: Westminster, 1964. German orig. 1946.
———. *The Christology of the New Testament*. Philadelphia: Westminster, 1959
Daley, B. E. *The Hope of the Early Church*. Peabody, MA: Hendrickson, 2003.
Delgado, Mariano, et al., eds. *Europa, Tausendjähriges Reich und Neue Welt: Zwei Jahrtausende Geschichte und Utopie in der Rezeption des Danielbandes*. Stuttgart: Kohlhammer, 2003.
Dodd, C. H. *The Parables of the Kingdom*. London: Nisbet, 1935; repr. 1961.
Flusser, David. *Jesus*. New York: Herder & Herder, 1969. German orig. 1969; revised German, 1999.
Grappe, Christian. *Le Royaume de Dieu*. Geneva: Labor et Fides, 2001.
Gray, John. *The Biblical Doctrine of the Reign of God*. Edinburgh: T. & T. Clark, 1979.
Gunkel, Hermann. *Genesis*. Macon, GA: Mercer University Press, 1997. German orig. 1901.
Gutierrez, Gustavo. *A Theology of Liberation*. Maryknoll, NY: Orbis, 1973.
Harnack, Adolf von. *History of Dogma*. New York: Dover, 1961. German orig. 1885.
———. *The Sayings of Jesus*. London: Williams & Norgate, 1908. German orig. 1907.
Hengel, Martin. *Studies in Early Christology*. Edinburgh: T. & T. Clark, 1995. See esp. pp. 181-86.
Henning Paulson, *Der zweite Petrusbrief und der Judasbrief*. KEK 12:2. Göttingen: Vandenhoeck & Ruprecht, 1992.
Horsley, Richard A. *Jesus and Empire*. Minneapolis: Fortress, 2003.
———. *Jesus and the Spiral of Violence*. San Francisco: Harper, 1987.
———. *Religion and Empire*. Facets. Minneapolis: Fortress, 2003.
Hurtado, Larry W. "New Testament Christology: A Critique of Bousset's Influence." *TS* 40 (1979) 306-17.

———. *One God, One Lord*. Philadelphia: Fortress, 1988.
John Paul II, Pope. *Mission of the Redeemer*. 1990. Dialogue and Proclamation. Vatican, 1991.
Jeremias, Joachim. *New Testament Theology*. New York: Scribner, 1971.
———. *The Parables of Jesus*. Translated by S. H. Hooke. 2nd ed. New York: Scribner, 1972.
Kant, Immanuel. *Groundwork of the Metaphysics of Morals*. Cambridge: Cambridge University Press, 1998.
———. *The Metaphysics of Morals*. Cambridge: Cambridge University Press, 1996.
———. *Religion within the Boundaries of Mere Reason*. Cambridge: Cambridge University Press, 1998.
Käsemann, Ernst. *Jesus Means Freedom*. London: SCM, 1969.
———. *New Testament Questions of Today*. London: SCM, 1969.
———. "The Problem of the Historical Jesus" In *Essays on New Testament Themes*, 15–47. London: SCM, 1964.
Klatt, Wilhelm. *Hermann Gunkel*. FRLANT 100. Göttingen: Vandenhoeck & Ruprecht, 1969.
Kloppenborg-Verbin, J. S. *Excavating Q*. Minneapolis: Fortress, 2000.
Kümmel, Werner Georg. *The New Testament: The History of the Investigation of Its Problems*. Nashville: Abingdon, 1972.
———. *Promise and Fulfillment*. London: SCM, 1961.
Küng, Hans. *Eternal Life? Life after Death as a Medical, Philosophical, and Theological Problem*. New York: Doubleday-Image, 1985.
Larcher, Chrysostome. *Le Livre de la Sagesse; ou, La Sagesse de Salomon*. EBib, n.s., 1, 3, 5. Paris: Gabalda, 1983, 1984, 1985.
Lagrange, M.-J. *Le messianisme chez les juifs*. Paris: Gabalda, 1909.
Lüdemann, Gerd. "Die Religionsgeschichtliche Schule." In *Theologie in Göttingen*, edited by Bernd Moeller, 325–61. Göttingen: Vandenhoeck & Ruprecht, 1987.
———. *TRE* 28 (1997) 618–24.
Manual, F. E., and F. P. Manual. *Utopian Thought in the Western World*. Cambridge, MA: Belknap, 1980.
Massey, M. C. *Christ Unmasked: The Meaning of the Life of Jesus in German Politics*. Chapel Hill: University of North Carolina Press, 1983.
———. "The Literature of Young Germany and D. F. Strauss's Life of Jesus." *Journal of Religion* 59 (1979) 298–323.
Meeks, M. Douglas. *Origins of the Theology of Hope*. Philadelphia: Fortress, 1974.
Meier, John P. *A Marginal Jew*. 3 vols. Garden City, NY: Doubleday, 1991, 1994, 2001.
Merklein, Helmut. *Die Gottesherrschaft als Handlungsprinzip*. Würzburg: Echter, 1978.
Metz, J. B. *Followers of Christ*. New York: Paulist, 1978.
———. *Theology of the World*. New York: Herder & Herder, 1969.
Montagnes, Bernard, ed. *Exegese et obeissance: Correspondance Cormier-Lagrange (1904–1916)*. Paris: Gabalda, 1989.
———. *Le Pere Lagrange 1855–1938*. Paris: Cerf, 1995.
Moltmann, Jürgen. *A Theology of Hope*. New York: Harper, 1967.
Neill, Stephen. *The Interpretation of the New Testament 1861–1961*. Oxford: Oxford University Press, 1964.
Neufeld, K. H., and Adolf von Harnack. *Theologie als Suche nach der Kirche*. Paderborn: Bonifacius, 1977.

Niebuhr, H. Richard. *Christ and Culture.* New York: Harper, 1951.
Neyrey, Jerome H. *2 Peter, Jude.* AB 37C. Garden City, NY: Doubleday, 1993.
Pannenberg, Wolfhart. *Theology and the Kingdom of God.* Philadelphia: Westminster, 1969.
Perrin, Norman. *Jesus and the Language of the Kingdom.* Philadelphia: Fortress, 1976.
———. *The Kingdom of God in the Teaching of Jesus.* Philadelphia: Westminster, 1963.
Rad, Gerhard von. *Holy War in Ancient Israel.* 1991. Reprinted, Eugene, OR: Wipf & Stock, 2001.
Ratzinger, Joseph. *Eschatology, Death and Eternal Life.* Translated by Michael Waldstein. Dogmatic Theology 9. Washington, DC: Catholic University of America Press, 1988.
Reimarus, H. S. *Fragments.* Philadelphia: Fortress, 1970. German orig. 1778.
Ricciotti, Giuseppe. *The Life of Christ.* Milwaukee: Bruce, 1947.
Robinson, J. A. T. *Jesus and His Coming.* London: SCM, 1957.
Sanders, E. P. *Jesus and Judaism.* Philadelphia: Fortress, 1985.
Schelkle, Karl Hermann. *Die Petrusbriefe, der Judasbrief.* 4th ed. HTKzNT 13/2. Vienna: Herder, 1976.
Schlosser, Jacques. *Le Regne de Dieu dans les dits de Jesus.* Paris: Gabalda, 1980.
Schnackenburg, Rudolf. *God's Rule and Kingdom.* New York: Herder & Herder, 1963. German orig. 1959.
Schweitzer, Albert. *The Quest of the Historical Jesus.* New York: Macmillan, 1969. German orig. 1906.
Scognamiglio, Edoardo. *Ecco: Io Faccio Nuove Tutte le Cose.* Padua: Messagero, 2002.
Strauss, D. F. *The Life of Jesus Critically Examined.* Philadelphia: Fortress, 1972. German orig. 1835–1836.
Theissen, Gerd, and Annette Merz. *The Historical Jesus.* Minneapolis: Fortress, 1998. German orig. 1996.
Vatican Council II. *Constitution on the Church.* Rome, 1964.
———. *Constitution on the Church in the Modern World.*
Viviano, Benedict T. "Apocalypse et Culture: L'interpre'tation de 1 Co 15:20–28." In *Mysterium Regni,* edited by Vittorio Fusco, 739–56. Bologna: Dehoniana, 2001.
———. "The Genres of Matthew 1–2: Light from 1 Timothy 1:4." *RB* 97 (1990) 31–53.
———. *The Kingdom of God in History.* Wilmington, DE: Glazier, 1988.
———. *Trinity-Kingdom-Church.* NTOA 48. Göttingen: Universitätsverlag, 2001.
Vögtle, Anton. *Das Neue Testament und die Zukunft des Kosmos.* Düsseldorf: Patmos, 1970.
Vorgrimler, Herbert. *Hoffnung auf Vollendung.* Vienna: Herder, 1980.
Weiss, Johannes. *Jesus' Proclamation of the Kingdom of God.* Philadelphia: Fortress, 1971.
Winkelhofer, Alois. *HTG* 1:327–36.
Wikenhauser, Alfred. "Die Herkunft der Idee des tausendjährigen Reiches in der Johannes-Apokalypse." *Römische Quartalschrift* 45 (1937) 1–24.
———. "Weltwoche und tausendjähriges Reich," *TQ* 127 (1947) 399–417.
———. *TDNT* 3:921–54 (Friedrich Büchsel and Volkmar Herntrich)
———. *TWAT* 8:408–28 (H. Niehr);
———. *ABD* 3:1104–1106 (T. L. J. Mafico).

10

The Adoration of the Magi

Matthew 2:1–12 and Theological Aesthetics

"*Magna est veritas et praevalebit*"; "Great is truth and it will prevail."
(1 ESDRAS 4:41)

"You are like whitewashed tombs, which appear beautiful (*horaios*) on the outside, but inside are full of dead men's bones."
(MATT 23:27)

"How beautiful (*horaios*) are the feet of those who bring [the] good news."
(ROM 10:15)

INTRODUCTION

The Epiphany story of the birth of Jesus, the jealous alarm of king Herod, the adoration and gifts of the magi, the slaughter of the innocents, is one of the most familiar passages in the Bible. Part of Matthew's dense, compact narrative of Jesus' origins, it has long been a favorite of artists because it gives them a chance to use their gold paint. Not only do the magi present a gift of gold; once they were understood to be oriental kings (based on Isa 60:3 and Ps 72:10–11, by Caesarius of Arles, ca. AD 520), their robes could be depicted as flecked with gold, and their crowns as made of gold.

The passage is often underinterpreted, because it is understood as a story for children. Yet there is an abundance of scholarly literature devoted to it so that one hesitates to add another essay. But since 1980 there has been a newer accent in theology called theological aesthetics. The purpose of the present article is to offer a fresh perspective on this well-known text, a reading energized by some of the questions raised by theological aesthetics.

"The heavens proclaim the glory of God" (Ps 19:1), but beauty is not regarded as an unmixed blessing in the Bible. Consider Prov 31:30: "Charm is deceitful, and beauty is vain, but a woman who fears the LORD is to be praised." Here we sense the biblical moral and religious reserve in regard to a predominantly aesthetic approach to people or to life, the tension between appearance and reality. In Matthew 2 we see the same tension between the beauty of the bright, splendid, shining star as it appears in the open sky, the great joy of the magi at it, on the one hand, and the royal estate of Herod as a mask for his abuse of power, his paranoid fear of rivals to the throne, his secret inquiry (Matt 2:7), his lie (2:8), his intent to murder (2:16–18) on the other hand.

There is thus a series of tensions in the story, between real beauty and beauty as a mask of abusive power, between truth and lie, between fair (pious) speech and hidden harmful intent, between goodness and evil. Terms for fear and warning abound in the text. To make matters more complicated, some of the good characters in the story, the magi, having implicitly agreed to Herod's request to inform him, break that agreement. Warned by a dream, they slip away undetected.

It comes as no surprise that both the Lucan and the Matthean "infancy" gospels have become favorites of liberation theology. So we note a tension in the reception of the text between regarding it as a beautiful story for children (nativity crèches, especially the elaborate Neapolitan ones) and regarding it as a political-theological struggle between two kings, king Herod and king Jesus son of David, for the right to the throne, a struggle characterized on Herod's side by deceit and bloodshed. The contrast in approaches could hardly be greater. Can theological aesthetics be of help to us in comprehending this diversity of readings?

II

Although there may always have been theologians who paid attention to the formal beauty of the texts and themes which they treated, theological aesthetics, as here understood, is a movement which can be dated to 1980, the year of first publication of Hans Urs von Balthasar's *Herrlichkeit* (The Glory of the Lord). Von Balthasar is the founding figure of the movement (b. Lucerne 1905, d. Lucerne 1988, named a cardinal just before his death). His innovative role can be seen at a glance, comparing the second (1963) and third (1996) editions of the *Lexikon für Theologie und Kirche*. The second (pre-conciliar) edition has no article under theological aesthetics, the third one does, and it presents von Balthasar as the main figure. To be sure, the second edition does have an article on beauty (*Schonheit*), but the treatment is purely philosophical.

To break out of the antitheses in postconciliar Catholic theology, von Balthasar decided to open a third front so to speak. He did so on a grand scale: seven volumes of the *Herrlichkeit* (The Glory of the Lord) series, five volumes of *Theo-drama*, and three volumes of *Theo-logic*. The sense of this project, in simple terms, was to circumvent the battles over truth and goodness (i.e. dogmatic or doctrinal and moral theology in the church) by choosing a new starting point: the element of beauty in the Christian faith. Besides the advantage of a fresh start, this approach could hope to reach a broader audience, to make a broader appeal. Novels, plays, and films reach more people than do works of professional, academic, technical theology. Reduced to slogans: "beauty will save the world"; "the beautiful is the true"; in English poetic terms: "'Beauty is truth, truth beauty"—that is all ye know on earth, and all ye need to know' (John Keats, "Ode on a Grecian Urn"). One should not forget that von Balthasar's doctorate was not in philosophy or theology but in German literature.

In a similar spirit, Malcolm Muggeridge could entitle a book about Mother Theresa of Calcutta *Something Beautiful for God*. The idea is that her life of caring for the homeless was not simply moral or charitable or holy, but beautiful. Again, one thinks of a group of English academics who tried to recreate the Christian imagination for modern times. Collectively known as The Inklings, they included J. R. R. Tolkien, C. S. Lewis, Dorothy Sayers, Charles Williams, Own Barfield, Gervase Mathew. Some of them have achieved cult status and cinematic success to an extent even they could hardly imagine.

Insofar as theology has to do with Scripture, von Balthasar, with this approach, could avoid all problems addressed by the historical-critical method. These problems had been troubling the churches since the seventeenth century, provoked by Spinoza, Hobbes and Richard Simon. The issues became more acute with Reimarus, de Wette, D. F. Strauss, Renan, Loisy, Lagrange, and the demythologizing program of Bultmann. Von Balthasar here chose a path of pneumatic (Karl Barth) or spiritual exegesis that reached back to the fathers of early Christianity. In this von Balthasar was pursuing a path laid out by two French Jesuits that influenced his initial theological studies: Henri de Lubac and Jean Daniélou, as well as the German priest Romano Guardini. American analogues would be Hans Frei, Brevard S. Childs, and the "Yale School" of a few decades ago. This side-stepping of modern biblical studies was a bold move. It related the Bible directly to a spiritual reception, without the need for university theology.

This move also allowed von Balthasar to oppose more easily the critical, reform-oriented theology of Hans Küng, a theologian from his home canton of Lucerne. Küng came to use the international journal, *Concilium*, as, to some extent, an engine of war in his campaigns for church reform; von Balthasar founded another journal, *Communio*, as an organ for the renewal of the church on a different basis, theological aesthetics. As the struggle wore on, von Balthasar's banner drew powerful adherents to itself. His theology became, in an unofficial manner, a dominant voice in the International Theological Commission. The church movement *Communione e Liberazione* adopted his theology as its own. Publishing companies like Jaca Books (Milan) and Ignatius Press (San Francisco) promoted his works. As the old masters of conciliar theology faded from the scene, some younger theologians turned to theological aesthetics as a way to the future.

From an earlier period we may consider the case of St. Thomas Aquinas. In his theology Thomas often uses arguments from *convenientia*, i.e., fittingness, appropriateness. This means that he is arguing: this affirmation is so fitting, so beautiful, that it ought to be so, even if it is not found explicitly in Scripture and early Christian tradition. Thomas argues thus when there is insufficient support in Scripture for a particular (secondary) point he wants to propose. At bottom, this is an argument from beauty, *bella figura*. (Cf. the book on the argument from fittingness by Gilbert Narcisse, *Les Raisons de Dieu* [Fribourg: Academic Press, 1997].) In this sense Thomas to some extent precedes and anticipates Hans Urs von Balthasar and his followers, with their program of theological aesthetics. It also means that Thomas uses rhetorical arguments, a sort of "public relations" point of view; not what is true, not what is clearly taught in Scripture and in the early Christian tradition, but what looks or sounds good now. In such cases, Thomas betrays his ideal of theology as a science, and accepts lower levels of argumentation in theological discourse. (This statement presupposes the four levels of discourse listed by Aristotle in the introduction to his *Posterior Analytics*:

poetics, rhetoric, dialectic, scientific demonstration.) This argument would be relatively harmless, were it not for the painful fact that, alongside the Platonic triad of transcendental values (truth, goodness, beauty; sometimes the One and Being are added to the list), there is also power. Power can easily exploit beauty, to undermine and to betray truth and goodness (goodness entails justice and charity for Christians). Beauty can be used to mask the injustice of the powerful. Thomas himself does not do this, but he offers a flank to this abuse.

Because theological aesthetics tended to ignore modern exegesis, modern exegesis tended to ignore it. This is probably an unhealthy, even dangerous, state of affairs. The present essay is intended as a small step in a larger effort to bring the two positions into some conversation, even if it is not always a serene conversation. To be sure, biblical studies have for a long time been discussing the crisis in biblical theology (Childs), the crisis in the historical-critical method (Levenson), the inclusion of literary-critical methods (Alter and Kermode). Even predominantly aesthetic approaches to the Bible have been developed. Yet these have not, to our knowledge, been put into dialogue with theological aesthetics. Before we undertake to do this in relation to Matt 2:1-12, it will be necessary to present some theoretical aspects of the long debate concerning the right relation of the Platonic triad of values and other values besides, to one another and to biblical revelation.

III

A. Beauty

From the time of Plato, thinkers have accepted that among the characteristics of being figure prominently the triad: the true, the good, the beautiful. But already Plato mistrusted art as mere appearance, as deceptive (*Gorgias* 479E), and rhetoric as sophistry. For Aristotle, beauty purifies the passions (*catharsis*) by art and trains humans to ethical conduct.

In the history of Western thought then, beauty is too massive, too present, a force to be ignored, yet it has never ceased to be regarded with suspicion, as a troublesome, even a dangerous, aspect of reality, an aspect which should be subordinated to and tamed or held in check by the surer, higher values of truth and goodness. It may be useful to list some of the ways in which beauty is a force in society, ancient and modern. There will follow another list of the basic objections to beauty as an emphasis in Christian life and thought. (1) When we think of the presence and power of beauty in our world, we may think first of all about the *physical beauty* of human beings.

This physical beauty attracts people to one another, leads to relationships, marriages, children. It has an aspect of biological programming. This beauty may be considered the prime analogate of all other forms of beauty, from the viewpoint of human beings. (2) Beauty is not identical with art or aesthetics, but is often associated with them. Beauty is found in nature as well as in human constructs called art. Art can choose to be deliberately ugly. Art is a big *business*, both fine art and commercial art. (3) Medicine. Beauty affects medicine through such activities as plastic/cosmetic surgery, control of weight, dieting, dietetics, fitness, body-building, liposuction, anorexia, boulemia, botox. (4) Religion. In its visible aspects, many religious practices involve beauty and art: architecture, music, the administration of the sacraments. (5) The media: handsome actors, beautiful actresses on screen and television, news broadcasters, the "star system," fan clubs, posters, value-free celebrities. (6) The beauty bonus in employment. Good looking employees are paid more highly. We could add the factor of a virility bonus: deep voice, heavy beard, and a tallness or height bonus. (7) Theological ideas can be beautiful: God, the risen Christ in glory, the transfigured Christ, the lives of the saints. The theological aesthetics movement holds that the crucified Christ is beautiful. (8) Cuisine. Food can be carefully prepared and beautifully presented. People are often willing to pay more for this. (9) Housing. People are willing to pay more to live in a cheerful rather than in a depressed neighborhood, when they can.

We will now add a list of objections to beauty as an emphasis in Christian life and theology. (a) From an intellectual point of view, beauty is often regarded as trivial, decorative, ornamental, pleasant, shallow, superficial, belletrist. Beauty is only skin deep; it prefers form over matter, style over substance. (b) Ethically, an accent on beauty can be viewed as offensive because (1) it can be elitist; (2) it is compatible with grave evils, e.g., SS uniforms were "smarter" than other armies' uniform, but their actions were gravely evil.; (3) an interest in beauty can distract from the pursuit of truth and goodness, what the rabbis call "neglect of Torah" *(betul Torah)*; (4) beauty can lead to immorality, e.g., adultery, divorce, damaged children, murder (David's indirect murder of his general Uriah over Bathsheba, 2 Samuel 11), war (Helen of Troy), poor use of economic resources (Lola Montez and the kingdom of Bavaria); (5) one could consider the beauty bonus in hiring a form of injustice.

We have just sketched some objections to the dangers posed by the power of beauty. There are also some reservations lodged against the program of theological aesthetics. First, although von Balthasar begins with the self-emptying *(kenosis)* of Jesus on the cross, some critics suspect that the reality of human suffering is not taken seriously enough in his theology. Von

Balthasar realizes that the kenosis of God, the lowly, formless figure of the suffering Christ, the heart of the New Testament gospel, differs from the Old Testament starting point, the glory of God in creation, and from the Greek idea of beauty. The *kenosis* requires a new definition of glory and beauty. There is a tension within the New Testament itself between the ugly fact of the shameful execution of Jesus (Mark 15:33–37) and the radiant exaltation of Jesus (Rev 1:12–18), his transfiguration and glory (Luke 9:28–36, esp. v. 32), the incarnation of the glory of God (John 1:14, *doxa* twice), the elevation of humans to participation in it (2 Pet 1:4). Still, the critics note that both in antiquity and today there is a reluctance to see the cross as the instrument of death that it is It has been covered with jewels and made a thing of beauty. (Already in the gospel according to John, one could think that Christ reigns from the cross as sovereign Lord.) For these critics the *kenosis* means God's going out of all tidiness into the status of the questionable. For them the concept of beauty must be freed from the Neoplatonic tradition and linked with modern art where negativity is included.

Next, the strongly moral emphasis of both testaments (the law, the prophets, the wisdom teachers, Jesus, and Paul) supports a hostility to an aesthetic approach to God.

Third, theological aesthetics sets out to present the joy of Christian faith convincingly against the grumbling discontent of the Enlightenment, its carping criticism and skepticism. Yet theological aesthetics in practice tends to an aprioristic impatience with the problems of modernity. It reacts to the modern competition of art with traditional religions as the religion of modernity and of the future (e.g., the Wagner cult of the last two centuries). Despite its effort to oppose aesthetical theology, theological aesthetics reflects a modern trend to aesthetisize the world in which we live, the perpetual quest of some Christians to find their ecclesial Bloomsbury. It seeks a return to wonder and to ecstatic contemplation, but this search should not rule out critical thinking.

Finally, the critics mentioned in note 2 judge that we need not only an aesthetics of the sacraments but also an aesthetical consideration of the church which would bring to light the connection between beauty, authority and power, and abuse of power.

B. Truth

Where does *truth* fit in the Bible, and in relation to beauty? In the Christian theological tradition there are four cardinal virtues (Wis 8:7) and three theological virtues (1 Cor 13:13). They are all great moral values. But there is also a Platonic triad of values: truth, goodness, beauty. Of these three only one is necessarily moral, goodness. But where do the other two fit in? The clearly moral part of truth is the cardinal virtue of prudence, i.e., practical wisdom. But what of scientific or historical or forensic or theological truth as an end in and of itself? Does it have a place in philosophy, in Christian life?

Biblical scholars distinguish between (1) Hebrew truth or *'emeth*, which has a primarily *moral* connotation of fidelity, reliability, and (2) Greek truth or *aletheia*, which has a more *intellectual* connotation of reality or knowledge of reality.[1] Often it is said that one is more aural (interpersonal), the other more visual, objective: there is a tree in the yard: true or false? In the NT, John is the main author or circle of authors interested in the theme, roughly two-thirds of the occurrences in the NT. Authors are divided on truth in John. Both tendencies are present, biblical and Hellenic. Bultmann and Dodd say that the Hellenic sense prevails in John, de La Potterie that the biblical sense prevails. Brown hesitates. Barrett tries to hold both together, as does Dodd to some extent, but Barrett's view is corrupted by Bultmannian Heideggerian decisionism and voluntarism. What is clear is that for John truth is primarily the person of Jesus (14:6) both as the revelation of the Father and as the means of salvation. Truth is thus a religious *saving* truth, related to faith. And faith for John has a doctrinal content (20:31), the person of Jesus as the Christ the Son of God.

As for an intellectualist, objectivist concern for truth as a value in its own right, it is present in the Bible, though not often using the *term* "truth." (1) Truth about nature and natural science, e.g., Gen 1–3; Sir 42:15–25; 43:1–33. (2) Historical truth, the story of the birth of the nation, e.g., Ps 77:5; Ps 7–8; Deut 6:6 and 7 = an educational program. (3) Political truth: Nathan confronts David on abuse of power: "You are the Man!," 2 Sam 12:7; Naboth's vineyard, 1 Kings 21; Amos 1; Pilate and Jesus John 18:36. (4) Forensic truth, Deut 16:18–20. Impartiality in judgement, *aprosopolepsia*.[2] (5) Theological truth, e.g., polemic against those who teach or practice otherwise: against Samaritans, Ezra 10; Jesus against people who do not believe

---

1. On truth in John see: Raymond E. Brown, *The Gospel according to John (I–XII)* (AB 29a; Garden City, NY: Doubleday, 1966), 499–501; C. H. Dodd, *The Interpretation of the Fourth Gospel* (Cambridge: Cambridge University Press, 1953), 170–78; *TDNT* 1:232–51, s.v. *aletheia* (Rudolf Bultmann); Ignace de La Potterie, *La vérité dans Saint Jean*, 2 vols. (AnBib 73–74; Rome: Biblical Institute Press, 1977; 2nd ed. 1999); C. K. Barrett, *The Gospel according to John*, 2nd ed. (Philadelphia: Westminster, 1978), 167, 218, 344ff, 458, 489, 537; Rudolf Schnackenburg, *The Gospel according to St. John* (New York: Seabury-Crossroad, 1980), 2:225–37.

2. *TDNT* 6:779–80, s.v. *prosopolepsis* (Eduard Lohse); Jouette Bassler, *Divine Impartiality* (SBLDS 59; Chico, CA: Scholars, 1982).

in his credentials, his mission, his heavenly origins: John 5, 7, 8, 9, 10; Paul against Peter, Gal 2:11–14; Paul against Judaizers, Galatians 1–4. So there is a biblical interest in truth or veracity in these areas, but often without a use of the *term* "truth." There is also a *delight* in the truth, marvelling in nature or the divine law, e.g., Ps 8 or Ps 104; Ps 1; Sir 38:34b; 39:1–11, the praise of the scribe.

An interest in beauty is present in the Old Testament,[3] but not much in the NT. Everyone is in favor of truth until it uncovers something embarrassing to their reputation or harmful to their interests. Then people begin to writhe and squirm. They become agents of untruth, liars. They try to cover the embarrassing fact up. But the hard issues come when we begin to treat what are known as messy or inconvenient truths of history or politics. This is the kind of truth that gets institutions irritated, defensive and feeling threatened. This is when public relations experts, propagandists, truth spinners go into action and earn their high salaries. This is when the principle that one is not always obliged to reveal everything is invoked. And the spinners are helped by the fact that reality is rich and many-sided. The presentation of uncomfortable truths, e.g., that Pius IX was a severe epileptic, that Vice President Richard Cheney has had a series of heart attacks, can pass into calumny or libel or mudslinging. This is where Hans Küng invokes the value of truthfulness or veracity.[4] "Truth is the cry of all, but the game of the few" as Bishop Berkeley said (*Siris*, par. 368).

The Bible, in an unsystematic way, manifests the normal human healthy interest in the reality of the world, of nature, of history, of politics, of God's presence and power to help, as well as in beauty. But the Bible's primary interests are moral and salvific. Yet the prophets seek political and religious reform, and to that end, invoke unpleasant facts or truths. So the Platonic triad of values is present in the Bible, with the accent on goodness (cf. Vatican II, *Gaudium et spes*, par. 76). Another related issue is the historicity of truth. On the positive side, this means that to understand a human reality, e.g., a nation or a religion, it is helpful to know its history. This has become in some circles a banality; it is the basis of encyclopedia articles. On the other hand, carried to extremes, this historicity of truth can mean the denial of any possibility of truth, a dissolving of all truth in pure relativism. This is a huge problem, the danger of hermeneutical nihilism or total relativism.[5]

---

3. Cf. concordances and Gerhard von Rad, *Old Testament Theology*, trans. D. M. G. Stalker (Edinburgh: Oliver & Boyd, 1962), 1:356–70, esp. 364.

4. Hans Küng, *Truthfulness: The Future of the Church* (London: Sheed & Ward, 1968).

5. Simon Blackburn, *Truth: A Guide* (Oxford: Oxford University Press, 2005); Jim

A related problem is the truth value and the truth danger of a philosophy of history. Such a philosophy typically tries to understand the meaning of the (historical) process of world history: politics, war, culture, religion. In its classic form, Hegel's *Philosophy of History*, it concludes that Prussia is the present and permanent incarnation of the Holy Spirit and that it is God's will that Prussia should conquer and govern the world. Or so it was understood. Such an understanding led to the First World War. Such folly led many to mistrust such grandiose attempts at a philosophical understanding of history (Popper and Sartre again), or to do it better (Toynbee), or to remain silent about it altogether (*Fides et Ratio*).[6]

From the English-speaking tradition of Catholic Christian theology, we may mention two contributions of John Henry Newman, later cardinal of the Roman church. On the one hand, in his masterpiece of 1864, *Apologia Pro Vita Sua*, he had to defend himself and his church from Charles Kingsley's accusation that truth for its own sake was not a value for the Roman Catholic Church. Newman succeeded brilliantly, by distinguishing between the value of truth in itself (this was upheld by the church), and the need for white lies and diplomatic ambiguities in certain, carefully defined, circumstances (this was also upheld by the moral theologians (casuists) like St. Alphonsus Liguori). On the other hand, in his *Essay on the Development of Christian Doctrine* (1845), Newman composed a masterpiece of historical theology. In this work he gave a detailed presentation of the evolution of dogma, and thus of the historicity of Christian truth. Whenever in the church there is a movement to deny or to veil this historicity, Newman's works can serve as a helpful tonic and guide to ecclesial reality, and as an encouragement to tell the truth. (N: Owen Chadwick, Aidan Nichols.)

IV

Thanks to our theoretical investigations of problems related to beauty and truth, problems also less directly related to justice and goodness, we turn now to Matt 2:23 with an awareness heightened by the program of

---

Holt, "Say Anything," *The New Yorker* (22 Aug 2005) 69-75.

6. K. R. Popper, *The Open Society and Its Enemies*, 2 vols. (Princeton: Princeton University Press, 1971; orig. 1945); J. P. Sartre, *Being and Nothingness* (New York: Washington Square, 1964; orig. 1943); Arnold Toynbee, *A Study of History*, abridgement of vols. I-VII by D. C. Somervell (New York: Oxford University Press, 1946); Toynbee, abridgment of vols. VII-X (New York: Oxford University Press, 1957); Pope John Paul II, encyclical *Fides et Ratio* (Rome: Vatican Press, 1998); G. F. Hegel, *The Philosophy of History* (Amherst, NY: Prometheus, 1991; orig. 1837); Friedrich von Schlegel, *The Philosophy of History* (London: Bohn, 1859; orig. 1829).

theological aesthetics. It can help us to see more sharply elements of beauty which really are present in the biblical text. Its insights will however lead us astray, if they are not combined with a sensitivity to the concerns of liberation theology which are also present in the text. The text is so rich that, granted its extreme brevity and compactness, a single method does not suffice to disclose all its facets.

Our analysis will be selective, rather than exhaustive. It is in the nature of a hermeneutical exploration rather than of a complete exegesis. The analysis will take particular note of elements of beauty and ugliness, truth and deceit (lying, deception, the double cross), goodness and evil, suffering and joy, cross and crown. When we attend to the play of both the light and the shadow, the careful balance of elements in the text, we begin to grasp it in the fullness of its powerful grip on reality, despite its initial air of a charming Oriental legend from the Arabian nights. Total originality here is out of the question.

Matthew's drama of the birth of Jesus contains three acts and six scenes. The three acts are 1:18–25 (the announcement to Joseph), 2:1–12 (the magi, the star, King Herod), and 2:13–23 (the flight to Egypt, the slaughter of the boys, the return from Egypt). The six scenes are: 1:18–25; 2:1–8, 9–12, 13–15, 16–18, 19–23. The drama is lively and agitated, moving quickly from Joseph's embarrassment and discretion to a mysterious pregnancy, to divine reassurance, to the birth of a son to a virgin, to the visit of some mysterious magi guided by a miraculous star. The magi meet a duplicitous king, rejoice at the star, bring gifts to the child, and disappear. The young family flees to Egypt, Herod goes on a murderous rampage in and around Bethlehem, the family finds a second refuge in Galilee. All this happens in 31 verses (48 verses with the genealogy). By contrast, Luke's infancy story, including its genealogy, runs to 148 verses; it is longer due especially to the hymns and to the story of John the Baptist. Matthew's drama is also characterized by many references to the Old Testament: direct quotations, allusions, and typological patterns.[7] The first two chapters of Matthew form a tight unity, especially chap. 2, despite some rough edges. (For example, Herod and the magi are informed of the child by two sources of information: the star and the Scriptures. Would not one have sufficed?) The total effect is one of dramatic intensity and theological density. We see here a good example of Meir Sternberg's idea of the "foolproof" method of biblical composition: a text so simple a child can understand it, yet so rich that a scholar can explore, mutter, puzzle, marvel, and delight over it.[8] Thus the text can be read on two

---

7. R. D. Aus, *Matthew 1–2 and the Virginal Conception* (Lanham MD: University Press of America, 2004).

8. Meir Sternberg, *Poetics of Biblical Narrative*, cited note 16 above.

levels, as a story and as a subject of scholarly investigation and theological reflection.

From a scholarly point of view, some preliminary background questions are important. The question of the literary genre of Matt 2 I have treated elsewhere.[9] The text as we have it bears every sign of Matthean composition, yet Matthew did not compose it freely. He put down, fused, and arranged for the first time oral traditions he had received.[10] The text contains not only history, but also abundant elements of theological typology, midrash, the fulfillment of scriptural prophecies understood as messianic. Moses typology and the messianic interpretation (based on Num 24:17) are especially striking. The prophecies cited range from Isaiah, to Micah, Hosea, Jeremiah, and the enigmatic "he shall be called a Nazorean" (possibly a reference to Isa 11:1 and/or to Judg 13:5, 7).[11]

Three explanations of the magi have been proposed: (1) they are Zorasatrian priests from Persia; (2) they are Chaldean astrologers from Babylonia; (3) they are Nabatean merchant princes from Northern Arabia (including modern Jordan and Syria). A good case can be made for each of these options: the *word* magi meant Persian priest; the star supports the astrological line; the gifts of gold and spices support the trade caravan option.[12] (Herod Antipas was in conflict with Nabatean king Aretas IV, at a slightly later period; cf. Mark 6:14-29 parr; 2 Cor 11:32.)[13] Matthew leaves the matter so open that perhaps the best solution is to conclude that: (1) in general the evangelist strives for a maximum of suggestivity within the framework of extreme concision; (2) in the case of the magi he intends the informed reader to think of all three backgrounds. In any case, in his text they are (Gentile) dignitaries who worship the Jewish messiah; they also defy the rival king Herod. The magi also concretize narratively the pilgrimage of the nations to Israel prophesied by Isaiah (2:2-5; Mic 4:1-4). In addition, they remind the biblically literate of the pilgrimage of the Queen of Sheba to King Solomon (1 Kgs 10:1-29).

The devout reader of Matthew normally does not realize that Herod the Great (reigned 37-4 BC) is one of the best known figures of ancient history, nor even that he is called Great or why. Yet we are informed about the most intimate details of his life thanks to the memoirs of his grand vizier,

---

9. See n. 1 above.

10. See the works of Brown and Luz cited in n. 1 above.

11. M. J. J. Menken, *Matthew's Bible* (BETL 173; Leuven: Peeters, 2004) and the earlier works there cited there.

12. R.E. Brown, *Birth of the Messiah*, 167-71.

13. R.S. Kraemer, "Implicating Herodias and Her Daughter in the Death of John the Baptizer," *JBL* 125 (2006) 321-49.

Nicolas of Damascus, as they are incorporated into the histories of Flavius Josephus.[14] He is called great because of his military successes and because of his political astuteness, as well as because of his long reign and his ambitious cultural programs. He rebuilt the Jerusalem Temple on a grand scale for the Jews and pagan temples for others. The most beautiful and impressive masonry in the Holy Land is still called "Herodian," even though some of it could just as well be called Roman. Herod was cynical, devious, and cruel, effective but unloved, especially because of his high rate of taxation. He grew increasingly jealous as he grew older, and killed three of his ten wives and three of his sons. His interest in beautiful architecture and his murder of suspected rivals are both relevant to our investigation of Matthew 2. The slaughter of the innocents in and around Bethlehem is not recorded as such by Josephus, but Matthew's story reflects accurately enough one aspect of Herod's character. With these background issues in mind, we can approach the biblical text anew, in the conviction that a combination of the methods of theological aesthetics and historical criticism will enable us to see more clearly certain aspects of the gospel. To be sure, these aspects were always present in the text. But they were not always sharply perceived, because the sensitivities of readers had not been raised by these methods. When combined, these methods or lines of interrogation can also disclose more problems, for example, how beauty can mask deceit and abuse of power. Did the Magi intentionally deceive Herod? The text requires us to pay attention to both the magi and Herod, to both beauty and ugliness. In 2:1-2 we meet two kings: "in the days of Herod the king" (v. 1); "where is he who has been born king of the Jews?" (v. 2). Herod is again called king in v. 3. The title shifts in v. 4 to "Christ," presumably the anointed royal messiah (Jesus is called son of David in 1:1). In the biblical citation in v. 6 the terminology changes again to *hegemon* (rulers of Judah) and *hegemenos* (ruler) and *poimanei* (he will shepherd, that is, govern). Herod is referred to without a title in vv. 7 and 12, as king in v. 9. From these data, we conclude that a contrast is set up by the evangelist between two kings, one old, one just born (the death of Herod is mentioned in vv. 15 and 19). This contrast is only rather gently suggested, except for the fear and anxiety of Herod mentioned in v. 3 (literally, "he is shaken"). Matthew constructs this contrast with both a political and a religious motive in mind. The question is implicit

---

14. Josephus, *B.J.* 1:18-33; *Ant.* 15;16; 17:1-8; Emil Schürer, *The History of the Jewish People in the Age of Jesus Christ*, rev. G. Vermes and F. Millar (Edinburgh: T& T Clark, 1973) 1:287-329; Abraham Schalit, *Köinig Herodes: Der Mann und sein Werk* (SJ 4; Berlin: de Gruyter, 1969); Peter Richardson, *Herod: King of the Jews* (Columbia: University of South Carolina Press, 1996); Nikos Kokkinos, *The Herodian Dynasty* (JSPSup 30; Sheffield: Sheffield Academic, 1998); R. S. Kraemer, art. cit. in n. 34 above.

in the text: which of these two persons is the true king of the Jews? Herod's fear expresses his awareness that a threat to his power lurks in the wings. The text suggests a struggle for the succession to the throne. This is not a gospel for children only.

Verses 4 and 5 present a question and a clear answer. The high priest and scribes of the people (perhaps the scribes were the educated elite of Hue various parties in Jewish Palestine at the time) quote a mixed passage from Scripture (v. 6): a mixture of Mic 5:2 and 2 Sam 5:2 (= 1 Chr 11:2). The quotation includes an apostrophe to the town of Bethlehem, a litotes added by the evangelist, and an interpretation of the future ruler as a shepherd, implicitly a gentle ruler in contrast with harsh lictrod. The matter is a bit tangled. The quotation is part of the court experts' answer to Herod, so it is not introduced by Matthew's fulfillment formula. On the other hand, even if the quotation, with its deviations frorn the Hebrew and Septuagint text types, for the most part derives from Matthew's sources, as many think, nevertheless the gentle shepherd interpretation at the end betrays the hand of the evangelist and weakens *the* narrative plausibility. Thus, while it is generous of Mathew to portray the experts as so knowledgeable, it is improbable that they would give such a Christian twist to the quotation.[15] The secrecy motif is v. 7 (cf. 1:19) heightens the dramatic interest.

The next verse (8) is crucial for our purpose, because, under the most unctuous of pious pretenses, Herod's statement of his intention to worship the newborn rival king, there stands the big lie. His love of power brooks no rivals. As the reader will learn in v. 16, Herod will try to have the Christ child killed, even if it means taking the lives of innocent infants. This is a far cry from devout prostration. It is a striking literary illustration of the gap that can exist between fair words and promises and the brutal realities of politics, a gap that can exist in any era. This is a gap that has made people wary of beautiful rhetoric, that has led them to ask what is the reality behind the rhetoric. The magi (v. 9) are said to "hear" the king. Biblically, the verb "to hear" often means "to obey" (*obaudire*, the Latin original of English "obey," also means to listen hard). If we translate "The magi obeyed the king," we take this to mean that the magi made an implicit promise to Herod or an implicit contract with him. This would be a natural reading, but then it would create difficulties later on (vv. 12 and 16).

The star (vv. 2, 9, 10) leads the magi to the house where the Christ child dwells; the star then stands over it; the star is the occasion of great joy for them. The behavior of the star, rising, leading, stopping, is probably inspired by the behavior of the pillar of fire in the cloud, which leads

---

15. M. J. J. Menken, *Matthew's Bible* (see n. 32 above), 255-63.

the Israelites in their Sinai desert wanderings and campsites. This behavior is most thoroughly described in Num 9:15-23, especially v. 17. In Jewish tradition, the pillar of fire, the cloud and the star (cf. Wis 10:17; 18:3) are understood as folins of the presence of God, the Shekinah, among human beings, on earth. So understood, the joy of the magi at an object of beauty, bright, shining and pleasing to the eye, includes a religious dimension, and, in relation to "the child with Mary his mother" (v. 11), a Christological and Mariological dimension as well.[16] The phrase "the child and his mother" occurs five times in chapter two: vv. 11, 13, 14, 20, 21. This repetition is a narrative necessity, yet the evangelist follows the biblical style of composition wherein repetition also often serves as.a means of emphasis.[17]

Matthew uses five verbs to describe the behavior of the magi in v. 11: they see, kneel or fall down, adore or pay homage, they open (their treasure chests) and they offer their gifts. They are portrayed as model worshippers, according to the often repeated Pentateuchal principle, "No one shall appear before me [the Lord] empty-handed" (Exod 23:15; 34:20; Deut 16:16). The three gifts, derived from Isa 60:6; Ps 72:10-11, 15; Cant 3:6; 4:6, 14; 5:1, 5, 13, regarded on the surface level, have a beautiful, pleasing quality: gold is valued because it shines; incense gives off a sweet smell; myrrh is an ointment or body lotion, used as a perfume, or to ease physical pain or to embalm a corpse (John 19:39; cf. Luke 23:56). Over the centuries gift giving at Christmas has taken on enormous comercial, economic significance. Today's merchants, worthy successors of their Nabatean forebearers, recognize that the gifts have an aspect of sensual delight, a basis for their religious role as appropriate for a king, the Son of God, the crucified Savior.

With v. 12, the magi are warned in a dream not to return to Herod. They return to their own country by another route. Here the pretty surface of the oriental tale begins to crack. Herod's cruel scheme, veiled in declarations of pious intent, begins to be unmasked. One warns against a danger, however discreetly the danger is here insinuated by the text. But troubling moral issues arise from more than Herod's lie. The Magi here break their implicit agreement with Herod. They do so in obedience to a higher authority. The dream warning comes from God. Does this mean that God commanded them to break their promise? We are here in treacherous waters. Kant said that Abraham should have disobeyed God's command to sacrifice his son Isaac.[18] John Hus was burned at the stake at the Council of

---

16. B. T. Viviano, "The Movement of the Star, Matt 2:9 and Num 9:17," see n. 1 above; D. C. Allison, *Studies on Matthew* (Grand Rapids: Baker, 2005), 17-41.

17. Martin Buber, *The Prophetic Faith* (New York: Harper-Macmillan, 1949), 8, 9, 21; cf. Richard Wagner's musical technique of the Leitmotif.

18. Immanuel Kant, *Religion within the Boundaries of Mere Reason* (1793),

Constance on the grounds that promises made to heretics do not bind (in this case, the promise he could go free even if he were condemned by the council). But this argument does not receive much favor today. The exegete cannot solve all theses problems. Suffice it to say that the text raises some perplexing moral issues.[19]

The rest of the chapter (2:13–23) consists of three short scenes. They are less beautiful than vv. 1–12, less used in the liturgy, less frequently depicted in great art (Breughel is the great exception, moved as he was by the horrors of the wars of religion in his own time). We could con elude that they are less important (liturgically, the eon imentoration of the lioly innocents is as a feast day, less than a Sunday or Solt:4)1114y, ws loss well known to the faithful), But these scones arc important for our second concern, that an interest in beauty be balanced by a concern for truth, including the truth of the horror of abuse of power. This section anticipates the cross of Christ, his kenosis, and so enables chap. 2 to be called the gospel in a nutshell, that is, the kerygma gospel of salvation through the suffering, death and rising of Jesus the Christ. These verses are full of dream warnings (vv. 13, 19, 22), fear (vv. 22), anger (v. 16), death (vv. 16, 19, 20), and flight, first to Egypt, then to Galilee. The verses contain a catalogue of bitter truths, but also of fulfillments of biblical prophecy (vv. 15, 18 [a sad fulfillment], and in some sense, 23).

Verse 13 repeats vocabulary (return, dream), from the transitional or hinge v. 12. Geography continues to play an important role in this story of origins. The flight into Egypt is also rather well served by artists, although the scene is not in itself beautiful. In the Bible, Egypt suggests land of idolatry, sorcery and slavery (Exodus 1–15), but also of safety and refuge (e.g., for Jacob and his sons and their families in danger from famine, Genesis 41–50).[20] Verses 13 and 14 are structured according to the biblical pattern of command and execution; the second echoes or mirrors or realizes the first, adding only the evocative detail "by night."[21] The angel of the Lord, who reveals Herod's murderous intent, the dream, and the quotation from Hosea (11:1) are all elements which heighten the religious character of the passage. The evangelist also plays on the double sense of "my son," since biblically God's son is both his people Israel and the Messiah. Here the two senses

---

translated Allen Wood and George di Giovanni (Cambridge: Cambridge University Press, 1998), p. 100 (6.87); p. ISO (=6.187), reflecting on Genesis 22.

19. Tim Schramm and Kathrin Löwenstein, *Unmoralische Heiden: Anstössige Gleichnisse Jesu* (Göttingen: Vandenhoeck & Ruprecht, 1986).

20. Jan Assmann, *Moses the Egyptian* (Cambridge: Harvard University Press, 1997).

21. Rudolf Pesch, "Eine alttestamentliche Ausführungsformel in Matthäus-Evangelium," *BZ* 10 (1966) 220–45; 11 (1967) 79–95.

overlap in the child Jesus. The individual and the collective perspectives are fused. The angelic message to wait until the tyrant dies contains the wisdom of historical experience: tyrants fall, bad times pass, everything depends upon surviving until the tide turns, until the moment becomes favorable.

Now comes the slaughter itself (v. 16). First, it dawns on Herod that he has been treated as a fool by the magi. The Greek here is important: *empaizo* (from *pais*, child or slave) means: to be played with as with a child; then, to mock; then, more seriously, to deceive, trick, dupe. For the able politician that was Herod, who had survived many turns of the political wheel, by knowing when to change sides (notably from Mark Anthony and Cleopatra to Octavian after the battle of Actium), this was hard to take. The magi are here mentioned twice and then disappear from the text (cf. Acts 13:6, 8). Older translations shied away from the idea of the magi deliberately deceiving Herod; recent translations are less shy. Have the magi narratively doublecrossed Herod by a deceit contrary to his own big lie in v. 8? Or is Matthew here only intending to display Herod's paranoid sensibility? In any case, Herod falls into a jealous rage and orders the slaughter of the *paidas* (children). Perhaps Matthew here deliberately plays with the etymology of *empaizo*. There is also the delicate euphemism in the verb *aneilen* (from *anairo*, literally "take away," here however it means "to kill"). Under the veil of language the horror is told. This particular slaughter is elsewhere unattested, but it is in character with the Herod narrated by Josephus. The pericope, mercifully brief, concludes with a moving citation from the sorrowful prophet Jeremiah. In the mother's poignant, inconsolable, weeping for the loss of her children, the poet says more than would a detailed catalogue of gore. Here again biblical honesty about pain, suffering, misery, cruelty, injustice, and death as an evil, goes hand in hand with a terse literary finesse. But it is not art for art's sake. It is a cry of protest. The echo of the killing of the Israelite boys in Exodus 1 and 2 adds a depth dimension that would have been fairly evident to the first Jewish-Christian hearers-readers of the gospel, without undermining the painful reality that Herod also had young people killed. Sin has a history too. (For H. U. von Balhasar, dramatic tragedy is the highest of all artistic achievements.)

The final pericope (vv. 19–23) brings some closure, while adding some enigmas. After the death of the children, Herod's death is announced. (His rampage is understandable as a reaction to his declining powers, as is his drowning two of his own sons two weeks before his own death.) The plural in v. 20 is initially enigmatic: "those . . . are dead." It is an echo of LXX Exod 4:19, where it refers to the Midianites who had been seeking Moses' life. Here it suggests Herod and his most active entourage. There is a balance of terror, some retribution, some khanna, some hope that evil does not prevail forever and always. Yet there is also a continuity of evil: with Arehelaus succeeding Herod in Judea, however briefly, the coast is not yet completely clear; hence the withdrawal to Galilee. In vv. 19-21 we have another example of the command and execution pattern, and more briefly again in v. 22. Verse 22 echoes v. 12. Verse 23 calls little Nazareth a *polis*, a city. For Matthew its dignity is enhanced by its serving as the residence of the true king; it is theologically a city. The last verse contains another enigma, a formula citation, in proper form, of a phrase fro an unidentifiable source, "he shall be called a Nazorean." Of the many proposals to solve the puzzle, perhaps the best is to find an echo here of Matt 1:21, "You are to call him Jesus, for he will save his people . . ." Thus Nazorean here suggests "nazir," a consecrated savior figure, a strongman judge like Samson (Judg 13:5, 7), Jesus as a new Samson; both win as they die (cf. Judg 16:23-30).

After what we hope has been a close reading of Matthew 2, it remains to draw up a balance sheet of elements which could be called beautiful in the narrative, and ugly elements as well. On the beautiful side we can put first the narrative art with which the story is told: its brevity, surface simplicity, and intertextual depth, its dynamism (rapid changes of scene and character); the chatin of an Oriental legend, to which the largely unidentifiable magi from the mysterious east make a major contribution. The miraculous star also fascinates. The birth of a child, followed by the repose of the child in its mother's arms or lap is normally regarded as a joyous event, although the actual delivery may be frightening or even life-threatening. (It is a delicate matter how far the Bible wants to go in the cult of Lady Wisdom, the Madonna and child, the woman crowned with twelve stars [Rev 12], the eternal feminine, Robert Graves' white goddess.[22] The Bible exercises great restraint, yet the feminine is usually there.) With a little imagination, aided by Josephus and archaeology, one can imagine the splendor of Herod's court, his and the priests' palaces, the Citadel and Antonia fortresses, the restored Temple itself.[23] There is also the lure of the question, the mystery: "Where is the child who has been born king?" with which the chapter begins and to which all that follows is an answer. Finally, there is the noble intent of the magi to worship the Messiah, supported by the generosity of their elegant gifts. This side of the story is edifying, it is good business, but it is also the delight of artist and families. This beautiful side is, however, negatively balanced by ugly elements, embarrassing, painful truths. These are primarily Herod's great lie in v. 9; the broken promise and double cross by the magi

---

22. Robert Graves, *White Goddess* (1948; reprinted New York: Vintage, 1958).
23. J. H. Charlesworth, ed., *Jesus and Archaeology* (Grand Rapids: Eerdmans, 2006).

(vv. 12, 16); the slaughter of the children (v. 16); the fear, flight, and exile (vv. 19-22) of Joseph, Mary, and the Christchild.[24]

V

Matthew's second chapter has undoubtedly been a great "success": it is loved by parents and children, by artists and merchants, by believers and unbelievers. It is a tale well told and colorful. Like any well told story, it contains a few enigmas. Artistically, the scenes most often represented by artists are the adoration of the magi and the flight of the holy family into Egypt.

This essay has been in the nature of an exploration. It has tried to wrestle with the approach of theological aesthetics as a relatively recent lens through which to read the biblical text. This approach concentrates on the aesthetic, artistic, beautiful aspect of Christian theology as a first step toward an appreciation of its truth and its moral significance (goodness, holiness). Yet our task has been complicated by a deep suspicion on our part of the validity of this approach. Our suspicion concerns the risk that this approach will help us to see the beauty in the text (which is, to be sure, really there) at the expense of ignoring or neglecting the bitter, the ugly, the social-critical, the historical and legendary elements that are also present. That is, we are suspicious of the very method we are trying to apply.

This suspicion is rooted in another, far older one: the suspicion, since the Bible and Plato, that beauty, while in itself a blessing, an expression of the goodness of God the Creator and Redeemer, remains dangerous. Beauty is moreover in many circumstances unavoidable, even at times omnipresent, not only in nature but also in the world of human culture and the arts, in religious rite and song, in the encounter with other people. Because beauty can have such a powerful effect on us, we need to make a special effort to be wary, lest it blind us to underlying evils it can mask: shallowness, deceit, abuse of power. The same Plato that made beauty a transcendental characteristic of all being, alongside oneness, truth, goodness, insisted that the poets be banished from his republic. The same Bible that praises God for the wonders of his creation (e.g., Ps 104) warns that beauty is fleeting and superficial, that moral and religious values are important and enduring (Prov 31:30; Matt 23:27). Beauty ought not to be allowed to distract us from

---

24. Cf. David Satran, "Deceiving the Deceiver: Variations on an Early Christian Theme," in *Things Revealed: Studies in Early Jewish and Christian Literature in Honor of Michael E. Stone*, ed. E. Chazon, D. Satran, and R. A. Clements (Leiden: Brill, 2004), 357-64; Boniface Ramsey, "Two Traditions on Lying and Deception in the Ancient Church," *The Thomist* 49 (1985) 504-33; M. E. Stone, *Adam's Contract with Satan* (Bloomington: Indiana University Press, 2002).

these more fundamental values. (Another aspect of this endless subject is that people in power can abuse younger, socially weaker people who happen to be beautiful.)

When applied to Matthew 2, this twofold approach, theological aesthetics and suspicion of, even hostility to, theological aesthetics, has led us in this study, we hope, to see more sharply, more precisely, both the elements of beauty in the narrative which make it attractive, as well as its historical and literary honesty. This honesty does not conceal but rather sets forth the mendacity inherent in power, the mendacity, duplicity, and cunning needed to resist the abuses of power, the horrible cruelties to which a jealous hold on power can lead, the obligation to unmask the abuse, to tell the truth about it. In this way our appreciation of both elements in the text is deepened: the beauty, as well as that truth which includes a dimension of justice and goodness.

True Christian theological aesthetics begins with a *kenosis*, the self-emptying of Christ on the cross, shameful and horrible. This starting point must not be forgotten or lost in ecstasy at the splendor of the risen Christ. He still bears the scars of his unmerited suffering.

From an earlier period we may consider the case of St. Thomas Aquinas. In his theology Thomas often uses arguments from *convenientia*, i.e., fittingness, appropriateness. He does this when there is **insufficient** support in Scripture for his theological position. In effect, he argues: this affirmation is so fitting, so beautiful, that it ought to be so, even if it is not to be found explicitly in Scripture and tradition. At bottom this is an argument from beauty, *bella figura*.[25] In this sense Thomas to some extent precedes and anticipates Hans Urs von Balthasar (and his followers) with their program of theological aesthetics. It also means that Thomas uses *rhetorical* arguments, a sort of "public relations" point of view; not what is true, not what is clearly taught in Scripture and the early Christian tradition, not what looks or sounds good now. In such cases, Thomas betrays his ideal of theology as a science, and accepts lower levels of argumentation in theological discourse. (This presupposes the four levels of discourse listed by Aristotle in the introduction to his *Posterior Analytics*: poetics, rhetoric, dialectic, scientific demonstration.) This would be relatively harmless, were it not for the painful fact that, alongside the Platonic triad of transcendental values (truth, goodness, beauty; sometimes one and being are added), there is also power. Power can easily exploit beauty, to undermine and betray truth and goodness (i.e., justice and charity) and to mask its injustice.

---

25. Cf. the book on this by Gilbert Narcisse, *Les Raisons de Dieu* (Fribourg: Academic Press, 1997).

11

The Christian and the State in Acts and Paul (Acts 25:16 and Rom 13:1–7)

Roman Fairness Revisited

I. ACTS 25:16

Toward the end of the Acts of the Apostles, Paul is held as a prisoner in Caesarea maritima, where he makes his appeal to be sent to Rome, to be tried before Caesar. Before this happens, the Roman governor Festus arranges for a hearing of Paul by King Agrippa and his sister Berenice. (Agrippa II was a minor ruler with little influence on the Jewish population of Palestine.) In presenting Paul to the Herodian royal siblings, Festus explains that the Jewish authorities in Jerusalem had demanded Paul's condemnation by him. Festus then makes this proud, noble declaration: "It is not Roman practice to hand over an accused person before he has faced his accusers and had the opportunity to defend himself against their charge" (Acts 25:16). Whether Festus actually said these words cannot be confirmed from external witnesses, but they do correspond to a Roman juridical principle (the ancient Law of the Twelve Tables) and to a Roman legal ideal. This ideal principle was often violated in practice, as occurs even in the context in Acts. For Festus and Felix do not hold to this practice (Acts 24:19) perfectly. (The ideal is partially illustrated in 24:1–10, but the original accusers, from Asia Minor are absent [24:19]. Luke is not blind to flaws in Roman justice. He mentions

Felix's expectation of a bribe [24:26]; delays in procedure [24:27; 25:9]; the conclusion in 26:31–32 could be read as a failure of justice.) One could thus regard Festus' words here as those of a hypocrite and a liar. However that may be, Luke certainly thought that the words were important and valuable in themselves and for his missionary purpose.

It is one of the less well known or appreciated redactional traits of Luke that he has a feel for and an interest in legal procedure.[1] For example, only Luke gives a list of three charges against Jesus, at the beginning of Jesus' trial before Pilate (Luke 23:2). Luke is also careful about the exact titles of authorities and assembles in Asia Minor and in Achaia. Although it is not customary to connect the writing of Luke-Acts with the city of Rome, it is noteworthy that he concludes Acts with Paul preaching the kingdom of God announced by Jesus (Acts 28:23, 31) and doing so precisely in the imperial capital, the seat of central government. This is both politically bold and intentionally motivated by a missionary strategy. The Christian gospel is intended for the whole Roman Empire.

II. ROMANS 13:1-7

In Paul's great letter to the Romans, his last will and testament as it has been called,[2] he offers a fine synthesis of his ethical instruction in chaps. 12 to 15. This instruction is for the body of Christ (12:3) and presupposes the gifts of the Spirit (12:6-8). It includes a short passage of eschatological hope and urgency (13:11-12), a sense that the time is short before the return of Christ and the Kingdom of God arrives in its fullness. In these and other ways, the instruction is original, creative, dynamic, a masterpiece of pastoral theology.

---

1. J. Dupont, "*Aequitas Romana*: Notes sur Actes 25,16," in *RSR* 49 (1961) 354–85, reprinted in Dupont, *Études sur les Actes des apôtres* (LD 45, Paris: Cerf, 1967), 527–52. This remains the classic study of the verse's vocabulary and classical parallels, but it does not treat the verse's relation to Paul or to the Synoptic Gospels. Dupont presents Luke's interest in the law on pp. 540–41, 551–552. Dupont does not emphasize the gap between the historical Festus and Luke's edifying picture of him. This is done by other authors, notably E. Haenchen, in his *The Acts of the Apostles: A Commentary* (Philadelphia: Westminster, 1971), *in loco*. See also J. J. Taylor, *Les actes des deux apôtres* 6 (EBib, n.s. 30; Paris, Gabalda, 1996), 190–94; G. Schneider, *Die Apostelgeschichte* 2 (HTKNT 5, Freiburg: Herder, 1982), 360–64; J. A. Fitzmyer, *The Acts of the Apostles* (AB; New York, Doubleday, 1998), 748–53.

2. G. Bornkamm, "The Letter to the Romans as Paul's Will and Testament," *ABR* 11 (1963) 2–14, repr. in K. P. Donfried, ed, *The Romans Debate* (Peabody MA: Hendrickson, 1991), 16–28; German orig. in his *Geschichte und Glaube* 2 (BEvT 53, Munich: Kaiser, 1971), 120–39.

Yet, the instruction, granted its originality, also builds upon earlier life wisdom traditions: Stoic philosophy, Israelite wisdom and law (e.g., the quotations of Prov 25:21–22 in Rom 12:20, of the Decalogue in 13:9), perhaps even the Jesus tradition (the love of enemies, the primacy of the love command, the duty to pay taxes). This drawing upon the wisdom of the past is only to be expected, once it has been transformed and recontextualized by Paul's Christology, pneumatology, and eschatology. Nevertheless, the reader is astonished to the point of disorientation by the intrusion of a passage (Rom 13:1–7) altogether devoid of Christological, pneumatological, or eschatological references. It is a straightforward piece of theological instruction and diatribe, expressed in general terms, to subordinate yourself to the civil authorities. At the time it was written, that meant submission to a pagan government, the Roman principate, of which Paul was a citizen.

The text reads:

> (1) Let every person be subject to the governing authorities, for there is no authority except from God, and those authorities that exist have been instituted by God. (2) Therefore whoever resists authority resists what God has appointed, and those who resist will incur judgment. (3) For rulers are not a terror to good conduct, but to bad. Do you wish to have no fear of the authority? Then do what is good, and you will receive its approval, (4) for it is God's servant for your good. But if you do what is wrong, you should be afraid, for the authority does not bear the sword in vain! It is the servant of God to execute wrath on the wrongdoer. (5) Therefore one must be subject, not only because of wrath but also because of conscience. (6) For the same reason you also pay taxes, for the authorities are Gods servants (*leitourgoi*), busy with this very thing. (7) Pay to all what is due to them—taxes to whom taxes are due, revenue to whom revenue is due, respect to whom respect is due, honour to whom honour is due. (NRSV)

To many modern readers whose political experience is democratic, this passage is an occasion of scandal. The problem lies in the absolute, sweeping nature of its assertions, undifferentiated, without qualification or limit as they seem to be (see vv. 1, 2, 3a, 4a, c, d, 5, 6b). Little wonder then that the commentator J. C. O'Neil could write the harsh assessment: "These seven verses have caused more unhappiness and misery in the Christian East and West than any seven verses in the New Testament *by the licence they have given to tyrants*, and the support for tyrants the church has felt called on to offer as a result of the presence of Romans 13 in the canon."[3] Little wonder either that some have suggested that the passage is a late interpolation.[4] Yet, amazingly, most commentators accept the Pauline authenticity, both because of the vocabulary and because of the close weave between vv. 7 and 8, a hook word link between *opheilas* and *opheilate*. The silence in the text about Christ, the Spirit, and the eschaton are troubling but not unprecedented in Paul: e.g., Christ is absent from Rom 9:6-33; 11:1-36. We will proceed as though the text were authentic. In fairness to Paul we should note that four terms in the text provide an explicit basis for some limits to the sweeping statement. The repeated word *hypotasso* (submit, subordinate) contains the idea of *taxis*, order. That is, the obedience serves the purpose of public order. The authority is for good (*to agathon*), not for evil. Paul appeals to human conscience (*syneidesis*), that is, a capacity for personal moral judgment. One is to render what is due (*opheilas*), not what is not due.

Given these built-in limits, the modern reader might be tempted to add some implicit or desirable further limitations. But these do not prove to be workable. For example, we might think that Paul should have written: be subject to the *legimate* authorities. But since the Roman emperors arrived at power by manoeuvres within the army and senate, without popular elections, how could one tell if they were legitimate or not? In Paul's day they were pagans. They appointed the provincial governor. From Paul's monotheistic point of view, God forms light and creates darkness, makes weal and creates woe (Heb. rʿa, evil) (Isa 45:7). The question of legitimacy ceases to be meaningful.

Another example of a useless attempt at improvement is to suggest that Paul write: whoever resists *with armed violence* . . . resists what God has appointed. But Paul could count on passive resistance in any case, e.g., resistance to taxation, at least by paying the minimum necessary. He did not need to encourage that. Armed resistance had failed in the past and would fail again three times after Paul's death (Jews against Vespasian, Trajan, Hadrian). It served Paul's pastoral purpose better to insist on paying all due taxes, because that would make a good impression on the authorities and would gain their good will. Therefore, when Paul warns not to resist authority, he has in mind, given the brewing events, primarily violent resistance.

---

3. J. C. O'Neil, *Paul's Letter to Romans* (Harmondsworth, UK: Penguin, 1975), 209. It is important to note that Rom 13:1-7 is not read to the faithful in the Catholic liturgy; it is not used in the Roman lectionaries.

4. E. Barnikol, "Römer 13: Der nichtpaulinische Ursprung der absoluten Obrigkeitsbejahung von Römer 13,1-7," in *Studien zum Neuen Testament und zur Patristik: Erich Klostermann . . . dargebracht* (TU 77, Berlin: Akademie-Verlag, 1961), 65-133; J. Kallas, "Romans XIII. 1-7," *NTS* 11 (1964-1965) 365-74.

To say so explicitly however would have been dangerous. Even to mention sedition in order to denounce it was to lay oneself open to suspicion. (Sauffenberg, Bonhoeffer, and Delp would have to relie on other texts when they tried to assassinate Hitler on 20 July 1944.)

Since the text is traditionally taken to treat of the Christian's relation to the state, it will be well to look at the broader biblical and extrabiblical background of this striking teaching, and to do so in a broader way than is customary, even if we can only do so briefly. The Hebrew and deutero-canonical Scriptures provided Paul with a rich supply of political instruction, legal, prophetic, and sapiential, as well as with historical exemplifications. Revolts, rebellions, and touching loyalty to kings are all part of the biblical heritage on which Paul could draw.

Israelite political consciousness could be said to begin with the Passover liberation from Egyptian slavery, a sort of slave revolt, unarmed but enforced by the muscle of the ten plagues, according to the Exodus narrative.[5] This liberation from Pharaoh's tyranny was led by the God of the Patriarchs, but also by his servant Moses. Already in Exod 14:31, the identity and authority of God and Moses begin to be blurred. This is a dangerous blend. It leads to a series of revolts: the people, aided by Aaron, worship the Golden Calf (Exod 32–34); Aaron and Miriam revolt against Moses' exclusive authority (Num 12:1–16); Korah, then Dothan and Abiram, revolt (Num 16); another sinful revolt takes place in connection with the Baal of Peor (Num 25). All are severely punished. Israel is no stranger to resisting authority. From the complex period of Israel's monarchies, as recounted in Samuel and Kings, especially in the historically more reliable succession narrative (2 Samuel 9–20; 1 Kings 1–2), let us select only two relevant traditions. It is twice related that when Saul was seeking to take David's life and David had it within his grasp to kill Saul, he spared his life (1 Samuel 24 and 26). "The Lord forbid that I should do this thing to my lord, the Lord's anointed, to raise my hand against him; for he is the Lord's anointed" (1 Sam 24:6; cf. 26:11). Sedition is not to be undertaken lightly. Judea will enjoy another period of political independence, between the Seleucids and the Romans, thanks to the *armed* revolt of the Maccabees.

From Israel's *legal codes* we may note that legislation is provided for a king (Deut 17:14–20). Moreover, great emphasis is placed on the pursuit of justice in the courts (Deut 16:20) and on the need for impartiality in judgment (Exod 23:2–3; Lev 19:15; Deut 1:17; 16:18–20; cf. Rom 2:11).

---

5. Not necessarily historical. Exodus 7:8–11:10; for critical discussion see for example W. H. C. Propp, *Exodus 1–18* (AB 2; New York: Doubleday, 1999), 286–345.

From the early *prophets* we may cite Hosea (8:4), where the Lord complains: "They made kings, but not through me; they set up princes, but without my knowledge." This implies the existence of Israelite kings without divine legitimacy, a sharp contrast with Rom 13:1-7. Micah 3:1-4, 9-12 warns kings about their abuse of power in their unjust and cruel treatment of the people and prophesies the loss of their territory.

Of the prophets that experienced Israel's loss of political sovereignty Jeremiah did the most to help the deportees adjust realistically to their new situation under foreign rule in Babylon. "Build houses and live in them; plant gardens and eat what they produce" (Jer 29:5). At the same time Jeremiah is told to warn the overlords: "It is I [God] who by my great power . . . have made the earth" (Jer 27:5-7). Your time will come to suffer.

This view of divine supremacy is echoed, without the warning, in Israel's *wisdom literature*. "By me kings reign, and rulers decree what is just" (Prov 8:15). Daniel interprets king Nebuchadnezzar's dream so: "You, O king, the king of kings — to whom the God of heaven has given the kingdom, the power, the might, and the glory" (Dan 2:37). The king's second dream includes this interpretation: "The Most High is sovereign over the kingdom of mortals; he gives it to whom he will and sets over it the lowliest of human beings" (4:17). Sirach adds: "The government of the earth is in the hand of the Lord . . . it is he who confers honor upon the lawgiver" (10:45). Commentators more and more stress the role of Wis 6:1-11 in shaping Paul's thought here. The author affirms, as does Paul, that ruling power has been given by God to some humans, but, unlike Paul, he adds that earthly rulers will be severely judged if they do not rule justly and according to law. This threat of divine vindication of the abused and the oppressed is an important balancing note that Paul's text needs. At the conclusion of this survey of Paul's biblical predecessors we may still note two things. In Bar 1:11-12 the exiles in Babylon send money so that sacrifices and prayers may be offered for the life of their pagan king. The apocryphal *Letter of Aristeas*, stemming from the exiles in Ptolemaic Egypt, offers the king a mirror or list of virtues suitable for rulers.

The Hebrew Bible already shows influence from Ancient Near Eastern legal tradition and law codes (e.g., that of Hammurabi), but Paul did not know them directly. Their influence on him was through the Bible, so there is no need to go deeper into them. But, from the surrounding pagan cultures, Greco-Roman philosophers represent a special case. Paul had passing acquaintance with them by growing up in Tarsus, but especially through his knowledge of the Wisdom of Solomon. That he knew this book is fairly clear from his condensation of its central section in Romans.[6] This Hellenistic

---

6. See the chart in W. Sanday and A. C. Headlam, *The Epistle to the Romans* (ICC;

Jewish work manifests a knowledge of Plato's *Republic* and *Laws*, as well as Aristotle's *Politics*.[7] These great philosophers wrestled at length with issues of true justice and right government.[8]

We may detect an allusion to Aristotle's classical definition of justice (*Rhet.* I.9, 1366b) in Paul's statement (Rom 13:7): "Pay to all what is due to them." This definition was later formulated for the Roman law code by the jurist Ulpian as *suum cuique tribuere*, to pay to each his own.[9]

Commentators also emphasize the role of Stoic philosophers, especially of Seneca, on Paul's view of the laws of nature, but also on the policies of the emperor Nero.[10]

Some early Christians felt that the affinity of thought between Paul and Seneca was so great that they invented an apocryphal correspondence between the two contemporaries, as well as a legend that Paul converted Seneca to the Christian faith. In reality, Seneca fatalistically committed suicide.[11]

Although none of the canonical gospels was written before the death of Paul, the Jesus tradition did circulate orally and perhaps in the private notes of disciples, as was the practice with the rabbis.[12] This explains why some scholars have seen a knowledge by Paul of Jesus' teaching preserved in all three synoptic gospels in his verse seven: "Pay . . . taxes . . . revenue . . . respect . . . honor." Jesus had said: "Give to the emperor the things that are the emperor's" (Mark 12:17; Matt 22:22; Luke 20:26). It could well be the case that Paul knew this teaching. It is a memorable logion. Similar in subject matter is the story of the stater in the fish's mouth. This however is found only in Matthew (17:24-27) and could be a midrash inspired by a post-AD 70 situation and principles derived from Jesus and Paul.

Edinburgh: T. & T. Clark, 1895), 51-52.

7. See D. Winston, *The Wisdom of Solomon* (AB 43; Garden City, NY: Doubleday, 1979; C. Larcher, *Etudes sur le livre de la Sagesse* (Paris: Gabalda, 1969); C. Larcher, *Le Livre de la Sagesse*, 3 vols. (Paris: Gabalda, 1983, 1984, 1985); M. Gilbert, *La critique des dieux dans le livre de la Sagesse* (AnBib 53; Rome: Pontifical Biblical Insitute, 1973).

8. W. Jaeger, *Paideia: The Ideals of Greek Culture*, 3 vols. (Oxford: Oxford University Press, 1939, 1943, 1944; German orig. 1933, 1944, 1947).

9. Justinian's Code, *Institutiones*, I. i: I.

10. H. Koester, "*Nomos physeos*: The Concept of Natural Law in Greek Thought," in *Religions in Antiquity: Essays in Memory of E. R. Goodenough*, ed. J. Neusner (Numen Sup 14; Leiden: Brill, 1970), 521-41.

11. See J. N. Sevenster, *Paul and Seneca* (NovTSup 4; Leiden: Brill, 1961).

12. S. Lieberman, *Hellenism in Jewish Palestine* (New York: Jewish Theological Seminary of America, 1962), 83-99, esp. p. 87; B. Gerhardssohn, *Memory and Manuscript* (Lund: Gleerup, 1961; repr. 1998), 160-61.

Having come so far, it is now time to look at other pertinent passages in Paul himself. It is not so easy to bring all his teaching on the state into a simple unity. For example, in Rom 13:4-5 the authority is the servant of God to execute wrath, but in 1 Thess 5:9, "God has destined us not for wrath but for obtaining salvation." In 1 Cor 2:6-8 the rulers of this age are doomed to perish, the very rulers who crucified the Lord of glory. In 1 Cor 15:24-25 Christ destroys the rulers and subjects them to God (not us to them, as in Rom 13:3). Both in 1 Cor 15:20-28 and in the earlier 1 Thess 4:13-18, Paul expresses the apocalyptic hope of the early church that Jesus will return in glory to bring the kingdom of God in its fullness to earth (cf. also Rev 20:1-10; Mark 13:26-27 and parallels; John 14:3). These passages suggest that Paul hoped for an eschatological-political solution on earth as in heaven. Yet in Phil 3:20 Paul says that our citizenship or commonwealth (*politeuma*) is in heaven. This could seem apolitical.[13] Yet he continues: "It is from there that we are expecting a savior." That means, he still hopes for a return of Christ to earth, where he will make all things subject, to himself (v. 21).[14] So here Paul does not abandon his apocalyptic political hope for this world; he hopes the world ("our humble bodies") will be transformed by the power of Christ.

There is one other proto-Pauline text that has been brought into the discussion of our passage, Rom 12:2. It is of particular importance for the right understanding of Rom 13:1-7, because it belongs to the heading of the entire section of ethical teaching (Rom 12:1-2). This heading provides the general principles which should determine and characterize all that follows. Here Paul says, "Do not be conformed (*syschêmatizesthe*) to this world." Now the passage Rom 13:1-7 seems to be telling its readers the exact opposite: be subject (*hypotassesthô*) to the orders of the governing authorities. This is a serious problem. Once felt, the tension is so glaring that the student is tempted to the conclusion that Rom 13:1-7 is a late, post-Pauline, interpolation. If this temptation is once more resisted and the passage continues to be regarded as proto-Pauline, the tension calls for some hard reflections. To begin with, we should not expect absolute consistency from Paul (or from any other author).[15] One can hardly speak ten sentences in a row without contradicting oneself at least once. But these contradictions can actually be part of a dialectical zigzag that unfolds gradually the many facets of a jewel, in this case, the text of Paul. Observing the tension within a text can

13. Pope Benedict XVI, *Jesus of Nazareth* (London: Bloomsbury, 2007), 339.

14. E. Peterson, *Das Buch von den Engeln* (Leipzig, Hegner, 1935); Eng. trans. *The Angels and the Liturgy* (New York Herder & Herder, 1963).

15. "A foolish consistency is the hobgoblin of little minds" (R. W. Emerson, "Self-Reliance," in *Essays* [Boston: Houghton Mifflin, 1844]).

be a heuristic device to open the text up so that one can see further dimensions. Not every tension needs to be resolved by positing a new and different source or an interpolation. So, in this case seeing the tension between Rom 12:2 and 13:1–7 may support the widespread view that Paul is here speaking tactically (others say: opportunistically).[16]

But before we arrive at the historical context that would render this tactical explanation plausible, let us continue our survey, now of post-Pauline reception. First of all, then, in Ephesians, we find an apolitical view that "our struggle (*pale*) is not against enemies of blood and flesh, but against . . . the spiritual forces of evil in the heavenly places" (Eph 6:12; cf. also 5:21). Therefore, our only sword is "the sword of the spirit, which is the word of God" (6:17; cf. Luke 22:36–38, where Jesus advises the apostles to buy swords). Next in the Pastoral letters, the author urges that prayers be offered for kings and all who are in high positions (1 Tim 2:1–2). In Titus (3:1) we find a clear echo of Rom 13:1–7: "Remind them to be subject to rulers [and] authorities, to be obedient . . ." This echo supports the view we have adopted, that Rom 13:1–7 belongs to the original letter. (Either that, or else the author of Titus himself wrote Rom 13:1–7.) 1 Peter 2:13–17 also restates the teaching of Rom 13:1–7. In fact, one could even speak of a careful *rewriting* of the Pauline text. But the author inserts a verse in which he reminds his readers of their freedom (v. 16). He feels authorized to do so because Paul had said something similar in Gal 5:13, but in a context that had nothing to do with civil authorities. "As servants of God, live as free people, yet do not use your freedom as a pretext for evil" (1 Pet 2:16). This is an interesting case of a creative application of Pauline material to "correct" or soften a troublesome Pauline text. (We are not the first then to find the text problematic.) The author of 1 Peter adds a new clarification of Paul's teaching in 1 Pet 3:13—4:2 when he addresses the issue of unmerited suffering, implicitly including persecution by the state. He counsels following the example of the suffering Christ (cf. also 1 Pet 2:21).

In many ways the gospel according to John is a mature synthesis and meditative reflection on both the Synoptic Gospels and Paul, to be sure with its own selective accents. In John 19:11 Jesus replies to Pilate: "You would have no power over me unless it had been given you from above . . ." This is a fair summary of Rom 13:1, now in the crucial context of Jesus' own trial and death.[17] This verse suggests that the evangelist accepts the God given authority of the governor precisely when he is about to commit the greatest

---

16. R. A. Harrisville, *Romans* (Minneapolis: Augsburg, 1980), 203–8.

17. In H. Schlier's essay, "Der Staat nach dem Neuen Testament," in his *Besinnung auf das neue Testament* (Freiburg: Herder, 1964), 193–211, John 19:11 in this basis for the whole New Testament teaching on the state.

imaginable crime. The evangelist does not flinch before the horror. Recent exegesis has tried to limit the range of Jesus' statement by restricting it to the immediate situation, based on the phrase "power over *me*," but it is not clear that this observation solves all the problems. It does not establish a world of difference between Rom 13:1-7 and John 19:11, even though it does accentuate the place of the death of Jesus in the divine plan.[18]

One senses a greater distance from Paul in the book of Revelation. Here, in chap. 13 the author presents, in the form of apocalyptic animal symbols inspired by Daniel's vision of four empires (Daniel 7), the Roman empire as (a) exercising authority (vv. 2, 4, 5, 7, 12), (b) encouraging idolatrous worship of itself (vv. 4, 8, 14, 15), and (c) as persecuting those who refused to commit idolatry, i.e. who refused to worship the beast (vv. 7, 15). Yet violent resistance is to be avoided (v. 10), although this teaching is so expressed that violent resistance is not forbidden. It is simply said to be highly risky. While some of the details of the chapter remain unclear, it is commonly said that the author has in mind the persecuting emperors, Nero (in his last, manic phase) and Diocletian. To be sure, the author intends to provide a text that will express God's disapproval of any such idolatrous, persecuting state, not just of his own time. Nevertheless, his text can be and has been used as a counterweight to Rom 13:1-7, to show that there are regimes which have lost their divinely given legitimacy.[19] Indeed, the opportunistic interpretation of Rom 13:1-7 entails that Paul would have agreed with Revelation 13, had he survived the Neronian persecution. (These brief remarks are not intended to exhaust the subjects of idolatrous states or persecution or divine disapproval of such in the book of Revelation. They are only meant to be suggestive. Cf. for example Revelation 18, esp. vv. 6-8.)

In Acts 5:29 Peter and the apostles are reproached by the high priest for violating the order of the council not to teach in the name of Jesus. The accused reply, "We must obey God *rather than* men" [NRSV: human authority; Gk. *anthropois*]. This verse has been called the *clausula Petri*, whereas the biblical text speaks of Peter *and the apostles* as giving this answer. What is striking is the opposition of God *rather than (mallon è)* men. Romans 13:1-3 implies an identity between God and human authority, a harmony or symphony between them. So this verse represents a real contrast with or correction of Rom 13:1-7. It is also an intended echo by Luke of what Socrates says in Plato's *Apology* (29c): "I will obey God more than you."[20]

---

18. R. Schnackenburg, *The Gospel according to St John* 3 (New York: Crossroad, 1982; orig. 1975), 261-62.

19. O. Cullmann, *The State in the New Testament* (New York, Scribner, 1956); D. E. Aune, *Revelation 17-22* (WBC 52B; Nashville: Nelson, 1998), 961-1012.

20. G. Schneider, *Die Apostelgeschichte*, vol. 1 (HTKNT 5, Freiburg: Herder, 1980), 395.

Since at least Lagrange, exegetes have tried to pin down the exact historical context of Rom 13:1–7 as located between on the hand the experience of the expulsion of the Jews from Rome under the emperor Claudius (ca. AD 49) and on the other hand the persecution of the Christians in Rome under Nero (AD 64). Between these dates Paul may have seen a window of opportunity to extend the Christian mission in Rome during the early years of Nero's reign (AD 54–58), which were relatively enlightened and benevolent. Exegetes suggest that, had Paul lived beyond the Neronian persecution, he would have written differently about the higher authorities. As it is, in his epistle as a whole, he tries to show the difference between Christian faith and Jews faithful to the ritual details of the Torah. Their fidelity to the Torah led some Jews to acts of rebellion against the Roman Empire. Paul was trying to avoid that danger. When he wrote the letter to the Romans, ca. AD 56–58, he thought he still had a chance to prevent persecution. By AD 64, it was too late.[21]

If this historical contextualization is correct, it would mean that Paul wrote Rom 13:1–7 for strategic missionary reasons, as indeed he wrote all his letters as a function of his apostolic mission. This is the truth in the "opportunistic" interpretation of the pericope. Once however Romans had been accepted as canonical inspired scripture, it had to be looked at in another way. Jülicher and Legasse emphasize that in peaceful times, when the state does not overstep its bounds in religious matters but maintains peace, justice and civil order, this pericope serves a legitimate role as encouraging Christians to accept their responsibilities and duties as part of their conformity to the will of God.[22] As we have noted, Paul includes some limitation in the text: for the good, as conscience allows, and so on.

The recent commentary by Robert Jewett takes up an idea put forth by the Jewish philosopher Jacob Taubes.[23] According to this view Paul is here expressing a certain Jewish impudence or *hutzpah* by requiring obedience to the state in the name of the God of Israel, a God who is far above all earthly states and overturns them at will. This subversive interpretation, if

---

21. See most recently S. Schreiber, "*Imperium Romanum* und römische Gemeinden: Dimensionen politischer Sprechweise in Röm 13," in *Die Bedeutung der Exegese für Theologie und Kirche*, ed. U. Busse (QD 215; Freiburg: Herder, 2005), 131–70, esp. 145–46 and note 45, citing Tacitus, *Annales* 13,50–51 (LCL, pp. 88–91) and Suetonius, *Lives*, VI, Nero 10 (LCL, p. 101).

22. A. Jülicher, *Der Romerbrief*, 78–80, in *Schriften des Neuen Testaments*, vol. 2, ed. J. Weiss, (Göttingen, Vandenhoeck & Ruprecht, 1907); S. Legasse, *L'épitre de Paul aux Romains* (LD 10; Paris: Cerf, 2002), 810–34.

23. R. Jewett, *Romans* (Hermeneia; Minneapolis: Fortress, 2007), 780–803, esp. p. 790; J. Taubes, *Die politische Theologie des Paulus*, ed. A. Assmann et al. (Munich: Fink, 1995), 24–27, 73–75.

true, would be a variant on the strategic or opportunistic line we have been pursuing.

III. CONCLUSION

In conclusion, we may state the relation of Acts 25:16 to Rom 13:1–7 in this way. On the one hand, Luke shares Paul's trusting optimism in the Roman state. Luke in this verse echoes Rom 13:1–7 in general terms. To this extent he shows himself as a faithful disciple of the great missionary. Both of these passages are silent on the story of the crucified, a glaring example of the failure of Roman justice. The crucifixion of Jesus is a contradiction and thus a partial refutation of the truth of these two passages. It is an embarrassment.

According to tradition Paul is beheaded in Rome.[24] If this is true, it undermines both Rom 13:1–7 and Acts 25:16. By going to Rome, Paul is no longer able to face his accusers. So the Festus principle fails to operate. Luke sacrifices the story of Paul's violent end. It too is an embarrassment. These narrative sacrifices or silences serve the pragmatic goal of the Christian mission. In this matter there is a perfect harmony and fit between Paul and Acts, *pace* P. Vielhauer.

On the other hand, the harmony does not stop there. Both Paul and Acts contain the gospel of the crucified and risen one at the center of their message. So the idealistic picture presented in these two texts is not naïve or uncritical. Luke for example states plainly that the governor Felix sought a bribe (Acts 24.26), shortly before Festus' noble declaration. Irony remains present. In both of our two texts, the idealistic picture serves two goals. First, it teaches an ethical and juridical value which is as relevant and necessary today as it was then, for both state and church. Today it is as often abused as it was then. The second goal of the idealistic picture is the pursuit of a missionary strategy, to permit the crucified truth and goodness of Christ to speak to beautiful, cruel and abusive power.

---

24. *I Clement* 5; for discussion, see O. Cullmann, *Peter* (London: SCM), 1962, 91–93; M. Smith, "The Report about Peter in Clement 5, 4," *NTS* 7 (1960–61) 86–88; K. Beyschlag, *Clemens Romanus und der Frühkatholizismus* (BHT 35; Tübingen: Mohr/Siebeck, 1966); J. D. Quinn, "Seven Times He Wore Chains," *JBL* 97 (1978) 574–76; M. Hengel, *Der unterschätzte Petrus* (Tübingen: Mohr/Siebeck, 2006); my review appears in *CBQ* 69 (2007) 581–83; J. Gnilka, *Petrus und Rom* (Freiburg: Herder, 2002); C. Bötrich, *Petrus* (Leipzig: Evangelische, 2001); A. F. Gregory and C. M. Tuckett, eds., *The Reception of the New Testament in the Apostolic Fathers* (Oxford: Oxford University Press, 2005).

12

Apocalypse and Culture

The Interpretations of 1 Corinthians 15:20–28 in German Protestant Exegesis from 1870 to 1960, a Hypothesis on the Sociology of Exegesis

I. THE APOCALYPSE IN 1 COR 15:20–28

Paul's most important statement on the Kingdom of God and apocalyptic eschatology merits some attention. Here is the passage, 1 Cor 15:20–28:

> But in fact Christ has been raised from the dead, the first fruits of those who have died. For since death came through a human being, the *resurrection* of the dead has also come through a human being; for as all die in Adam, so all will be made alive in Christ. But each in his own *order[tagma]*: Christ the first fruits, then at his coming [*parousia*] those who belong to Christ. Then comes the end, when he hands over the *kingdom* to God the Father, after he has destroyed every ruler and every authority and power. For he must *reign* until he has put all his enemies under his feet (Ps 109:1). The last enemy to be destroyed is death. For 'God has put all things in subjection under his feet' (Ps 8:7). But when it says, 'All things are put in subjection', it is plain that this does not include the one who put all things in subjection under him. When all things are subjected to him, then the Son himself

will also be subjected to the one who put all things in subjection under him, so that God may be all in all.

This crucial text in the first place presents the positive side of the faith in the resurrection of Christ and of Christians. But it also develops the broader apocalyptic dimensions of the resurrection of Christ, i.e., its socio-political, cosmic and universal consequences, its relationship with the Kingdom of God and with the history of salvation until the end of time. By means of this text, the resurrection is put into such a vast framework that it encompasses simultaneously the believers, all humanity, the universe and the future.

This article will be in three parts: (1) Exegetical remarks on this apocalyptic passage, to recall its interest and to show its problems. This touches the apocalyptic element in the title. (2) A sketch of the history of the exegesis of Paul by German Protestants in the last two preceding centuries. This touches the cultural aspect of title. (3) Some examples of the interpretation of our passage by German-speaking commentators to illustrate a thesis on the relations between apocalyptic and culture. In the conclusion we will try to draw some ecumenical lessons.

1.1 Exegetical Remarks

Without trying to offer an exhaustive analysis of a text which is practically inexhaustible, we may note first its structuring according to four Old Testament citations: (1) Gen 3:17-19, the punishment of the first Adam by death. For St. Paul as for many of his fellow Jews of the period, protology is the model and the basis for eschatology. *Urzeit wird Endzeit*, in the phrase of Hermann Gundel.[1] (2) Daniel 2:44: toward the end of time, God will establish an eternal kingdom for his people. In Dan 7:13-14, the apocalyptic text par excellence, this kingdom will be transferred to one like a son of man; here we speak of a *translatio regni*, a transfer of the kingdom from one king to another. In our text, Paul envisages a final transfer of the kingdom. At the end of time, Christ will "hand over the kingdom to God the Father" (v. 24). (3) Psalm 110:1, a psalm important for the interpretation of the resurrection of Christ by the early Christians. "The LORD said to my Lord: Sit at my right, that I may make your enemies a footstool for your feet!," that is, "that I place all your enemies under your feet," according to the Septuagint, and

---

1. H. Gunkel, *Schopfung und Chaos in Urzeit und Endzeit: Eine religionsgeschichtle Untersuchung uber Gen 1 Ap Joh 12* (Göttingen: Vandenhoeck & Ruprecht, 1895); Gunkel, *Creation and Chaos in the Primeval Era and the Eschaton: A Religio-Historical Study of Genesis 1 and Revelation 12* (Grand Rapids: Eerdmans, 2006).

the quotation made by Paul. Here Paul places the accent on the combative, struggling, agonistic aspect of the verse, in relation with or against the demonic enemies of the Kingdom of God and especially against personified Death. (4) Psalm 8:7b: "You have put all things under his feet." Here Paul interprets the *ben Adam* of the Psalm as the Son of man to whom the Kingdom has been transmitted in Dan 7:13–14, and, for Christians, the Son of man identified with Jesus Christ.

Beyond this Old Testament structuring, what interests us in this passage is the order (*tagma*) given to the events of the last times, and the link made between the theme of the Kingdom of God and that of the resurrection. On this last point at least, and perhaps even on the first point, Paul goes beyond the data provided by the Synoptic Gospels. The question of the order of the events of the last times is perhaps the most difficult and the most disputed of all eschatological questions.

1.2 Questions Raised

Before addressing these two problems, it will be well to provide a list of questions raised by this text in the minds of theologians after Paul.

1. According to the majority of modern exegetes, the major problem in Corinth that Paul had to face in this chapter was this. A part of the Christian community of Corinth shared a "overrealized" eschatology, that is, they believed too much, in a way common to converts of every era. They believed not only that Jesus had been raised, but that they too had already been raised. It was a type of proto-Gnostic belief.

2. In the era of the great Trinitarian and Christological debates, the Arians justified their subordinationism by referring to these verses, which speak of a (voluntary) submission of the Son to the Father at the end of time. Because of the arguments of Marcellus of Ancyra based on 1 Cor 15 that the Kingdom of the Son is limited in time, the Fathers of the first council of Constantinople added to the creed of Nicea the words: "and of his Kingdom there will be no end," based on Luke 1:33, itself quoting Dan 7:14.

3. During the Enlightenment, drawn by the Spinozist renewal of ancient pantheism, there were some minds troubled by the apparent pantheism of the last words of our passage, "so that God may be all in all."

4. In the era of Romanticism, scholars like David Friedrich Strauss were scandalized by the apparently mythological eschatology of Jesus and of

Paul, at least as Paul expresses himself here. This mythology remains a difficulty for more recent interpreters like Bultmann and Conzelmann.

5. Among Catholics, Lemonnyer and Spicq found in this passage a solution to the classic theological question of the motive of the incarnation.[2]
6. Finally, and this is one of the sources of our discussion, Jean Hering, Modernist Protestant professor at Strasbourg, sought to eliminate the idea of an eternal hell from the teaching of Christianity.[3] He felt himself therefore obliged to oppose, or at least to refine, the interpretation given to our passage by the history of religions school of Johannes Weiss and Hans Lietzmann.

1.3 Word Studies

This last point leads us back to the details of this text, and, to begin with, its vocabulary. In vv. 23-24 are found the words which give the order of the events which make up the end of the ages or the last days, in other words, the resurrection in the broad sense of the term. We begin with the word *tagma*, order or rank. Then follows Christ as *aparche*, the first fruits [offering, sacrifice], he who holds the chronological primacy as well as the primacy of rank or dignity. Then (*epeita*) the believers will rise. Up to this point the meaning of the terms causes no difficulty. But the meaning of the word *telos* has provoked controversy. The history of religions school (Johannes Weiss, Hans Lietzmann, Albert Schweitzer), obsessed, not without reason, by the desire to respect the orientation toward a sort of apocalyptic timetable, have opted for the meaning "the rest." In context, this would suggest the sense: those who remain after "the resurrection of the believers," that is, the non-believers, those condemned. The resulting meaning makes excellent sense from the viewpoint of an apocalyptic timetable. Unfortunately, the word *telos* does not normally mean "the rest." Its normal meaning is "the end, the completion." Jean Hering insisted passionately on this point. He wanted to eliminate any reference to an eternal hell for the non-believers. (He would no doubt have preferred the annihilation of the non-saved, like many modern theologians, notably Edward Schillebeeckx).[4] Jean Hering's

---

2. C. Spicq, "Epitre aux Corninthiens," in L. Pirot-A. Clamer, eds., *La Sainte Bible*, (Paris, 1948), vol. 2.2, 282-85; A. Lemonnyer, "Cur Deus Homo," in Sadoc Szabo, ed., *Xenia Thomistica* (Rome, 1925), 2:311-18.

3. J. Hering, *The First Epistle of Saint Paul to the Corinthians* (London, 1962) 164-68; Hering, "Saint Paul a-t-il enseigne deux resurrections?," *RHPR* 12 (1932) 300-320.

4. E. Schillebeeckx, *Church* (New York, 1991), 134-39; see also J. Moltmann, *The Coming of God* (Minneapolis, 1996), 96-101, 105-6, 108, 116-18.

firm position has had a great influence.[5] What should we think? Hering is probably right about the meaning of *telos*, the end, and not the rest. This has as a result for the viewpoint of exegesis of the text that Paul does not speak explicitly of the resurrection of unbelievers and of their final destiny. On the other hand, Johannes Weiss was right about the general meaning of the passage as an apocalyptic timetable. But for him to arrive at the final destiny of the unbelievers, he must appeal to a parallel passage, Revelation 20, especially vv. 5, 13, 15. "The rest (*hoi loipoi*) of the dead did not come to life until the moment when the thousand years were ended" (v. 5). Weiss can therefore deduce analogically from the parallel that the same meaning is implicit in Paul. This exegetical conclusion is not without a certain plausibility, but it is not explicit in the words of Paul.

If we try to compare the three parallel texts, we note the following similarities and divergences:

1 Cor 15:20-28	1 Thess 4:13-18	Rev 20:1-15
a. The resurrectiion of Christ, vv. 20, 23.	a. The resurrection of Christ alone, v. 14.	a. Binding of Satan, vv. 1-3.
b. The sin of Christians, at the Parousia, v. 23. [Kingdom of God on earth]	b. The Parousia of Christ, the resurrection of Christians, vv. 14-16.	b. First resurrection of martyrs and of apostles, vv. 4-6. Millennial kingdom, vv. 1-7.
c. The final battle, vv. 24-26. [General resurrection?]	c. Rapture of Christians alive at the Parousia, v. 17. [Joyful arrival on earth] [kingdom of God on earth]	c. The final battle, vv. 7-10. Eternal damnation of the devil, v. 10.
d. Handing over of the Kingdom to the Father, submission of the Son to the Father, vv. 24-28.	d. Union forever with the Lord, v. 17b.	d. Last judgment, of all the death, saved and damned, vv. 11-15. [Second resurrection, v. 13.]

On the basis of the similarities between these three texts, Bousset and Weiss were convinced that there existed a common scheme as the background, shared by the early Christians. To be sure, the inspired authors were free to add different aspects, to develop this or that detail. This liberty explains the divergeneces, but that does not eliminate a common eschatological hope, for this world and for the world to come. Among these

---

5. For example, W. D. Davies, *Paul and Rabbinic Judaism* (London 1948), 291-98; H. Conzelmann, *I Corinthians* (Hermeneia; Philadelphia, 1975), 267-75.

divergences, it is that Paul does not show an interest in the fate of unbelievers, or for eternal damnation, and this is the capital fact for Hering.

For this scheme to be adequate for systematic theology, it would need to be rounded out by a teaching on the end of the world (see the conflagration or *ekporosis* of 2 Pet 3:10), and by a statement on eternal, heavenly life with the beatifying vision of God (see 1 John 3:2). But our three texts do not enter into these considerations. Paul remains satisfied with a conprehensive formulation, "so that God may be all in all" (1 Cor 15:28).

Continuing our study of the vocabulary of the passage, we note the variety of terms which refer to the kingdom of God: *parousia, basileia,* and the related verbs *basileuein, tithenai, hypotassein.* This last word, which means "to submit," occurs not less than six times. The heaping up of recurrences is based in part on the quotation from Ps 8:7. The root *pan*, "all," which is repeated eight times, undergoes a somewhat complicated shift of meaning: *all* Christians (v. 22), *all* the hostiles powers (vv. 24, 25, 27), the whole universe (*ta panta*) (vv. 27c, 28), God the Father (v. 28).

We see already the theological importance of this text, in itself, and in the history of its interpretation. We also see the problems with which it swarms.

2. CULTURE

Before we undertake the detailed history of interpretation of this passage by Protestant exegetes who write in German, I would like to present a brief survey of Pauline exegesis in the last two centuries. A study of the history of interpretation implies the phenomenon of social confidence and concessions to the opposition, a phenomen present among Prussian exegetes. This phenomenon can be explained by a sociological rule: societies which feel themselves to be under siege tend to resist change, while societies which feel themselves to be strong and self-confident accept to undertake necessary changes with greater ease. On the intellectual level, these changes can include concessions on the level of historical truths, granted to groups with which the society in question has had a polemical relationship for centuries. (The opposite can also occur, to be sure. A society may feel itself forced to changes, to resist an attack.)[6]

---

6. B. J. Hodge and W. P. Anthony, *Organization Theory* (Boston, 1979), 376–405; A. Downs, *Inside Bureaucracy* (Boston 1967), 261–80; G. E. Berkley, *The Craft of Public Administration* (Boston 1975), 84–101; H. Kaufman, *Are Government Organizations Immortal?* (Washington DC, 1976), 3–22, 68–70. I would like to thank Professor George D. Wendel for his help with research on this point.

I have the impression that this law is operative in German studies of Paul. Before the First World War, in the Wilhelmine period, 1870–1918, North German Protestant studies of Paul exhibit a great self-confidence, an openness to other points of view, a desire to search for the historical truth (in this case, the meaning of Paul) as objectively as possible. But, after the military catastrophe of 1918 and the political humiliation of Versailles in 1919, the German Protestant scholars lost this self-confidence, at least in regard to Paul. They retreated to a more strict and narrow confessional position, more defensive, sometimes even fearful and hostile, certainly more self-absorbed. Here are some illustrations which concern the theme of justification by faith.

2.1 The First Half of the Nineteenth Century

The first half of the nineteenth century was dominated by Romantic idealism. The great event in New Testament studies was the large *Life of Jesus* (1835–36) written by David Friedrich Strauss.[7] (Paul would have to wait another century for a similar shock-therapy. This shocking treatment was done by William Wrede in 1905.) During this first period, the interpretation of Paul was still dominated by the dogmatic and polemical interests of the Reformation and the Counter-Reformation. In such a context, Paul was reduced to his letters to the Galatians and to the Romans, and above all to the theme of justification by faith alone. Paul's other letters were neglected or else interpreted in the light of this dominant interest.

Nevertheless, some progress may be noted in the field of Pauline exegesis. In this area, the main innovating figure of the era was Ferdinand Christian Baur. For the most part, Baur wrote as a disciple of Hegel. He applied the Hegelian dialectic to the New Testament in such a way as to see in the Jewish-Christian writings of Matthew and James the "thesis," in Paul and his writings the Gentile "antithesis," and in Luke-Acts the attempt at a "synthesis," however inadequate. Finally, John was considered the masterpiece, idealist and triumphant, of a "higher synthesis," as *Geist*, that is, the absolute Spirit incarnate in a book (rather than as the solitary combatant which John became in the research of the period 1864–1964). In addition, the start of a critical approach to Paul can be found, in this period, in the suspicion of Schleiermacher who attributed to the Pastoral Epistles a post-Pauline origin, as well as in the hypothesis of Semler, according to whom

---

7. D. F. Strauss, *The Life of Jesus Critically Examined* (Philadelphia, 1972); A. Schweitzer, *The Quest of the Historical Jesus* (New York, 1910; orig. ed. 1906).

the letters of Paul consisted of genuine fragments, put together or assembled in their present form by church editors.[8]

For the rest, it was Baur who was the first to evoke the threefold division of the Pauline corpus of letters, a division well known to students, and presented in introductions of the New Testament: proto-Paul (for Baur only the four main letters: Galatians, 1-2 Corinthians, Romans); deutero-Paul or the antilegomena (the Captivity Letters Ephesians, Colossians, Philippians, Philemon, plus the first and second letters to the Thessalonians); and trito-Paul (the Pastorals and the writing to the Hebrews).

2.2 1850–1918

Introduction. After the failure of the liberal revolution of 1848, the intellectual movement of Romantic idealism was seriously weakened, and was replaced by historiographical positivism, and by neo-Kantian philosophy. Positivist historiography used the inscriptions and papyri recently published, a sober, dry tone in the evaluation of primary sources, a method formulated by the French historians Langlois and Seignobos. The neo-Kantians were characterised by a mistrust in regard to speculation, by a rather negative or at least minimalizing, prudent and moralizing tone, by a resolute rejection of metaphysics, mysticism, and eudemonism in ethics. This last point led logically to a negative perception of the Law, as if it would automatically lead to legalism. The bias against legalism often slipped into a theological anti-Judaism. Later still, in this period there developed real social-Darwinist pseudo-biological racial anti-Semitism (Sir Francis Galton for example). Among the neo-Kantian thinkers were Lotze, Dilthey and Ritschl. Students often found this neo-Kantian philosophy boring, and were soon ready for a rebellion against it. Among these discontented students, the more moderate tried to make Kant more flexible, basing themselves on his third Critique, the *Critique of Judgement*. (The example of a bold student is the case of the young Hermann Gunkel, of whom we will speak below.) All these positivist and neo-Kantian tendencies were summed up theologically in the thought of Albrecht Ritschl. His ideas were then popularized by his most famous student, Adolf von Harnack. But in the period 1850–1870, the situation was still favorable to changes, and the main lines were not yet fixed. The next generation was groping its way forward.

Before speaking directly of the history of religions school (*Religionsgeschichtliche Schule* = RGS; in French and English, sometimes called the

---

8. A. Schweitzer, *Paul and his Interpreters* (New York, 1912; original German ed. 1911).

Comparative Religions School or *Ecole comparatiste*), associated with the universities of Göttingen and Berlin, I would like to recall briefly the general framework of these universities.

a. The university of Göttingen had been founded in 1737, that is, it had a late start. It owed its inspiration to the scientific ideas of G. W. Leibnitz, a man from liberal Hanover, whose king-elector resided most of the time in England. The Hanoverian state church embraced a moderate form of Lutheranism, which made it easier to undertake theological innovations. It was an Enlightenment university. It rapidly acquired a reputation for excellence, in the natural sciences, in classics and in comparative mythology, in the fight for academic freedom (the Göttingen Seven), but especially in theology (see below).

b. The university of Berlin was founded in 1808, in an atmosphere of revolutionary awakening, the fight against Napoleon. It was founded later even than Göttingen, and was intended from the start to become a showcase of Prussian culture. The older universities, Erfurt and Wittenberg, were closed, and then sold, to pay the expenses of the new foundation in Berlin. The loss of Erfurt grieved the Catholics in the kingdom, the loss of Wittenberg grieved the Lutherans. The goal of being the cultural showcase was quickly attained thanks to a stupifying succession of philosophers, beginning with Fichte and continuing with Hegel and then Schelling, without mentioning Fries and Schopenhauer. In this transitional period, church and state joined their efforts (they were hardly separated) to allow greater liberties at Göttingen and Berlin than elsewhere.

c. The intellectual fathers of the comparative religions school in this period of transition in Göttingen and Berlin were Albrecht Ritschl for the New Testament and systematic theology , Julius Wellhausen. Bernhard Duhm and Paul de Lagarde for the Old Testament, Carl Mirbt for church history, Ulrich Maria von Wilamowitz-Moellendorff for classics (first at Göttingen, then at Berlin), Hermann Lotze in philosophy and Fritz Leo for modern literature. The scene is now set for the footlights to go up.

The Religionsgeschichtliche Schule at Göttingen

The main persons who devoted energy to understanding Paul were Hermann Gunkel, Wilhelm Bousset, Wilhelm Heitmueller, Johannes Weiss, and William Wrede, with the help of Alfred Rahlfs for the Septuagint and of Ernst Troeltsch for systematic theology and social and political ethics. The nursery of these young research scholars was the preachers' seminary at Loccum near Göttingen, where just after finishing their doctorates, their teaching loads were light, so that the young scholars could pursue deeper research for their next degree, the *Habilitationsschrift* which qualified them to receive a professorial appointment, under ideal circumstances.[9]

a. **Hermann Gunkel**, in 1888, published his thesis on *The Manifestations of the Holy Spirit in the Popular View of the Apostolic Era and in the Teaching of Paul*.[10] This rather provocative little work was intended as an attack on neo-Kantian ethics. It tried to show that the Holy Spirit, as he was manifest in the first Christian communities to whom Paul was writing, was not always dressed in white tie and tails, producing discourse in the style of Hegel's metaphysics and harmonies like those of Beethoven's ninth symphony; the Holy Spirit was not even always ethical, but revealed himself in wild ecstasy and dithyrambic enthusiasm. The Holy Spirit sometimes dressed in war paint and loincloth, tomahawk in hand, so to speak. Once he had shown himself to be a naughty boy, Gunkel had to wait many years before he found a suitable academic post, and then not in his preferred field of work, the New Testament, but in the Old Testament. In that field he became the founder of form criticism.[11]

b. **Wilhelm Bousset**. His studies of the Jewish backgrounds to the New Testament helped to overcome the naïve overspiritualization of Paul's theology, and began the process of our rejudaization of our way of understanding the New Testament. He was aware of the fact that we only possess fragments of Paul's thought. Bousset was moreover sensitive to the social justice dimension of historical research. His commentary on the Apocalypse of John made explicit the connection between 1 Cor 15:20–28 and Revelation 20.[12]

---

9. G. Lüdemann, "Die Religionsgeschichtliche Schule," in B. Moeller, ed., *Theologie in Göttingen* (Göttingen 1987), 325–61; the same author wrote the article on this subject in *TRE* 28 (1997) 618–24.

10. H. Gunkel, *The Influence of the Holy Spirit* (Philadelphia, 1979; orig. ed 1888).

11. W. Klatt, *Hermann Gunkel* (FRLANT 100; Göttingen, 1969).

12. W. Bousset, *Die Offenbarung Johannis* (Göttingen, 1896); A.F. Verheule, *Wilhelm Bousset: Leben und Werk* (Amsterdam, 1973); L. W. Hurtado, "New Testament Christology: A Critique of Bousset's Influence," *TS* 40 (1979) 306–17; Hurtado, *One God, One Lord: Early Christian Devotion and Ancient Jewish Monotheism* (Philadelphia, 1988).

c. **Wilhelm Heitmueller**, one of Bultmann's teachers, reconstructed a pre-Pauline Hellenistic Jewish Christianity. This brilliant reconstruction (of a church which may never have existed) suffered from chronological difficulties pointed out later by Martin Hengel. This reconstruction can be abused as a convenient means of getting rid of aspects of Paul which a modern reader might find distasteful; it becomes a sort of trash can or dust bin. Such an abuse throws historical understanding into disorder. Heitmueller explained the sacraments of baptism and eucharist in Paul by means of the mysteries of the pagan cults (Mithras, Attis, the taurobolium or bull blood bath) and shocked his contemporaries with his earthy approach. Later historical scholarship would not be able to follow Heitmueller in all this suggestions.[13]

d. **Johannes Weiss** achieved something more lasting. It was he who in his little book of 1892, *Jesus' Preaching of the Kingdom of God*, rediscovered and even more importantly took seriously the apocalyptic kernel of the preaching of Jesus.[14] This affirmation upset his older contemporaries, who thought that such a belief in the apocalyptic coming of the Kingdom would render Christianity barbarian and unacceptable to sophisticated moderns. (They had been raised in a neo-Kantian view of the Kingdom as the ethical commonwealth.) The hue and cry raised by his little book obliged Weiss to refrain from a full development of his historical discoveries for modern theology. His message was however widely spread by Albert Schweitzer, and it resounds to our own day. His discovery has stood the test of time. In his day Father M.-J. Lagrange accepted Weiss's view with caution.[15] Ernst Käsemann and J.C. Beker have used it as the basis for their own studies of Paul in more recent times.[16] Weiss was able to apply his insight exegetically in a series of New Testament commentaries, published before his premature death. His great commentary on First Corinthians was published in 1910. His synthesis *Early Christianity* was particularly well designed.[17] Among other things, Weiss pointed out that, despite

---

13. W. Heitmueller, "Zum Problem Paulus und Jesus," *ZNW* 13 (1912) 320–27; Heitmueller, *Taufe und Abendmahl im Urchristentum* (Göttingen 1911).

14. J. Weiss, *Die Predigt Jesu vom Reiche Gottes* (Göttingen, 1892), English translation, *Jesus' Proclamation of the Kingdom of God* (Philadelpha, 1971).

15. Lagrange, *RB* (1904) 106–8.

16. E. Käsemann, *New Testament Questions of Today* (London, 1969); Käsemann, *Perspectives on Paul* (London, 1971); J.C. Beker, *Paul the Apostle* (Philadelphia, 1980); Beker, *Paul's Apocalyptic Gospel: The Coming Triumph of God* (Philadelphia, 1982).

17. J. Weiss, *Der Erste Korintherbrief* (Göttingen, 1910, reprinted 1977). This commentary is often considered the model for what a commentary should be. J. Weiss,

their common eschatological hope, Paul and Matthew were often in disagreement, and that Matthew dared a direct polemic against the theology of Paul, for example, Matt 5:19 and 16:17-19, against 1 Cor 15:9 and Gal 1:15-16 respectively.[18]

e. **William Wrede.** Influenced by Ernest Renan as well as by his Göttingen teachers, Wrede published a little book on Paul in 1905 which marked a breakthought in the historical understanding of the Apostle.[19] He showed that the usual Western view of Paul was a dogmatic reading, which began with the later phases of Saint Augustine's life, when he was at loggerheads with the Pelagians. This reading was pushed even further with the Reformers. Wrede's approach was quickly and correctly seen as a dangerous threat to Lutheran doctrine. His book on Paul could be said to have had the same galvanizing effect on Pauline studies as Strauss' *Life of Jesus* had been in its days on the study of the gospels. Several recent anthologies show clearly that the modern historical study of Paul begins with Wrede. [20] According to Wrede, Paul's theme of justification by faith was only a *Nebenkrater*, a subsidiary theme, in the Apostle's teaching. It was a polemical doctrine (a *Kampflehre*) against the Judaizers in the church. It was intended to keep the Gentile converts free from circumcision and the ritual precepts (while still maintaining the ethical precepts, Rom 13:8-10). When Paul was not fighting the Judaizers, he hardly ever mentioned this theme. That is the thesis presented in Wrede's little book. Wrede's breakthrough would not have been possible without a spirit of self-confidence and strength within Prussian Protestantism at this time. Wrede shared the conviction that that church could face this sort of revolutionary criticism. He even thought that the church could flourish and be even stronger than before, thanks to this criticism. This bold spirit withered after the military defeat of 1918.

Early Christianity (New York, 1959; original edition *Urchristentum*, Göttingen, 1914).

18. J. Weiss, *Das Matthaeus-Evangelium* (Göttingen, 1907), 266-69, 344-45. Cf A.-M. Denis, "L'investiture de la fonction apostolique par "apocalypse." Etude thematique de Gal, 1, 16" *RB* 64 (1957) 335-61; 492-515; J. Dupont, "La revelation du Fils de Dieu en faveur de Pierre (Mt 16,17) et de Paul (Gal 1, 16)," *RSR* 52 (1964) 411-20.

19. W. Wrede, *Paul* (London, 1907; original 1905); R. Morgan, "Re-reading Wrede," *ExpT* 108 (1997) 207-10.

20. K. H. Rengstorf, ed., *Das Paulusbild in der neuren deutschen Forschung* (Darmstadt, 1969), 1-97; W.A. Meeks, ed., *The Writings of St. Paul* (New York, 1972), 363-64.

OUTSIDE THE HISTORY OF RELIGIONS SCHOOL (RGS) OF
GÖTTINGEN, THERE WERE OTHER SCHOLARS WHO FOLLOWED THE
SAME HISTORICAL-CRITICAL LINE:

a. **Adolf Deissmann.** In his 1892 thesis on the Pauline formula In Christ, Deissmann was able to show that this formula and related formulas was more widespread and more central to Paul's theology than his formula justification by faith. He also renewed Pauline studies by his recovery of the concrete contexts and associations of Paul's theological vocabulary in the daily life of antiquity. This recovery was due to the recent discovery of papyri written in the *koine* (common) Greek of Egypt. His life of Paul had a great freshness, free of any apologetic bias, with its joyous evocation of the civilization of the olive tree and with its brilliant explanation of five Pauline metaphors for salvation, namely, redemption, reconciliation, adoptive sonship, justification and the forgiveness of sins, an explanation rooted in the lived experience of ancient man. It was a feat of strength and skill; its result was to relativize the importance of justification. Justification was no longer the center of everything, it was only one of five metaphors for salvation in Christ.[21]

b. **Hans Lietzmann** applied the new method in a series of commentaries on the four main letters of Paul (Galatians, Romans, 1–2 Corinthans). The commentaries were outstanding, even if too concise and learned for the average reader. (You had to switch from German to Latin to Greek to Hebrew or Aramaic, sometimes all in the same sentence.) [22] They are still in print, and rightly so, because they are mines of objective information. Karl Barth did them the honor of continuously attacking them (plus Juelicher's commentary on Romans) in his great commentary on Romans, great but ahistorical.[23]

c. **Albert Schweitzer.** This Alsatian outsider became the historian and the promoter of this exegetical shift. His own book on the *Mysticism of the Apostle Paul* (1932) was published late due to the disruption caused by the war; it was not warmly received, because the theological

---

21. A. Deissmann, *Paul* (New York, 1957; original German 1912), especially pp. 168–77.

22. H. Lietzmann, *An die Galater* (HNT; Tübingen, 1906; Lietzmann, *An die Roemer* (HNT; Tübingen, 1906); *An die Korinther* (HNT; Tübingen, 1907).

23. K. Barth, *The Epistle to the Romans* (Oxford, 1933; German original 1919; revised 1921).

climate had changed in the meantime.[24] It was severely criticized by no less than Martin Dibelius.[25] The work remains a brilliant apocalyptic reading of Paul and doubtless the best book Schweitzer ever wrote. Schweitzer sought a compromise: Paul had two doctrines of salvation, one consists in salvation by incorporation into the body of Christ by faith and baptism, the other consists in the "subsidiary crater" of justification by faith. But that compromise did not satisfy confessional Lutherans.

d. **Richard Reitzenstein** was another outsider, since he was not a theologian but a professor of classics at Göttingen. He developed the idea of a gnostic redeemer myth in a study on the Hermetic treatise *Poimandres*. This theory held sway for a long time, but today one prefers to explain the New Testament doctrine of redemption by means of wisdom texts from the Old Testament.[26] Reitzenstein was a wild figure, sowing disorder both in classical and theological studies. He was a pioneer on roads which led nowhere. He was however right to draw attention to the Hermetic literature, even if he dated the texts wrongly and made a poor use of them.

2.3 1918–1960. The retreat to the ghetto, or, the journey inward

After the collapse of German resistance in 1918, a new tone of self-defense emerged in the German interpretation of Paul. It aimed at a restoration of Reformed theology, accompanied by a feeling of isolation and by that most insidious of psychological poisons, self-pity. One circled the wagons and adopted a lager or siege mentality. We grasp the atmosphere is a remark made by Otto Proksch, in the preface to the 1924 edition of his commentary on Genesis: "Wir Deutschen sind auch in der Wissenschaft immer mehr auf uns *allein* gestellt." (We Germans must rely even in scholarship more and more on ourselves *alone*.)

---

24. A. Schweitzer, *The Mysticism of the Apostle Paul* (New York, 1931; German original 1930).

25. M. Dibelius, "Paul und die Mystik," *EHK* 22 (1941), reprinted in his *Botschaft und Geschichte* (Tübingen, 1956) vol. 2, 134–59; also, "Glaube und Mystik bei Paulus," in his *Botschaft und Geschichte* 2:94–116.

26. M. Hengel, "Jesus als Messianischer Lehrer der Weisheit und die Anfaenge der Christologie," in *Sagesse et Religion* (Colloque de Strasbourg), Paris, 1979), 147–88; A. Feuillet, *Le Christ sagesse de Dieu d'apres les epitres pauliniennes* (EBib; Paris, 1966).

2.3.1 1918–1944. BETWEEN THE TWO WARS

a. **Karl Barth**. During the First World War, the Swiss pastor Karl Barth broke his ties to his former master Adolf von Harnack, whose approach was primarily historical. In his commentary on the letter to the Romans of 1919, Barth criticized mercilessly the commentaries of Lietzmann and Jülicher for their inadequate theology. Barth's positive contribution was no doubt a renewal of supernatural faith and of the belief in the authority of scripture as divine revelation. But he also led a timid retreat away from apocalyptic eschatology, toward an existentialist escape-hatch, toward a kingdom devoid of personal decision. Barth accepted verbally the eschatological aspect of the New Testament, in a famous phrase: "if Christianity were not entirely, completely eschatological, there would not remain the least relationship with Christ."[27] But this sentence, placed in its context, is nothing but rhetoric. When later on Karl Barth and Oscar Cullmann were colleagues at Basle, they were in disagreement precisely on this point. Cullmann was waiting for a real return of Christ to earth, which would bring the Kingdom of God in its fullness and glory. Barth did not share this hope.

b. **Rudolf Bultmann** followed Barth in his rhetorical and existentialist eschatology. Radical in other areas, for example, in the form criticism of the synoptic gospels and in the interpretation of John, Bultmann remained rather traditional in his studies of Paul, strongly attached to the Lutheran dogmatic line. In this sense he remained orthodox and even on the defensive. He conceded that most of the New Testament was early catholic (*fruehkatholisch*), and therefore useless for the faith. In the last part of his *Theology of the New Testament*, he pursues this program of rejection with even greater intensity, as he deals with the last books of the New Testament and with the Apostolic Fathers.

c. **Martin Dibelius** was especially a great historian and commentator, but in a long essay of 1941 he attacked Schweitzer for his book *Mysticism of the Apostle Paul*, affirming that Paul was not a mystic (and therefore Paul was not comparable with other figures in the history of religions), but a unique and incomparable prophet (like Luther). In this position Dibelius was following the views of Nathan Soederblom and Friedrich Heiler.[28]

---

27. K. Barth, *The Epistle to the Romans* (London, 1933), 314.
28. See above, notes 24 and 25.

2.3.2 From 1945 to 1960

The period after the second world war was dominated in New Testament exegesis by Bultmann, then by his students. After the division of Germany and after the domination of the western part of Germany by Konrad Adenauer and his Christian Democratic party, the Protestants of this country were weakened and divided, partly in the east and partly in the west. A great part of their traditional strength was in East Germany. The feeling of being drowned by a sea of Catholics in West Germany and in its dominant party only increased during the first years of the Common Market, since five of the six member states had Catholic majorities, and were often governed by Christian Democratic parties. An effort to cut down the prestige of the Catholic church was effectively launched by Rolf Hochhuth in his play *The Deputy* (*Der Stellvertreter* 1963), much discussed at the time, even though not often staged and performed. The play condemned the silence of Pope Pius XII during the deportation of the Jews of Rome, and tried to make Catholics share the blame for the Nazi genocide or holocaust of Europe's Jews.

a. During this period, **Philipp Vielhauer**, professor of New Testament at Bonn, boasted of having never crossed the Main river, so as to spare himself contact with Catholic culture. At least that is what was said of him.

b. Among the post-Bultmannians, the one who most intensely devoted himself to the interpretation of Paul was probably **Ernst Käsemann**. In 1960 he published an important essay, "The Righteousness of God in Paul," a desperate attempt to save the predominance of justification by faith (alone) in the theology of the Apostle. Käsemann does this by removing this doctrine from its anthropological limits and situating it in the whole cosmos and in an apocalyptic reinterpretation. Later, Käsemann was able to develop this apocalyptic point in detail, in a very dense commentary on the letter to the Romans. (One could say that in his struggle with each verse of this great letter, Käsemann was fighting once again every battle of the Thirty Years War.) In the final analysis, Käsemann showed convincingly that there was an apocalyptic background to the justice/righteousness of God in Paul, namely the victory of God over his enemies, that is, the victory of the kingdom of God. But Käsemann did not succeed in saving the centrality of the metaphor "the righteousness of God."[29]

---

29. E. Käsemann, "Gottesgerechtigkeit bei Paulus," *ZTK* 58 (1961) 367–78. There are several English translations, especially in his *New Testament Questions of Today*

Käsemann wrote another important essay on the canon of the New Testament as a basis and a cause of the division of the churches.[30] This essay led to an interesting exchange with the Catholic theologian Hans Küng on the chances of an ecumenical reconciliation of the churches.[31] Käsemann adopted a hyper-Lutheran position. The criterion set up by Luther to determine the "canon within the canon," that it, to determine in the Holy Scriptures what is really authoritative, was this: *Was Christum treibet,*" whatever promotes Christ. By this he meant what promotes the doctrine of justification by faith alone, justification of the impious who remains impious even after justification. Käsemann takes this criterion with total seriousness. The result is that he rejects a large part of the New Testament as "early catholic," almost exactly like his teacher Bultmann. At the end of this essay only a few verses of Galatians 1-4 pass the examination. That is, they "promote Christ," that is, justification by faith. Like his master, Käsemann remains a Lutheran *sui generis*.

The apparently anti-ecumenical attitude of Käsemann was increased by the fact that his fellow student, Bultmann's favorite student, Heinrich Schlier, became Catholic. The biblical basis for Schlier's conversion concerned the authenticity or inauthenticity of the epistle to the Ephesians. The cosmic ecclesiology of the epistle was unacceptable to Käsemann and seemed to him unPauline. The polemical fronts remained impenetrable to a calm search for historical truth.

At the conclusion of this part, I would simply like to point out that the Bultmannian school remained reserved or hostile in regard to those who pursued a more historical approach to Paul, for example, Krister Stendahl, E. P. Sanders, James D. G. Dunn, Heikki Raisanen and Karl P. Donfried.[32] We see therefore that the German Protestants were still hesitant when one spoke of the historical Paul in the post-war period.

(London, 1968).

30. Käsemann, "Begrundet der neutestamentliche Kanon die Einhseit der Kirche?," *EvTh* 11 (1951) 13-21.

31. H. Küng, "Early Catholicism as an Ecumenical Problem," in his book *The Council in Action* (London, 1966).

32 K. Stendahl, "The Apostle Paul and the Introspective Conscience of the West," *HTR* 56 (1963) 199-215; Stendahl, *Paul among Jews and Gentiles* (Philadelphia, 1976); Stendahl, *Final Account: Paul's Letter to the Romans* (Minneapolis, 1995); E. P. Sanders, *Paul and Palestinian Judaism* (Philadelphia, 1977); J. D. G. Dunn, *Romans* (Dallas, 1988); H. Raisanen, *The Torah and Christ* (Helsinki, 1986); K. P. Donfried, *The Romans Debate* (Peabody, MA, 1991); Donfried, "Justification and Last Judgment in Paul," *ZNW* 67 (1976) 90-110.

3. FOUR EXAMPLES

In this third section I would like to give some examples of the interpretation of our passage in 1 Corinthians 15 by German language commentators. For the period which precedes the first world war, I have already given the essential. I will therefore summarize the data in a few words.

One can read this passage as a sort of apocalyptic timetable. This is the point of view of the history of religions school and of a few authors more attentive to the apocalyptic details. This reading can base itself on parallels in Rev 20:1–10 and 4 Ezra 7:29. In this hypothesis we can propose the following big picture analysis (the numbers in parentheses are the verses of 1 Corinthians 15): first comes the resurrection of Christ (vv. 20 and 23). This event should be followed by the time of the church, between the eons, even though this period is not mentioned. Second, the parousia or the coming of Christ in power and glory (23), accompanied by the first resurrection, that of the elect (23). Third, the reign of Christ, an interim messianic kingdom (25, 24). Fourth, the second resurrection or general resurrection (26), after which Christ will hand over the restored and purified creation to his Father who will then reign as Lord of the whole universe. This is on the whole the view point of Hans Lietzmann, Johannes Weiss, Albert Schweitzer, H. D. Wendland and of Walter Bauer.

We turn immediately to the period after 1918. I will only treat four authors: Adolf Schlatter, Karl Barth, Budolf Bultmann and Hans Conzelmann. The Swiss Free Churchman Schlatter represents a continuity with the past. He says:

> *hekastos* presuppose the *pantes* of the preceding phrase. Life comes for all but not for all at the same time. Humanity is divided by the resurrection in *tagmata*, in different groups, and each participates in the resurrection in its proper group. Jesus to be sure has a special place, because he has gone before us all as first-born from the dead. Those who belong to him come next, at the moment when he will again become visible. It is impossible that the enumeration stops there. Jesus is not a *tagma* (rank) in himself, because an individual cannot be a *tagma*. The community is this *tagma*, but it is only one of the *tagmata*, and Paul speaks of several groups. Consequently, he continues the enumeration. "Then comes the end." Thus is named not only the moment in time but also the event by which a new division of humans who will come to life. Paul is waiting for the resurrection of Christians first, then that of all mankind.[33]

---

33. A. Schlatter, *Paul der Bote Jesus* (Stuttgart 1934), 412.

We see with what simplicity he reasons on the text to arrive at the same conclusions as the exegetes of the comparatist school had come, but without forcing the meaning of the word *telos*. Here we are in the presence of a master of exegesis.

We turn now to Karl Barth. I cite:

> Paul did not develop here an eschatological mythology, but, with the help of metaphorical language, he expresses the following ideas: Christ as the second Adam is the beginning of the resurrection of the dead. Perfection is the resurrection also of his own, and thus the fundamental thing which had been denied at Corinth. This perfection is, like the abolition of death in general, his highest act of sovereignty and also the last act. Up until now it has not been completed, his power is still in conflict with other powers, the second-to-last powers, and so we are already in his kingdom, waiting for this final act. When Jesus will have triumphed, then will his kingdom, in so far as it is a particular kingdom alongside of God's kindom, have come to its end. His kingdom means the period of hope. To this goal or end the kingdom has been given to him, so that God may be all in all. This "God all in all," and therefore the resurrection of the dead, is the meaning, badly understood at Corinth, the meaning of Christian faith.[34]

We see how, according to this rhetorical interpretation, there is no longer a clear distinction between the death of Christians and the death of others. There is no more talk of *tagmata* or *telos*. Much less is there talk of a kingdom of God on earth, still to be realized by a new divine intervention in history. All this is set aside as eschatological mythology. We remain here with a Platonizing, classical Augustinianism. The apocalyptic perspective of the Bible is lost. The works of Weiss and Lietzmann count for nothing.

Of Bultmann I will only cite two phrases, from his *Theology of the New Testament*: "The drama described in 1 Cor 15:20–28 does not come from the tradition of the creation narrative, but from the cosmology and eschatology of the Gnostics. 1 Cor 15:28 treats of the final battle against the powers hostile to God." We see here clearly to what extent Bultmann is always looking for a way to avoid explaining the New Testament by Jewish sources, even the Old Testament. He prefers as much as possible a souce of pagan origin, in

---

34. K. Barth, *Die Auferstehung der Toten* (Munich, 1924), ad loc.; K. Barth, *The Resurrection of the Dead*, trans. H. J. Stenning (New York, 1933), 164–65. See also M. Kirwan, *The Resurrection of the Dead: Exegesis of 1 Cor 15 in German Protestant Theology from F.C. Baur to W. Kuenneth* (Basle, 1972); J. A. Moses, "The First World War as Holy War in German and Australian Perspective," *Colloquium* (Auckland, N.Z.) 26 (1994) 44–55.

this case Gnostic. He does this even here in a passage where there are three explicit references to the Old Testament! The biblical point of view is lost.[35]

The commentary of Hans Conzelmann on the first letter of Paul to the Corinthians was published in 1969.[36] It falls outside the period we are considering. I mention it to conclude our study. Conzelmann was probably the most faithful of Bultmann's disciples. In his commentary however he admits the presence of a Jewish apocalyptic scheme behind this text of Paul. But he always tries, and in a very subtle way, to distinguish Paul from the other early Christian authors, for example, the author of the Apocalypse of John. On this view, the other authors are victims of mythology, but Paul is spared such an indignity. Conzelmann, faithful to his master, tries to explain the text as much as possible by means of Gnosis, and by Judaism only as a last resort. The kingdom of Christ belongs to the present time and is identical with the church. His eschatology is in fact wholly realized. By torturous efforts, he reinterprets each element of future eschatology in existentialist terms. Everything is reduced to an interpretation of human existence in the immediate present. In this way Paul becomes a sacred cow, untouchable by the history of religions. We can see a clear backward slide from the historical exegesis of Weiss and Lietzmann toward an existentialist and confessional interpretation of the Bultmann school.

4. CONCLUSION

We return to the thesis of this essay: the spirit of social confidence in the period 1870–1918 enabled German-speaking Protestant interpreters of Paul to make concessions to their opponents in the matter of justification by faith and to attain to a high degree of historical objectivity in admitting an apocalyptic schema in Paul's thought. In contrast with that, there was a lack of confidence in the period 1919–1960 which contributed to shutting the exegetes up in their traditional positions and to rein in historical and ecumenical concessions. This was my impression as a student in the 1960s, as I was writing a thesis on Paul. There was a disparity, it seemed to me, between on the one hand Wrede, Deissmann, Lietzmann, Gunkel, Johannes Weiss, Albert Schweitzer, that is the comparative religions school, and, on the other hand, Karl Barth, Rudolf Bultmann, Ernst Käsemann. The difference between a predominantly historical approach and a rather confessional approach can be explained at least in part by the confidence felt by the scholars of the Wilhelmine period, and the contrast with the anxiety of

35. R. Bultmann, *Theology of the New Testament* (New York, 1951), 228.
36. Conzelmann, *I Corinthians*, 267–75.

the generations after each of the two world wars. To be sure, the historical survey we have given is a bit hasty. It is justified by the desire to explore a sociological hypothesis.

Some recent examples can be added. In 1963 the Lutheran World Federation met at Helsinki to evaluate and to vote on a short document entitled "Justification Today," which the Federation had taken ten years to prepare. The document was quite moderate. It only made small corrections in the Reformation formularies concerning justification and the sacraments. The preparatory consultation had been very prudent, balanced and careful. Nevertheless, the document was rejected, voted down. Why? We could easily multiply hypotheses to explain it. In any case, this rejection calls for a reflection and an effort to understand it. In so far as the explanation can be found in social fears and anxieties, it is probable that such fears impeded the progress in other domains of ecumenical and interreligious dialogue.

Later, in 1971, a study commission, composed of members of the Lutheran World Federation and the Roman Catholic Church, worked out a joint declaration on justification at Malta. (Hans Conzelmann withheld his signature at the last minute.) In October 1999, at Augsburg, a more detailed agreement was signed in Augsburg by delegates of the two churches. One could say that the fears of the past had been reduced by the reunification of German and by German economic strength and leadership in the European Union.

We see the same phenomenon in the interpretation of the two series of Pauline texts, those which concern apocalyptic and those which concern justification. The cultural context into which exegesis fits plays a role in the process of interpretation of biblical texts.

13

Hakeldama, the Potter's Field, and the Suicide of Judas (Matt 27:3–10; Acts 1:16–20)

One of the outstanding examples of the confluence of biblical narrative, theology, intertextuality (multilayered midrash) and the typography of Jerusalem is the story of Judas Iscariot's suicide as recounted in Matt 27:3–10 (with a partial parallel in Acts 1:18–19). In his great Jerusalem book, our honoree, Prof. Max Küchler, has devoted fourteen pages to the putative site of Judas' last moments on earth,[1] which for precision and drama could hardly be bettered. It was a pleasure and a challenge to revisit the site at my desk in the company of his work.

It is an odd fact that in the biblical witness, the site is named Hakeldama in the Acts of the Apostles; it is an Aramaic name which Luke translates as Field of Blood, whereas in Matthew the Aramaic name is avoided. Instead, Matthew gives the site two names and a purpose: the potter's field (based on the potter's house (not field!) in Jer 18:2–3), the field of blood, and the goal of burying foreigners. This goal can be understood so: as a mass grave (later at least understood as a pit or roofed cistern) which could be used to bury all those who did not possess a proper private family tomb in Jerusalem. This group would include not only foreign visitors (often pilgrims), but also local paupers, victims of the plague and executed criminals). As such a mass grave, with its stench of rotting bodies and its reputation as a place of infectious diseases and as the final dishororable resting place for criminals, it contributed to the local imagining of what hell was like (see below).

During my twelve-year residence in Jerusalem (as student for one year and later as a professor) I would recommend that newly arrived students

---

1. Küchler, *Jerusalem*, 766–79.

read Pierre Benoit's classic essay "The Death of Judas."[2] The reason for my recommendation was that this essay and the biblical texts it examines well illustrate the value of studying the Bible where much of it took place. the stories of the death of Judas, while not to be artificially harmonized in detail, are a remarkable example of the fusion of local popular-historical tradition, intertextual interpretation of Scripture, and Jerusalem topography. That there may also be present an element of bleak or hopeful theology, not to mention creative narrative imagination, only adds to the fascination and value of the texts.

Why did Matthew include this story in his gospel, while Luke saves his version for his second volume? In the case of Matthew, the answer to this question lies in the fact that Matthew did not write a second volume, so whatever post-paschal matters he wished to transmit, he had to find a place for in his one main work. Luke could wait to tell his story of Judas in a work devoted entirely to the apostles and their destinies. As Donald Senior has shown, Matthew was concerned to fill in narrative gaps in his narrative source text, Mark. Readers of Mark wanted to know how Judas ended his life. Matthew satisfies their curiosity.[3] This attention to the Marcan source makes a valuable contribution (cf. Mark 14:21b and Matthew's addition to it, Matt 26:24–25). But this attention to Mark should not be permitted to flatten out the Matthean innovations. These should not be reduced to their Marcan source, thereby impoverishing our appreciation of Matthew's contribution.

The death of Judas has received excellent analysis in recent reference commentaires on Matthew,[4] as well as in R. E. Brown's comparative study of the Passion narratives, *The Death of the Messiah*.[5] This level of detail need not be repeated here. In the remainder of this essay, I will dwell on two points: (1) the topography and geography of hell; (2) the ultimate fate of Judas. In the late Middle Ages St. Vincent Ferrer, Dominican, apocalyptic preacher, wrong on many things, was accused of heresy because he preached the ultimate salvation of Judas. Vincent Ferrer was acquitted. It has taken the general consciousness of the Church a long time to catch up with Vincent, in part because believers were too influenced by the negative portrait of Judas in John; cf. John 6:70–71; 17:12b. Vincent had read his Matthew carefully and his view is now in the ascendant. We will try to support it.

2. Benoit, "The Death of Jesus."

3. Senior, "The Fate of the Betrayer."

4. Gnilka, *Das Matthausevangelium*, vol. 2, 442–50; Davies and Allison, *The Gospel according to Matthew*, vol. 3, 557–73; Luz, *Matthew 21–28*, 466–90.

5. Brown, *The Death of the Messiah*, 565–67 (bibliography), 636–60 (comment and analysis), 1394–418 (appendix on Judas).

THE TOPOGRAPHY AND GEOGRAPHY OF HELL

Despite their independence from one another, Matthew and Acts share the idea that Judas came to a sudden, speedy and unhappy end, and that his end is somehow connected with a field or place where the dead are buried, a place or field of blood. Local Jerusalem tradition located this place in the Hinnom valley at the confluence of three alleys southwest of the city, the Hinnom, the Tyropoean and the Kedron valleys. Because cold winds would rush south from the Lebanon mountains in the north, at least in winter, the place was a pocket of air turbulence. The winds whistled and howled there. As such it was an ideal site for an ancient industrial zone, for baking pottery, for iron foundries (smiths and metal working), large fulleries (textile work) and laundries. These crafts all needed fires and furnaces to melt the metals, to bake the pots, to heat the water for the cloth making (thickening and cleansing). The wind helped to supply the kilns and bellows and open fires with oxygen. Hence came Matthew's idea of a potter's field, even though his prophetic source in Jeremiah speaks of a potter and of a field, but not of a potter's field.

This spot lay south of what is called the Dung Gate. The gate is so called because the city refuse was collected, deposited and burnt there. The rotting and the burning of the waste matter (often animal droppings) contributed to a certain odor of the place and to the link with fire.

The New Testament texts we have mentioned suggest that there was a burial place, a field of blood. There had earlier been tombs there. But eventually there was a deep rectangular pit bricked over with an arched roof. This roof had a rectangular opening or slit. Through the opening the bodies of executed criminals, paupers and victims of the plague could be thrown. The stench of the rotting corpses and the vermin that fed on them added to the ill fame of the quarter. To this could be added the danger of pollution or contamination, but there was no center for disease control in those days. We must try to avoid anachronisms. Yet the Bible is aware of a connection between plagues and mice (1 Samuel 6), even if is is not our modern bacteriological notion of the connection.

To this sorry picture must be added one more note. Matthew refers to Jeremiah in his last formula citation (27:9). The quotation is in fact from Zechariah (11:13), yet behind Matthew's use of Zechariah there stand allusions to Jeremiah (18:2-3; 19:1-8; 32:7-9). These allusions refer to a potter's house, to the purchase of a field (at Anathoth, not Jerusalem) and then a potter's jug. Jeremiah is told by God to buy a jug and take it "to the valley of the son of Hinnom at the entry of the Potsherd Gate." There Jeremiah is to denounce the idolatry which has taken place at that spot and to declare a name change: the place "shall no more be called Topheth, or the valley of the son of Hinnom, but the valley of Slaughter" (Jer 19:1–2, 4, 6, *ge ha-haregah*, valley of murder or killing are other possible translations). In the Septuagint the proper name Tophet disappears and is replaced by Diaptosis, The Fall or Place of Falling. The term valley is replaced by *polyandrion*, a euphemism for cemetery or burial place, literally a place of many men. In the Septuagint *ha-haregah* (slaughter) is rendered literally sphage. This bundle of terms and associations already orients Matthew's allusions. But for Jeremiah the place is destined to disaster because it was a place of idolatry, of the shedding of the blood of the innocent, of the children, burnt as sacrifices to Baal. For Jeremiah there could be nothing worse than this. In the prophecy the result is that Judah will be defeated by its enemies. The dead bodies will be food for birds and wild animals and the city will be a horror, a thing to be hissed at (Jer 19:7–8). (The term 'son of Hinnom' may mean in Hebrew idiom "a tributary of the Hinnom wadi or winter river" because in Hebrew "son of" or "daughter of" can mean something little or inferior, as in the rabbinic expression *bath qol*, literally "the daughter of a voice" but in sense meaning "a little, soft, low voice," in usage referring to the whisper of God or his spirit.

These four elements (industry, waste-disposal, burial ground and idolatry) combine to characterize this place, the Hinnom valley or Gehenna. The flames, the stench, the dangers of death (through disease or contamination, ritual impurity) and of sin (through idolatry) merge to provide a vivid picture of hell, the place of eschatological punishment (*kolasis aionios*, Matt 25:46). But Matthew does not say that Judas was buried there. He is more concerned with the use of the thirty pieces of silver to help purchase the field as a place to bury foreigners. The silver is mentioned four times in the eight verses of Matthew's pericope. Matthew alludes to hell but does not say that Judas has gone there.

THE REPENTANCE AND SALVATION OF JUDAS

For a millennium and a half or more it was assumed that Judas was damned and had no hope of salvation. Dante put Judas in the icy pit of hell, reserved for traitors. How did this happen to the apostle from Iscariot in the gospel of mercy? It happened in stages.

First, the gospel according to John had to be accepted in the main churches. This took place between 100 and 200 AD. John has the most negative portrayal of Judas in the New Testament. Judas is a devil (John 6:70–71) and he was lost, to fulfill scripture (John 17:12b). John does not, however, say that Judas killed himself and not all modern exegetes are convinced that he is eternally damned even in John,[6] e.g., my colleague Luc Devillers, but that is not a subject we will develop here. It suffices to say that John's presentation led the early church to think that Judas was damned.

This conviction was reenforced by the contrast between Peter the denier and Judas the betrayer. In John, Peter's triple confession after Easter and the prediction that he would suffer martyrdom (John 21:15-19) led Christians to think that Peter was forgiven and rehabilitated. His martyrdom only increased his moral credit. In the dramatic logic, Judas was needed to provide a negative foil. People tend to think in binary oppositions.

Another contributing factor was the total condemnation of suicide by St. Augustine in the fourth and fifth centuries AD. He did this first in polemical debate with the Donatists, then more theoretically in *The City of God* (*Contra Gaudentium Donistarum* and *De civitate dei* 1:16-17). Augustine tended to dominate Western Christian moral thinking until the arrival of Jesuit moral theology in the seventeenth century. But even so, his views on suicide generally prevailed among both Roman Catholics and Protestants until the late twentieth century.

The first major precondition for the reopening of the question of Judas' fate was fulfilled by the Protestant Tübingen school led by Ferdinand Christian Baur in the period 1820 to 1848. Baur dared to suggest that there could be real conflict within the canon of New Testament books. The most obvious case is the opposition between Galatians and James, lucidly seen by Luther even earlier than Baur. Lutheran Bibles put the letter to the Hebrews and the letter of James out of the usual order toward the end of the canon as in a sort of quarantine, just before Jude and Revelation. The four together are considered of inferior worth. The fact of conflict was already narrated in the Acts of the Apostles, especially in chap. 15, the council of Jerusalem. But many Christians still resist the idea of substantive conflict within the New Testament on the basis that such an admission would undermine the doctrine of the divine inspiration of scripture. But in critical circles the Baur view has prevailed, even though efforts at easy harmonization never cease.

After the Second World War a second precondition for the reopening of the question of Judas' fate was provided by the development of what is called redaction criticism. This method puts an accent on the four canonical evangelists as true authors and theologians in their own right. This accent means that the scholar should carefully analyze the differences in the evangelists' tellings of the story of Jesus. Matthew, Mark, Luke, and John each have their own distinct theology, on this view. On a pastoral level, the

---

6. Stein-Schneider, "A la recherche du Judas historique," 415; Klauck, *Judas*, 24, 70-91; Kluack states that John 17:12b is a late addition, cf. ibid., 87; Klassen, *Judas*, 137-59.

redaction-critical approach was dramatically endorsed and applied by the Sunday lectionary introduced in the Roman rite liturgy in 1969-1970. It was designed as a three year cycle of pericopes. The first year provides readings from Matthew, the second from Mark (and John 6 during the summer to fill in for Mark's brevity), the third from Luke. John was introduced in the great seasons of Christmas, Lent and Easter. This system accentuates the specific characteristics of each gospel and encourages the production of books designed to help preachers with the details of each perspective. The result of Baur and redaction criticism is that Judas could be damned in John and saved in Matthew, if it came to that; that is, if you pressed the logic to that point.

In the meantime, in medicine and psychology, there has been a great development of understanding of people attempting suicide. Suicide attempts are now understood as cries for help, the result of depression or other mental conditions which reduce moral responsibility. These medical advances have in turn led to changes in pastoral policy. A funeral mass may be celebrated for the deceased and the corpse may be buried in consecrated ground.

The changed cultural mentality has freed theology and biblical scholarship to notice that "in the Bible suicide is nowhere explicitly forbidden."[7] The Old Testament tells us of five suicides. Abimelech (Judg 9:54); Saul and his armor-bearer (1 Sam 31:4-5; 1 Chr 10:4); Ahithophel (2 Sam 17:23), and Zimri (1 Kgs 16:18). These deaths are reported without comment or condemnation. Ahithophel the Gilonite was David's counselor. His story is entwined with the rebellion of Absalom against king David and stretches over 2 Samuel 15-17. Because he provides the closest parable to Judas' conduct in the Old Testament and may have influenced Matthew's narrative about Judas, we will cite the climactic verse. "When Ahithophel saw that his counsel was not followed, he saddled his donkey and went off home to his own city. He set his house in order, and hanged himself; he died and was buried in the tomb of his father."[8]

In both Matthew and Acts it is not clearly stated that Judas is eternally condemned. I would like to conclude this article by presenting a brief

---

7. Barth, *Church Dogmatics*, 3/4, 408-10 (new edition, vol. 20, 81-83; German ed., 3/4, 465-66).

8. Davies and Allison, *Matthew*, vol. 3, 565-66, provides an eight-point analysis of the parallels between Ahithophel and Judas. See further, Droge, *"Mori Lucrum"*; Whelan, "Suicide in the Ancient World"; Wick, "Judas als Prophet wider Willen"; Reed, "Saving Judas." Migaku Sato has given an oral presentation on the atoning value of Judas' death, but I have not been able to locate a published form. On the formula citation, Menken, *Matthew's Bible*, 179-99.

argument that within Matthew's theological framework Judas stands a good chance of being saved. Indeed, his desperate death contributes to the atonement for his sin of betrayal. We begin with a statement of God's salvific will according to the Matthean Jesus: "It is not the will of your Father in heaven that one of these little ones should be lost" (Matt 18:14). This comes at the end of the parable of the one sheep that went astray. It is not the point of this article to argue that Matthew taught an absolute universalism of salvation. But this verse points to the inclination of the divine will.

The next step in the argument is to note that Matthew holds a synergisitic view of the total process of salvation. We are judged not only on the basis of our faith but also of our works, our good or bad deeds (Matt 25:31–46).

The third step is to notice that in Matthew (as in the other gospels) those who lose their life for Jesus' sake will find it (Matt 10:39 = Q 16:25–26, from Mark). Before the main argument is reached it may be permitted to refer to a verse from outside the gospel but which Matthew may have known. The date of Colossians is debated, but in this letter Paul (or deutero-Paul) says: "I am now rejoicing in my sufferings for your sake, and in my flesh I am completing what is lacking in Christ's afflictions for the sake of his body, that is, the church" (Col 1:24). This is the sort of thinking that may lie behind Judas' action in Matthew.

My main argument is this. If we tqke the text of Matt 27:3–5 seriously, it expresses a fivefold project of repentance on Judas' part. To see this we must take note of the term Matthew uses in v. 3. He uses *metameletheis* (trom *metameleomai*, regret, be sorry), not *metanoeo*, to express Judas' repentance. This word choice could be explained as showing the weakness of Judas' repentance, as though it were only a mild regret. But classical authors distinguish the words differently: metanoeo refers to repentance of mind, intellect, *nous*; metameleomai refers to repentance of will, emotion. Even if this distinction is overdrawn, it may here help us to see the different stages of Judas' reaction. First, he sees (*idon*) the fact of the condemnation. He takes intellectual cognizance of the horrid judgment. This leads to ths change of will (*metameletheis*),[9] his sorrow and decision to try to undo the damage. The third stage is his effort of restitution (*estrepsen*) of the thirty pieces of silver. The fourth step is his public confession of his sin (*hemarton*) and its specification: "by betraying innocent blood." The fifth is his hanging himself (*apegxato*). Taken together these five steps suggest a complete and systematic repentance of Judas in mind, heart, word and deed. More could hardly be asked of him. That the high priests and elders refuse his

9. Cf. Michel, "*meameleomai*."

confession and refuse to stop the execution is not his fault. Even they are portrayed as nervous about handling the blood money. Our point however is that Martthew has done everything he could to portray the repentance of Judas as deep and sincere. Thereby the field of blod, Hakeldama, becomes also a place of mercy and atonement, despite its unsavory reputation.

BIBLIOGRAPHY

Barth, Karl. *Church Dogmatics.* Vol. 3, Pt. 4, *The Doctrine of Creation.* Edited by G. W. Bromiley and T. F. Torrance. Translated by A. T. Mackay. Edinburgh: T. & T. Clark, 1961.

Benoit, Pierre. "The Death of Judas." In *Jesus and the Gospel,* 1:189–207. Translated by Benet Weatherhead. New York: Herder & Herder, 1973. French orig. 1954.

Brown, Raymond E. *The Death of the Messiah: From Gethsemane to the Grave; A Commentary on the Passion Narratives in the Four Gospels.* 2 vols. Anchor Bible Reference Library. New York: Doubleday, 1994.

Davies, W. D., and Dale C. Allison Jr. *The Gospel according to Matthew.* Vol. 3. ICC. Edinburgh: T. & T. Clark, 1997.

Droge, Arthur J. "*Mori Lucrum*: Paul and Ancient Theories of Suicide." *NovT* 30 (1988) 263–86.

Gnilka, Joachim. *Das Matthäusevangelium.* Vol. 2. HTKNT 1/2. Freiburg: Herder, 1988.

Klassen, William. *Judas: Betrayer or Friend of Jesus?* Minneapolis: Fortress, 1996.

Klauck, Hans-Josef. *Judas—Ein Jünger des Herrn.* QD 111. Freiburg: Herder, 1987.

Küchler, Max. *Jerusalem: Ein Handbuch and Studienreiseführer zur Heiligen Stadt.* OLB 4/2. Göttingen: Vandenhoeck & Ruprecht, 2007.

Luz, Ulrich. *Matthew 21-28: A Commentary.* Translated by James E. Crouch. Hermeneia. Minneapolis: Fortress, 2005.

Menken, Maarten J. J. *Matthew's Bible: The Old Testament Text of the Evangelist.* BETL 173. Leuven: Peeters, 2004.

Michel, Otto. "*metamelomai.*" In *TDNT* 4:626–30.

Reed, David A. "Saving Judas": A Social Scientific Approach to Judas's Suicide in Matthew 27:3–10." *BTB* 35 (2005) 51–59.

Senior, Donald. "The Fate of the Betrayer: A Redactional Study of Matthew XXVII, 3–10." *ETL* 48 (1972) 372–426. Reprinted in Senior, *The Passion Narrative according to Matthew: A Redactional Study,* 343–97. BETL 39. Leuven: Peeters, 1975.

Stein-Schneider, Herbert. "A la recherche du Judas historique: Une enquête exégétique à la lumièree des textes de l'Ancien Testament." *ETR* 60 (1985) 403–25.

Whelan, Caroline F. "Suicide in the Ancient World: A Re-examination of Matthew 27:3–10." *Laval théologique et philosophique* 49 (1993) 505–22.

Wick, Peter. "Judas als Prophet wider Willen." *TZ* 57 (2001) 26–35.

14

A Woman's Quest for Wisdom and the Adoration of the Magi as Part of Matthew's Program of Solomonic Sapiential Messianism

> "The book of the genealogy [origin, birth] of Jesus Christ, the son of David
> ... David become the father of Solomon, whose mother had been the wife of Uriah."
>
> (MATT 1:1, 6)

The first son of David in the line of royal, anointed, messianic succession was king Solomon, Shlomo, whose name means peace and prosperity (1 Chr 22:8). This paper explores the concept of Solomonic sapiential messianism in 1 Kings, Matthew 1–2, and related texts. Building on a recent article on Matthew 2 and the abuse of power by Herod,[1] it will attempt to explore more thoroughly the role of 1 Kgs 10:1–13, the visit of the queen of Sheba, as the basic model in the composition of Matthew's narrative of the visit of the magi. The conclusion will stress the contributions of wisdom, including feminine wisdom, to Matthew's Christology and to his ethics of non-violent resistance to abuses of power.

---

1. B. T. Viviano, "The Adoration of the Magi: Matthew 2:1–23 and Theological Aesthetics," *Revue Biblique* 115 (2008) 546–67.

I. SOLOMONIC SAPIENTIAL MESSIANISM

Although studies of Matthew's portrait of Jesus as messianic son of David have abounded since the dawn of redaction criticism in the late fifties of the last century,[2] there seems to have been little interest in the specifically Solomonic character of his Davidic Christology. To be sure, there have been studies of wisdom Christology,[3] but to my knowledge, little has been said about Solomonic messianism, with the notable exception of Flander's glory, Eduard Schillebeeckx, in his great work on Jesus.[4] Schillebeeckx recognizes the relevance of the Solomonic sense in which Jesus is called son of David in Matthew, that is, Jesus is not simply genetically a son of David, nor is he his son solely as a healer, although that is also true and important. Jesus is also son of David in the sense that he is a wise leader, one who avoids violence in his teaching and in his actions (in regard to persons; cf. Matt 10:34-36; 11:12; 21:12-13). So let us look at the Solomon story as presented in the biblical tradition as it existed before Matthew released his gospel to the copiests.

Before we do so however we should first briefly look at similar sorts of typological research. The gold standard for such research was set by D. C. Allison with his book on Moses typology in Matthew.[5] Moses' immediate successor was Joshua. The late cardinal Jean Daniélou sketched a Joshua typology for Jesus in early Christian traditions.[6] Traits of the most famous of the judges, Samson, have been noted by Galbiati.[7] Jesus as son of David shepherd has been studied by many.[8] As already mentioned, Solomonic ty-

2. Wolfgang Trilling, *Das wahre Israel* (Munich: Kösel, 1964; 1st ed. 1959); G. Bornkamm, G. Barth, H. J. Held, *Tradition and Interpretation in Matthew* (Philadelphia, Westminster, 1963, orig. 1960); Georg Strecker, *Der Weg der Gerechtigkeit* (Göttingen, Vandenhoeck & Ruprecht, 1962); Reinhard Hummel, *Die Auseinandersetzung zwischen Kirche und Judentum im Matthäusevangelium* (Munich: Kaiser, 1966).

3. M. J. Suggs, *Wisdom, Christology and Law in Matthew's Gospel* (Cambridge: Harvard University Press, 1970); Felix Christ, *Jesus Sophia* (ATANT 57; Zurich: Zwingli, 1970); Celia Deutsch, "Wisdom in Matthew," *NovT* 32 (1990) 13-47; R. A. Piper, *Wisdom in the Q-Tradition* (SNTSMS 61; Cambridge: Cambridge University Press, 1989).

4. E, Schillebeeckx, *Jesus* (New York: Seabury Crossroad, 1979), 456-59.

5. D. C. Allison, *The New Moses* (Minneapolis: Fortress, 1993).

6. J. Daniélou, *From Shadow to Reality* (Westminster, MD: Newman, 1960).

7. E. Galbiati, "L'adorazione dei Magi," *Bibbia e Oriente* 4 (1962) 20-29.

8. Earlier bibliography in R. E. Brown, *Birth of the Messiah* (New York: Doubleday, 1993), 504-12; D. C. Duling, "The Therapeutic Son of David," *NTS* 24 (1978) 392-410; Duling, "Solomon, Exorcism, and the Son of David," *HTR* 68 (1975) 235-52; Duling, "Matthew's Plurisignificant Son of David in Social Science Perspective," *BTB* 22 (1992) 99-116; B. M. Nolan, *The Royal Son of God* (OBO 23; Fribourg: Editions Universitaires, 1979); L. Novakovic, *Messiah the Healer of the Sick* (WUNT II 170; Tübingen: Mohr/

pology has been neglected (except for Bruns and Galbiati)[9] in favor of Jesus as Wisdom incarnate.[10] Jesus has also been studied as the suffering servant of God as developed in Deutero-Isaiah[11] and as the suffering prophet like Jeremiah.[12] Finally there are the Christologically crucial studies of Jesus as the Danielic Son of Man.[13]

The main biblical narrative about Solomon is found in 1 Kings, chapters 1 to 11, closely followed by 2 Chronicles, chapters 1 to 9, and by Josephus, *Antiquities* 8.1-211; *Contra Apionem* 1.106-115.[14]

At this point let us go through the story as it is told in 1 Kings and read it on the surface level, noticing as we go possible or probable links with Matthew's story of Jesus. The story in 1 Kings begins with the struggle for succession to the throne of David. Adonijah, one of David's many sons, raises

---

Siebck, 2003); J. Willits, *Matthew's Messianic Shepherd-King* (BZNW 147; Berlin: de Gruyter, 2007); G. Garbe, *Der Hirte Israels* (WMANT 106; Neukirchen-Vluyn: Neukirchener, 2005); M. Konradt, *Israel, Kirche und die Völker im Matthäusevangelium* (WUNT 215; Tübingen: Mohr/Siebeck, 2007).

9. See notes 7 and 8 above. J. E. Bruns, "The Magi Episode in Matthew 2," *CBQ* 23 (1961) 51-54.

10. See note 3.

11. O. Cullmann, *The Christology of the New Testament* (Philadelphia: Westminster, 1963), 51-82; W. Zimmerli and J. Jeremias, *The Servant of God* (SBT 20; London: SCM, 1957); D. Hill, *Son and Servant: An Essay on Matthean Christology*, *JSNT* 6 (1980) 2-16; B. Janowski and P. Stuhlmacher, *The Suffering Servant* (Grand Rapids: Eerdmans, 2004), esp. 147-61.

12. M. P. Knowles, *Jeremiah in Matthew's Gospel* (JSNTSup 68; Sheffield: Academic, 1993).

13. The Son of Man figure has generated a large literature. My starting point as a student was Cullmann, *Christology*, 137-92. Useful surveys in J. J. Collins, *Daniel* (Hermeneia; Minneapolis: Fortress, 1993), 70-105; A. Yarbro Collins, *Mark* (Hermeneia; Minneapolis: Fortress, 2007), 187-89; R. E. Brown, *Introduction to New Testament Christology* (New York: Paulist, 1994), 89-102. Note also U. Luz, *Studies in Matthew* (Grand Rapids: Eerdmans, 2005), 83-112; H. E. Tödt, *The Son of Man in the Synoptic Tradition* (London: SCM, 1965).

14. Prof. C. T. Begg has a series of articles on Josephus's handling of the Solomon story. For our purposes the most relevant is "The Visit of the Queen of Sheba according to Josephus," *JSem* 15 (2006) 107-29. The bibliography on Solomon in OT studies is extensive. Among the chief monographs we note: J. B. Pritchard, ed., *Solomon and Sheba*, (London, Phaidon, 1974), outstanding for the history of interpretation; S. Wälchli, *Der weise König Salomo* (BWANT 141; Stuttgart: Kohlhammer, 1991); L. K. Handy, ed., *The Age of Solomon* (Leiden: Brill, 1997); P. Särkiö, *Die Weisheit und Macht Salomos in der israelitischen Historiographie* (Helsinki: Schriften der finnischen exegetischen Gesellschaft 60, 1994; and the same author's "Salomo I," in *TRE* 29 (1980) 724-32; recently A. E. Gardner, The Narratives of Solomon's Reign in the Light of the Historiography of Other Ancient Civilizations," *ABR* 56 (2008) 1-18; P. S. F. Van Keulen, *Two Versions of the Solomon Narrative (MT and LXX)* (VTSup 104; Leiden, Brill, 2005); C. Lichtert and D. Nocquet, eds., *Le Roi Salomon, FS. J. Vermeylen* (Brussels: Lessius, 2008).

a revolt to seize the throne before David is dead and before Solomon can claim it. Solomon's mother Bathsheba intervenes and the succession passes to her son. Here already we see a rough parallel with the opening chapters of Matthew, which depict a struggle between the aging Herod and the infant Jesus. Who is the true king of Israel? The slaughter of the children of Bethlehem shows to what lengths Herod will go to keep his hold on power. Jesus survives. He begins his peaceful ministry long after Herod is dead.

Twice in 1 Kings 1 it is stated that Solomon's throne is greater than David's (vv. 37 and 47). Yet Jesus is greater than Solomon (Matt 12:42). In 1 Kings 1:49 Adonijah's guests tremble. In Matt 2:3 Herod and all Jerusalem fear.

(At first Adonijah's life is spared by Solomon [1 Kgs 1:52–53] but then he is executed because of his arrogance [1 Kgs 2:24–25]. So too are Joab and Shimei put to death—for disobedience. Peace arrives in 2:33.)

Although there is no gospel parallel to Solomon taking an Egyptian wife, this detail (1 Kgs 3:1) is found embarrassing by later Jewish traadition; it is quietly suppressed in 2 Chronicles 1, some time before Matthew wrote. On the other hand, Jesus had several Gentile ancestors according to Matthew's genealogy: Rahab (1:5), Ruth (1:5), and possibly Bathsheba (1:6). Solomon loved the Lord (1 Kgs 3:3). In Matthew Jesus praises his Father (11:25). 1 Kings 3 continues with Solomon's dream at Gibeon. This contains God's question to Solomon, Solomon's prayer for a listening mind and God's friendly answer. Then Solomon goes to Jerusalem to offer sacrifice. This is followed by the exemplar story of Solomon exercising wisdom in judgment (on the two women and the one living baby). Here the parallels with Jesus are not close. Jesus experiences dreamlike temptations and he passes the tests. He prays to his Father in Gethsemani but his prayer is not answered in the way he had hoped. In Lucan special material Jesus refuses to act as judge between men (Luke 12:14), but in Matt 25:31 he presents the Son of man as eschatological judge.

The parallels between 1 Kings 4 and Matthew are much closer. In 1 Kgs 4:1 and 7, Solomon appoints twelve high officials. Compare Jesus' call and appointment of the twelve apostles (Matt 4:18–22 and 10:1–4). In 1 Kgs 4:20 the people eat, drink and make merry at the royal expense. Compare with that the feeding narratives in Matt 14:15–21 and 15:32–39. In 1 Kgs 4:29–34 the fame of Solomon's wisdom spreads; compare Matt 4:25 and 11:25–27; Jesus' fame spreads and people flock to him from a wide radius.

The next great section of the Solomon story concerns the building of the Temple and the royal palace (1 Kings 5–8). Solomon speaks to the delegates of king Hiram of Tyre. Solomon wants to include the Lebanese in the great project and praises the master carpentry of the Sidonians (1 Kgs

5:6). Jesus praises Tyre and Sidon indirectly while pronouncing woes on Galilean towns (Matt 11:21–22). More important still, Jesus withdraws to the region of Tyre and Sidon (Matt 15:2) and praises the faith of a local woman while healing her daughter. This does not mean that Jesus takes foreign wives, much less that he is an idolator. But he befriends Solomon's friends, of both sexes. On the other hand, the forced labor and heavy tax burden involved in the building of the Temple contrast with Jesus' offer of rest for the weary (Matt 11:28–30), although Jesus does counsel the paying of taxes (Matt 17:24–27; 22:15–22). The Temple is built in silence; its centerpiece is the Holy of Holies; within this is the Ark of the Covenant; on top of the Ark are the two cherubim; it takes them seven years to build the Temple (1 Kgs 6:7, 16, 19, 23, 37–38). Within the Ark are the tablets of the Law, the Decalogue. Jesus goes to desert places to pray alone (Matt 14:23), he teaches, comments on and summarizes the two tablets of the Decalogue (Matt 5:21–48; 22:34–40).

The building of the palace takes another thirteen years. It contains "the Hall of the Throne where he was to pronounce judgment, the Hall of Justice" (1 Kgs 7:1, 7). Jesus has a ministry in Jerusalem (Matthew 21–25). He enters the city solemnly and cleanses the Temple, declaring it to be a house of prayer (Matt 21:13; Jer 7:11). Jesus teaches in the Temple, answering a question about his authority, recounting three parables of judgment, and then answering questions about taxes, the resurrection, the greatest commandment and David's son as the Messiah and as David's lord. This pericope implies but does not state that Jesus is greater than both David and the original or historical Solomon.

Chapter 8 of 1 Kings recounts the dedication of the Temple. After the Ark has been brought into the Holy of Holies, a cloud of the divine glory filled the Temple. Solomon declares that the Lord will dwell in thick darkness. This contrasts with the cloud that covers Jesus and the three disciples at the Transfiguration which Matthew describes as *photine*, lightsome or bright (Matt 17:5). To be sure, this contrast may be more apparent than real, but for now we remain with the surface of the texts. The sequel of Solomon's dedication service consists of a speech, a very long prayer, a blessing and the offering of sacrifices. One of the surprising features of Solomon's prayer is that it does not mention sacrifice as part of the purpose of the Temple.[15] Matthean parallels would include Jesus' teaching of a short prayer (Matt 6:9–13), the blessing of the eucharistic elements in sacrificial terms (Matt 26:26–30) and his own death on the cross (Matt 27:33–56). In 1 Kings 9

---

15. E. Talstra, *Solomon's Prayer* (Kampen: Kos, 1993): L. J. Hoppe, "The Afterlife of a Text: The Case of Solomon's Prayer in 1 Kings 8," *SBFLA* 51 (2001) 1–30.

Solomon receives a second vision which announces the possibility of disaster in the future. This corresponds approximately to Jesus' great eschatological discourse in Matthew, chaps. 23–25, where there are woes, a lament over Jerusalem, and the announcement of calamities. The visit of the queen of Sheba to Solomon (1 Kgs 10:1–13) illustrates his international role, as the visit of the magi from the east illustrates the international role of Jesus (more on this later). Then the text notes that there were twelve lions around the royal throne, a feature which it insists is unique (10:20). Compare the twelve thrones for the judging disciples in Matt 19:28. A powerful summary statement in 1 Kgs 10:23–25 insists that Solomon surpassed all other kings in riches and wisdom, that the whole world sought his divinely given wisdom and brought him presents (gold and spices and other valuables) annually (cf. Matt 2:11). This could be called the high point of Solomonic Christology, a wholly positive picture.

First Kings 11 changes this rosy picture by listing Solomon's errors and his enemies. Jesus is free from the error of foreign, idolatrous wives. (This offence is eliminated in 2 Chronicles for the first Solomon.) Jesus has no foreign wives. Matthew does show Jesus as friendly with women (e.g., Simon Peter's mother-in-law, the Canaanite woman, Jairus' daughter, the woman with a hemorrhage, Pilate's wife, Mary Magdalene).[16] But, as Solomon is said to have Hadad and Rezon for enemies, so too the Matthean Jesus has Caiphas and Pilate as foes.

Solomon's legacy is mixed and complex. On the one hand, he had a long reign (forty years); he was renowned for wisdom and, true to his name (1 Chr 22:9), peace, even though there were a few hostilities. He died peacefully in bed. On the other hand, after his death the kingdom was divided. The ten northern tribes rebelled and served Jeroboam. The southern tribe of Judah remained loyal to Rehoboam and preserved the Temple in Jerusalem. In the Jesus story Judas could be seen as the rebel apostle, even though in Matthew he repents and is redeemed (Matt 27:3–10).[17]

We may now note that from a modern diachronic point of view, the Solomon story in 1 Kings, since it belongs to the Deuteronomic History, has been analyzed, on the basis of different ideologies or theological evaluations present in the text, into three strata. The first stratum is the Hezekian Deuteronomic History for which Solomon is the ideal monarch; he serves as the model for Hezekiah. The second stratum is the Josianic Deuteronomic

---

16. Cf. E. M. Wainwright, *Toward a Feminist Critical Reading of the Gospel according to Matthew* (BZNW 60; Berlin: de Gruyter, 1991).

17. B. T. Viviano, "Hakeldama, The Potter's Field, and the Suicide of Judas (Matthew 27:3–10; Acts 1:16–20)," in *Jerusalem und die Länder: Festschrift Max Küchler* (NTOA 70; Göttingen: Vandenhoeck & Ruprecht, 2009), 203–10.

History. In this layer Solmon is errant, and is corrected by king Josiah. In the third, post-exilic Deuternomic History, Solomon is a link in a long chain of miscreants that ruin Israel.[18]

This completes our survey of the Solomonic story in 1 Kings 1–11 and its bearing on Matthew's story of Jesus, with its many positive parallels and its also signicant differences. We have already referred occasionally to the modified version of the Solomon story to be found in 1 Chronicles 1–9. It is not to our purpose to mention all the differences between the two versions. But there is one major point that needs to be made. Given his priestly interests, the Chronicler attempts to tighten the links between Solomon's Temple and the desert tabernacle described in Exodus-Leviticus-Numbers. In line with this, the Chronicler develops a Moses typology for Solomon. The implications of this redactional tendency are great for our study of Matthew. We have already mentioned some of the many biblical typologies for Jesus present in Matthew. Such an abundance can lead to confusion and dispersal. It is therefore important to see how the many types tend to coalesce around one or two basic models, for example, Moses and David. In this sense Solomon for the Chronicler and for Matthew is both in continuity with David and at the same time in continuity with some of the religious significance of Moses, especially in regard to wisdom teaching (cf. Deut 4:5–8) and the service of worship.

Other biblical echoes of the Solomon figure will not delay us long . Psalm 72 is unusual as being attributed to Solomon in the title of the Psalm. This attribution is suggested by several features of the psalm, including his being a king's son and a wise judge (vv. 1–2), the broad extent of his rule (v. 8), rulers coming to him from afar, from Sheba and Seba, bearing gifts of gold (vv. 8–11, 15), and an abundance of peace (v. 7). The psalm concludes with a doxology which could remind one of David's prayer in 1 Kgs 1:48 but the wording is much more vague.

Although Solomon is not mentioned by name in Isaiah 60, this vision of Jerusalem's coming exaltation, from the prophet called Trito-Isaiah, has long been recognized as reflecting the Solomon story and as influencing the Matthean infancy gospel. In a proto-apocalyptic vision of a new dawn, Yahweh will arise [as the sun]. Kings will come , bearing on camels the wealth of the nations, gold, frankincense and flocks for sacrifice on the altar in the Temple (Isa 60:1–7). Sheba is explicitly mentioned, but again there is no

---

18. V. Fritz, *First and Second Kings* (Continental Commentaries; Minneapolis: Fortress, 2003), *in loco*; W. Dietrich, *The Early Monarchy in Israel: The Tenth Century B.C.E.* (Biblical Encyclopedia 3; Atlanta: Society of Biblical Literature, 2007).

mention of myrrh, a Matthean element derived from another part of the Solomon tradition, Cant 3:6 and Prov 7:17. [19]

The praise of Solomon in Sir 47:12–22 reiterates his wisdom in an age of peace, his building of the Temple, his composition of proverbs, songs, parables, the international range of his fame (perhaps an allusion to the queen of Sheba), his sin with women, and the division of the kingdom as a result of the sin. Sirach adds that the Lord will not abandon the Davidic line but will allow a remnant and a root to survive.

It is curious that the Septuagint of 1 Kgs 10:1–13 uses *epistemon* rather than *sophos* to describe Solomon in v. 12. In v. 14 it uses the verb *esophistheis* and the noun *syniesis* to refer to Solomon' wisdom and understanding, terms dear to Matthew.[20]

Intellectually the boldest exploitation of the tradition we are tracing is the Wisdom of Solomon. Written in good Greek between 30 BC and AD 70, probably in Alexandria, it represents the biblical message in the universal terms of Hellenistic philosophy. As the earlier wisdom books attributed to Solomon put him in dialogue with ancient near eastern wisdom (Babylonian, Canaanite, Egyptian, but including perhaps some debate with Epicurus in the cases of Qoheleth and Sirach),[21] so does Wisdom put Solomon in dialogue with Greek culture. The middle part of the book (6:22—10:21), written in the first person singular, retells Solomon's prayer for a listening mind as a passionately experienced spiritual odyssey in quest of divine wisdom. It seems to be a genuine personal religious experience, though attributed to Solomon. This combination of personal present and past traditional elements may seem an odd manoeuver psychologically, yet far from impossible. It shows that Solomon remained a living spiritual force long after his death, up to and including the time of Jesus.

The third and final part (11:1—19:22) of the book of Wisdom retells the Exodus story without proper names as in the Greek philosophical fashion. For us this implies that the author, like the Chronicler, wanted to tighten the link between Moses and Solomon. This procedure prepares for the more extensive fusion of biblical types in the figure of Jesus in Matthew (and in the rest of the New Testament). In the process the author of Wisdom introduces a list of Greek cardinal virtues (Wis 8:7) and a Greek argument for our knowledge of God by analogy from the beauty of created things (Wis 13:5). This inquiry is relevant to our project because it is likely that Matthew knew the Book of Wisdom (cf. Matt 27:43 and Wis 2:16; Matt 2:2 and Wis 18:1–3).

---

19. P. D. Hanson, *The Dawn of Apocalyptic* (Philadelphia: Fortress, 1979).
20. Bornkamm, Barth, and Held, *Tradition and Interpretation*, 105–12.
21. M. Hengel, *Judaism and Hellenism* (London: SCM, 1991), 115–75.

Even though Matthew does not use Greek philosophical concepts, he knew the bold extension of the Solomon type achieved by the author of this book. The Hellenized Solomon contributed to his gospel which begins with Jesus son of David, son of Abraham, and ends with a worldwide mission in the name of Jesus. [22]

(The reinterpretation of the Solomon tradition in Josephus' *Antiquities* was written a little late for it to be able to help us understand Matthew's intentions, so we leave it to the careful studies of Christopher Begg, mentioned above.)

Further echoes of the "school" of Solomon are found in the Psalms of Solomon, present in some manuscripts of the Septuagint. They are commonly said to have been composed in Hebrew, now lost, and give expression to a Pharisaic hope for the Davidic messiah in Psalms 17 and 18. They are dated around the middle of the first century BC. Most of these eighteen psalms are attributed to Solomon. The resemblances between Solomon and the Messiah figure include: "Each is called the son of David, . . . both were extenders of boundaries, restorers and beautifiers of Jerusalem, and defenders of the worship of [God]. They received tribute from foreign monarchs, who came to see their glory." The two last Psalms (17 and 18) mention wisdom alongside justice as characterisitics of the Davidic messiah's rule (17:25, 31; 18:8). [23]

The Odes of Solomon, first published in 1909, are Christian hymns that give thanks for the knowledge and light which come through baptism. Some scholars see in them a certain affinity with the gospel according to John.[24] They are composed later than Matthew, but they do indicate that in early Christianity even after Matthew there was an abiding interest in Solomon as a basic model of sapiential, intellectualist, messianic faith.

An ever stranger work is the Testament of Solomon, of uncertain date. It is thought to be a Christian reworking of a Jewish text. Most of chapters 1 and 2, and 20-25, are thought to be Jewish. It has a fairytale atmosphere, somewhere between the Niebelungenlied, the Brothers Grimm and The Lord of the Ring. It is full of named angels and demons, and includes a magic ring, astrology, signs of mental illness (split personality). It is a retelling of much of the story of the biblical Solomon in the mode of magic and Oriental fable. Solomon is powerful and wise, but above all he is building

---

22. C. Larcher, *Le Livre de la Sagesse ou La Sagesse de Salomon* (EBib, Paris: Gabalda, 1983, 1984, 1985); D. S. Winston, *The Wisdom of Solomon* (AB 43, New York: Doubleday, 1979); J. Barr, *Biblical Faith and Natural Theology* (Oxford: Clarendon, 1993); J. J. Collins, "Natural Theology and Biblical Tradition," *CBQ* 60 (1998) 1-15.

23. *OTP* 2:639-70, esp. 641 (R. B. Wright).

24. *OTP* 2:725-71 (J. H. Charlesworth).

the Temple. He is admired by the queen of Sheba and other rulers. But in the end he falls into idolatry because of his infatuation with a foreign woman and must hope for God's mercy. The author is interested in the technical problems of building the Temple: quarrying the stones, lifting the pinnacle stone. Solomon's wisdom here includes his mastery of the dark arts, his control of the (evil) spirits. This text is a striking example of how the Solomon story lived on in detail in the popular imagination among some Jews and Christians.[25]

To sum up the results of our survey of the Solomon tradition, we may take note of four constant elements. (1) Solomon stands for wisdom, creativity, worldwide culture. (2) Solomon's name (1 Chr 22:8) means "a man of peace, peaceable" and his reign is a forty year age of almost total absence of war, a time of non-violence, of peace and prosperity. (3) Solomon builds the Temple which is filled with the presence or glory of God. Although Solomon can function as a priest himself, there is no principled hostility to the priestly strand within Israel's traditions. (4) Solomon has a complex relationship with women. He takes an Egyptian wife at the outset. Then he is consulted by a royal woman who admires his wisdom. Finally, his good work is undone because of his foreign wives, and his kingdom is divided. This last negative point sets the stage for the coming of a new and even better Solomon. One could also say that Solomon has an open, friendly attitude to strong women. To that extent his type can serve some of the interests of modern feminism.

II. THE VISIT OF THE QUEEN OF SHEBA

Now let us take a closer look at the story of the queen of Sheba's visit to king Solomon as recounted in 1 Kgs 10:1–13. Two structures have been proposed. The first is linear: 1. The royal visit (vv. 1–3); 2. The praise of Solomon's wisdom (vv. 4–9); 3. The mutual exchange of gifts (vv. 10–13).[26] (Commentators generally agree that vv. 10–12 are an interpolation. One could argue against this, but it is not to our purpose.) The second structure is chiastic: A, narrative introduction (vv. 1–3); B, the queen observes Solomon's glory (vv. 4–5); B prime, the queen speaks about Solomon's glory

---

25. *OTP* 1.935–87 (D. C. Duling). For later Jewish reception, besides the appropriate essay in Pritchard (note 14 above) by L. H. Silberman, see L. Ginzberg, *The Legends of the Jews*, vol. 4 (Philadelphia: JPS, 1913), 123–76, with the notes, vol. 6 (1928), 277–303. The Second Targum to Esther plays an important role here. See the edition by P. Cassel (Leipzig: Friedrich, 1885).

26. S. J. De Vries, *First Kings* (WBC; Nashville: Nelson, 2004), *in loco*.

(vv. 6-9); A prime, narrative conclusion (vv. 10-13).[27] These proposals offer only a rough guide. The first has the merit of placing wisdom at the center of the passage.

If we ask what the point of the story is, where its accent lies, we find in the older reception history that the key to the interpretation is found in v. 13: "Solomon gave to the queen of Sheba every desire (*hafetz*) that she expressed." The word "desire" is interpreted as erotic desire. (Some see this erotic desire already in v. 2, "she came to Solomon," because this phrase sometimes has an erotic connotation.) This eros then becomes the stuff of legend. Solomon seduces her, then marries her. Their child Menelik is the beginning of the Ethiopian royal dynasty. For Rashi, she marries Nebuchadnezzar. For the Talmud she becomes Lilith the temptress. In sharp reaction[28] to this romantic version, modern exegetes tend to emphasize the commercial significance of the queen's visit. The goal of her mission is a trade pact. The meeting becomes a sort of early G-8 economic summit conference. This interpretation emphasizes the value of the gifts, the spice trade caravan routes, incense traffic. Volkmar Fritz combines the two lines of interpretation: it began with trade relations, but then blossomed into love.[29]

Over against these two popular reading strategies, I would like to argue for a reading which is at once intellectualist, feminist and religious. The text is primarily about a woman's desire for knowledge, for wisdom. The wisdom involved is multifaceted. On the basis of the surrounding culture and the earlier descriptions of Solomon's wisdom (1 Kgs 3:16-28; 4:29-34), we can say that this desired wisdom includes first of all ethical conduct, e.g., how to conduct oneself at court (Prov 23:1-3; 25:1-7). Then it involves an encyclopedic knowledge of natural history, so-called *Listenwissenschaft*, a science containing lists of species of plants and animals (1 Kgs 4:33).[30] Crucial for government, the ruler needs judicial wisdom as illustrated by Solomon's judgment in the case of the two harlots (1 Kgs 3:16-28), but the ruler also needs diplomacy and allies, illustrated by Solomon's friendship with king Hiram of Tyre (1 Kgs 5:1-18). On the level of philosophical and artistic creativity, Solomon composes proverbs, riddles, parables, psalms or songs both sacred and profane. Finally, there is the religious dimension: how to worship God in the Temple, the complex system of sacrifices and offerings,

---

27. J. T. Walsh and D. Cotter, *First Kings* (Berit Olam; Collegeville, MN: Liturgical, 1996), 126.

28. For example, J. Gray, *First and Second Kings* (London: SCM, 1970), 259; W. Brueggemann, *First and Second Kings* (Macon, GA, Smyth & Helwys, 2000), 131-35.

29. Fritz, *First and Second Kings, in loco*.

30. A. Alt, "Die Weisheit Salomos," in *Kleine Schriften* 2 (Munich, Beck, 1959), 90-99.

the rituals, incense rites, prayers and psalms, the experience of the presence of God in the Sanctuary. These elements are all explicit in the text and its context. I would like to add a speculation that the queen might have posed basic questions about the meaning and mysteries of life, its beginning, its ending, its goal or purpose; the meaning or lack of meaning of suffering; of aging; of death; what can we know about God or the gods?

This reading could be dismissed as modernizing or anachronistic, just as the commerical treaty could be so dismissed. But this sapiential approach can be substantiated by a glance at most of the eleven verses of the unit. The testing (*nassah*) and the riddles (*hiddoth*) (v. 1); her mind (*lebabah*) (v. 2); question, answers, explanations (v. 3); Solomon's wisdom (*hokmat*) is explicit in v. 4; the religious aspect of Solomon's wisdom is explicit in the burnt offerings and the house of the Lord which he had recently built (v. 5). But the verse also expresses the queen's interest in the domestic and court details of administration. Although such a fascination is not uniquely feminine, after all it is Solomon's court and Temple, here we see a note that fits well with a woman's way to wisdom too. The verse adds a remark about her breath, her spirit, her *ruach*, her *Geist*, an anthropological term which plays a great role in the biblical analysis of intellectual life.[31]

The next two verses (6 and 7) add precisions to the nature of wisdom. First it is paired with accomplishments (*debarecha*); it is thus a practical, active wisdom, not only an ivory tower learning. Then it is linked with prosperity (*tob*). This should be the result of a wise ruler's decisions. To be sure, an ancient prophet or a modern reader might want to ask whether the prosperity belongs only to Solomon or is it a properity shared by all the people. This question is not clearly answered in the text. Perhaps it is part of a panegyric by a court scribe who did not (yet) want to point out any flaws. But at least the people would benefit from a long era of peace, the so-called peace dividend. The two macarisms in v. 8 are a sapiential genre, here explicitly linked with the advantage of hearing Solomon's wisdom. For Ernst Würthwein[32] the folk story so far is wholly profane. For him v. 9 has been added to make it religious. Such a remark does not take into account the word of the Lord in v. 5 or the general religious tinge of biblical wisdom ("the fear of the Lord is the beginning of wisdom"). But certainly here a blessing is placed in the queen's mouth which twice names God Yahweh. This blessing is for both Solomon and the people Israel. But above all this

---

31. H. W. Wolff, *Anthropology of the Old Testament* (London: SCM, 1974), 32-39.

32. E. Würthwein, *Der erste Buch der Könige, Kap. 1-16* (ATD 11/1; Göttingen: Vandenhoeck & Ruprecht, 1985), 119-22.

refers to the royal duty to execute justice. This can be understood as the ethical, sociopolitical aspect of wisdom.

So these nine verses are easily understood as emphazizing the wisdom character of the unit, of the king and of the queen. This can be done without forcing. It is on this basis that we can argue that the desire (*haphetz*) of v. 13 should refer primarily to the queen's interest in wisdom, and only secondarily to eros or to commerce.

The three gifts of v. 10, gold, spices, jewels are not especially sapiential. To be sure, other biblical texts speak of wisdom as more precious than gold (Prov 8:19; cp. Ps 12:6). Wisdom is compared to myrrh and incense (Sir 24:15). We might ask whether the gifts are payment for instruction? No price is set for an invitation to wisdom's banquet (Prov 9:1-6). The rabbis hold that one should not make worldly use of the crown (of Torah study), but they allow indirect subsidies.[33] If not payment, which seems a consideration far from our text, what about v. 13, in which the king reciprocates in regard to the queen's generosity? Some commentators deny that Solomon gives her anything concrete in return.[34] Others hold that he outshines her in gifts.[35] The text says that Solomon satisfies her every desire and that he gave her gifts from the royal hand. This verse could be easily interpreted in context as satisfying her intellectual and religious curiosity first and then giving her material gifts. In the wisdom literature, wisdom is the most valuable treasure but is not usually opposed to material blessings. By giving the queen wisdom Solomon has surpassed her in generosity from this point of view. So there is a certain reciprocity but it is not exactly equal.

The meeting of the queen (a reigning monarch, not simply the wife of a king) with Solomon could theoretically be imagined as a private interview. But the text makes it clear that it is a matter of a public conversation or debate. The court is present. The mention of the food and the wine stewards (butlers) in v. 5 suggests that at least part of the encounter takes place at a banquet. It is a matter of a public display of wisdom (cp. Prov 9:1-6).

The presence of the queen, a foreign woman, at a sacrifice offered by the king is considered shocking by Second Chronicles.[36] The offerings are replaced by an ascent there (2 Chr 9:4). By his acquisition of gold, many wives and horses, Solomon is in violation of the law for the king given in

---

33. M. 'Abot 1:13; 4:5; B. T. Viviano, *Study as Worship* (SJLA 26; Leiden: Brill, 1978), 25-26; 92-97.

34. Brueggemann, *First and Second Kings*.

35. Walsh and Cotter, *First Kings*.

36. P. Buis, *Le Livre des Rois* (SB; Paris: Gabalda, 1997), 95-97.

Deut 17:14-20. The Bible can be critical of itself.[37] The queen's praise of God in v. 9 could be pressed to mean that she made a confession of faith in Yahweh, the God of Israel. (In the Qur'an she converts to the true religion, Sura 27:14-44.) Martin Noth reduces her prayer to the usual recognition of the local diety by a foreign visitor.[38] This however is too historicizing. The verse is due to a Deuteronomistic editor who expresses orthodox sentiments.[39]

III. THE ADORATION OF THE MAGI AND THE VISIT OF THE QUEEN OF SHEBA

It is our contention that the visit of the queen of Sheba as recounted in 1 Kgs 10:1-13 furnished the basic *narrative* model for the composition of Matthew's story of the visit of the magi (Matt 2:1-13). This study fits into the larger field of research called biblical intertextuality.[40]

In his study of 1962, Ernesto Galbiati breaks down Matthew's infancy gospel into five episodes after the initial genealogy.[41] Each of these episodes contains an explicit quotation from the Old Testament. These quotations are made explicit by the evangelist through formulas of citation. These citations have been the object of many fine studies.[42] Galbiati goes beyond these explicit quotations by noticing a parallel series of *allusions*. Thus in the first episode, there is a quotation from Isa 7:14 and an allusion to Samson in Judg 13:3-5. In the second episode there is a conflated citation from Mic 5:1-2 and 2 Sam 5:2, and an allusion to 1 Kgs 10:1-13, the visit of the queen of Sheba. There is a gap in the printing of Galbiati's third episode but it must be Hos 11:1 and an allusion to the exile and restoration of Israel. The fourth episode quotes Jer 31:5 and alludes to Exod 1:22. The fifth episode contains a mystery citation, "He shall be called a Nazarene," not found as such in the Bible. Galbiati decides for Judg 13:5 (Samson again) as the source of the quotation, a prudent view, and Exod 4:19 as the allusion.

---

37. T. E. Fretheim, *First and Second Kings* (Louisville: Westminster John Knox, 1999), *in loco*.

38. M. Noth, *Könige* (BKAT 9.1; Neukirchen-Vluyn: Neukirchener, 1968), 223-28.

39. Würthwein, *Der erste Buch*.

40. C.M. Tuckett, ed., *The Scriptures in the Gospels* (BETL 131; Leuven: Leuven University Press, 1997); D.C. Allison, *A New Moses*.

41. E. Galbiati, "L'adorazione dei Magi."

42. K. Stendahl, *The School of St. Matthew and Its Use of the Old Testament* (Lund: Gleerup, 1954); M. J. J. Menken, *Matthew's Bible* (BETL 173; Leuven: Peeters, 2004), refers to the many studies after Stendahl on 4-5.

Galbiati concludes from this complex intertextual weave that Matthew 1 and 2 are a narrative with a theological purpose. Jesus is thus presented as (1) a new Moses, (2) as an anointed nazir strong to save like Samson, (3) as the Davidic king messiah, greater than Solomon the royal sage; (4) Jesus condenses in himself the true Israel: (a) Moses and the Exodus; (b) the charismatic judges including Joshua and Samson; (c) Solomon; (d) exile and restoration. To be sure, these lists do not begin to exhaust Matthew's Christological repertoire. In a complete treatment the titles son of Abraham, Immanuel, and, for the whole Gospel, the apocalyptic Son of man would have to find a place.

Matthew's infancy gospel is extremely concise (only 48 verses). If we try to find some tighter coherence in the network of citations and allusions, we can say first, with Lagrange, that it is a "symbolic introduction to the action of Jesus."[43] It is however important to keep in mind that the diverse typologies can all easily be synthesized around Jesus as new and better Moses/David's son. These two key models are already beginning to be fused or merged in the Chronicler's retelling of the Solomon story. This fusion contains the elements of savior-liberator, sage and lawgiver, healer and builder (of the Church, not the Temple, Matt 16:18), prince of peace and friend of women (not as spouse but as sage).

If we compare the stories of the visit of the queen and the visit of the magi, we see first that they both come from a distance, the queen from the south (Matt 12:42), the magi from the east. In both cases the visitors are nameless. There is an air of mystery about them. They come in *quest* of the son of David, to admire, to worship. In both cases there is an element of adoration or prayer. The queen blesses God, the magi adore the child in the house which is thus treated as though it were the great house, the Temple. The visitors bring three gifts. They are identical, gold and incense, except for the third: jewels in one case, myrrh in the other. These gifts are appropriate for a king or a god. This bringing of the three gifts is the clearest indication of an intertextual connection between 1 Kings 10 and Matthew 2. (The parallel is so striking that it has been noticed, i.e., can be traced, in Christian interpretation and art since the sixth or seventh centuries, e.g., the venerable Bede. It continued to be a standard typology, like Isaac and Jesus, till around 1800. The nineteenth and twentieth centuries underplayed the parallel so as not to threaten the historicity of the Matthew 2.[44] On the historicity, see below.)

---

43. M.-J. Lagrange, *Matthieu* (Paris: Gabalda, 1922), 40.
44. J. B. Pritchard, ed., *Solomon and Sheba*, essay by P. F. Watson, 115–45.

Why does Matthew change the last gift from jewels to myrrh? It is impossible to be certain, but several answers come to mind. (1) Rather than a flat copying, the evangelist preferred an elegant literary variation. (2) He choose myrrh because he wanted to hint at a link with the Shulamite's love of Solomon in LXX Canticles (1:3,4; 2:5; 4:10,14). (3) He wanted to show the connection between the adoration of the magi and the anointing with myrrh by the woman at the end of Jesus' earthly life (Matt 26:7, 12; the word is slightly different: *smyrnon* in 2:11, *muron* in chap. 26. The sense is the same.). He thus creates an inclusion or framing bracket. (4) He or his source confused *libanon* (frankincense) with the Septaugint's third gift, *lithon timion*, precious stone.

There is a fourth common element in both stories but the fit is not perfect. It is the dream element. Solomon has two divine communications through dreams (1 Kgs 3:5; 9:2), but the queen is not said to have a dream. In Matthew, the magi have one dream (2:12) and Joseph has four (1:20-23; 2:13, 19, 22; cf. 27:19). Perhaps here the adult Joseph substitutes for the infant Jesus. The fifth parallel is the reposeful departure and return home (1 Kgs 10:13; Matt 2:12), though the Greek vocabulary is not identical.

Among the nonparallel elements, the strongest is the star.[45] There is no star in the Solomon story. Other differences are less sharp. There is in Matthew the terrible, murderous rage of Herod. This does not fit the peaceful reign of Solomon. Such cruelties and abuses of power are present in the Hebrew Bible, even in the David story, but not very strongly in the Solomon story. Solomon does with some reluctance have his enemies and rivals executed or exiled at the beginning of his reign (1 Kings 1-2). Matthew includes the Herod story because he had heard of Herod's insane jealousy and murder of some of his sons out of fear of their rivalry. (Matthew wrote before Josephus' detailed histories of Herod's reign were in circulation, but these crimes of Herod were notorious.)

On the historicity of the the magi episode let the following suffice. First of all, we take it for granted that the historical value of the infancy gospels is less great than, say, the teachings of Jesus as attested by the Matthean-Lucan overlap we call Q. Even D. F. Strauss did not contest the historicity of the sayings. [46] On the other hand, there are many historical elements in Matthew 2. Even if this specific episode is not otherwise attested, several of its constituent parts are well known, e.g., Herod did kill children he considered

---

45. B. T. Viviano, "The Movement of the Star, Matthew 2:9 and Numbers 9:17," *RB* 103 (1960) 58-64; repr. Viviano, *Matthew and His World*, 45-50; D. C. Allison, *Studies in Matthew* (Grand Rapids: Baker, 2005), 17-41.

46. D. F. Strauss, *Life of Jesus* (1835; Philadelphia: Fortress, 1977), 334-55.

rivals to his throne, including three of his own sons. [47] Foreign dignitaries did come to Herod's court for great occasions. Matthew sincerely believed that there was a rivalry between Herod's violent manner of governing and Jesus' non-violent teaching and normal behavior, not to mention that there was a difference in the legitimacy of their dynastic claims: Herod the half-Edomite, Jesus a full-blooded Judean Davidide.

Beyond these considerations, there is a good possibility that the germ of this chapter lies in Matthew's reflection on a saying of Jesus he reports in 12:42 (parallel Luke 11:31=Q): "The queen of the South will arise at the judgment with this generation and condemn it; for she came from the ends of the earth to hear the wisdom of Solomon, and behold, something greater than Solomon is here." This judgment saying of Jesus led Matthew directly to 1 Kings 10:1-13. The move from something greater than Solomon to someone greater was an easy one, since Jesus was the herald of the "thing," the kingdom of God. The rest came from contemporary history and the Bible. Matthew 2 could be understood in part as a putting into narrative of the teaching of Matt 12:42.[48]

Even more two-edged are the magi themselves. As usually conceived, they are males, members of a Persian religious caste, Zoroastrian priests; or else Chaldean astronomers. (I leave aside the later ideas that they were kings or were people of different races.) Narratively for Matthew they represent the non-Jewish distant nations. Their quest seems at first sociopolitical. They have come to find "the newborn king of the Jews . . . to do him homage" (Matt 2:2), that is, to perform the Persian court gesture of respect, the prostration. In Matthew, the religious connotations of worship of a divine being are clearly present (1:23).

Now if we read the magi story in the light of the Solomon-Sheba background as the closest biblical *narrative* parallel (as distinguished from motif parallels like the star) to it, some previously neglected possibilities open up: the sapiential and the feminine. On the one hand, in some languages it has long been customary to translate the unfamiliar term magi with the phrase "wise men." That Matthew would have understood the magi as some sort of Eastern sages is perfectly plausible. [49] On the other hand, the masculine plural *magoi* does not close the question of gender. *Magoi* could refer to both

---

47. Josephus, *Ant.* 16.361-394; 17.182-187; *B.J.* 1.538-551, 661-664.

48. On the historicity of issues such as the Davidic descent and birth at Bethlehem, see R. E. Brown, *Birth*, 505-516; on the literary genre of Matthew 1-2, see Viviano, *Matthew and His World*, 24-44; Viviano, "Making Sense of the Matthean Genealogy," in J. Corley, ed., *New Perspectives on the Nativity* (London: T. & T. Clark, 2009), 90-109.

49. For an argument that the magi were not wise, see M. A. Powell, "The Magi as Wise Men," *NTS* 46 (2000) 1-20.

male and female sages, if there were women among them. Grammar would not be an obstacle. The main reason to think of the presence of one or more women among the magi is the background story of the queen of Sheba, with her quest for Israelite royal wisdom, her reverent awe, and her three gifts fit for a king. A second reason to suspect the presence of the feminine is the Israelite tradition of personifying wisdom as a woman (Prov 8:22–30; 9:1–6; Sirach 24). The third reason is Matthew's presentation of Jesus himself later in the gospel in terms of Lady Wisdom, that is, with feminine traits (Matt 11:19, 25–30).[50] The presence of Jesus' mother Mary is an explicit statement of the presence of a woman at the time of the magi's visit. (The phrase "the child and his mother" is repeated five times in Matt 2:11, 13, 14, 19, 21.) It is a question of attending to the feminine resonances in the text.

These feminine resonances of awe and reverence contrast sharply with Herod's mendacity and abuse of power. His slaughter of the male children is an egregious abuse of power.[51] Matthew's story balances the beautiful elements of the star, the magi, the gifts, the mother and child, with a veracious report of royal unreason and ugly violence. The violent face of power is unmasked. The need for a non-violent wise lord is made more pressing. "At the judgment the queen of the south will arise with this generation and condemn it, because she came from the ends of the earth to hear the wisdom of Solomon; and there is something greater than Solomon here" (Matt 12:42).

---

50. See the works by F. Christ, J. Suggs, C. Deutsch, Piper, mentioned in note 3 above.
51. See article referred to in note 1 above.

15

Making Sense of the Matthean Genealogy

Matthew 1:17 and the Theology of History

Upon opening the New Testament, many readers are discouraged by its first page, the genealogy of Jesus (Matt 1:1–17). It seems at first glance to be a dry list of names, framed by some titles. Modern books do not usually begin in such an austere fashion. What first struck readers of old translations was the repetition of the verb "begat." The information that this sort of a list is a typical way to begin a book in the Near East—whether ancient (such as the biblical book of First Chronicles) or modern—is cold comfort. Even the idea that Matthew by this genealogy is trying to condense the whole of the Old Testament (Hebrew Bible and deuterocanonical books) as the indispensable background to the gospel story of Jesus only helps a little.

The thesis of this article is that the evangelist Matthew is here, in the three-part structure he provides for his genealogy, presenting the reader with the partial outline of one of the earliest recorded theologies of history. He is thereby further signaling to the alert reader that with the birth of Jesus a new era of salvation history has begun. The three-part structure is summarized by Matthew at the end of the genealogy: "Therefore all the generations from Abraham to David [are] fourteen generations, and from David to the exile of Babylon [are] fourteen generations, and from the exile of Babylon to the Christ [are] fourteen generations" (Matt 1:17). This verse is a statement not only about dividing the past into historical periods but also about Christology, the role of Jesus in God's plan. These are subjects worthy of an adult person's attention. It is a mistake to relegate the infancy narratives to the children's nursery. They are full of adult themes and interests. To be sure, this does not rule out a child's interest in stars, camels, and gifts—though the camels come from Isaiah (60:6), rather than from the text of Matthew.

Let me explain. Students of my generation learnt a simple three-part division of the past into historical periods: ancient, medieval, and modern. This structure is supported by a certain ideology, stemming from Voltaire, and is not neutral. But people need some sort of structure to break up the endless flow of the historical continuum. Otherwise history is rejected as meaningless—or in Oliver Wendell Holmes' phrase, "one damned thing after another."

Wherever people have experienced a major upheaval in history, they become hungry for some sort of overall explanation. Thus, after the French Revolution and the wars of Napoleon the philosophies of history offered by Hegel and Schlegel were eagerly devoured, and their works were widely translated.[1] The same thing happened after the First World War, when Oswald Spengler's turgid *Decline of the West* became an international bestseller.[2] Again, after the Second World War people bought and read Arnold Toynbee's *A Study of History* (in abridged form) to find out the meaning of the drama through which they had just lived.[3] After the sudden collapse of Communism in Eastern Europe and the end of the Cold War (without even a shot being fired), Francis Fukuyama was the first in the field to offer an explanation of what had happened and its future implications (*The End of History and the Last Man*).[4] His vision was so optimistic that it threatened the Pentagon's activities. To save their budget (it is alleged), Samuel P. Huntington wrote *The Clash of Civilizations* and thereby, with a little help from Osama bin Laden, created some of the impetus for the long war in Iraq.[5] In brief, people hunger for explanations of major events, explanations which relate them to significant happenings of the past and, to the extent possible, also foresee the future. In other words, they want a philosophy or a theology of history.

---

1. G. W. F. Hegel, *The Philosophy of History* (New York: Dover, 1956); Friedrich von Schlegel, *The Philosophy of History* (London: Bohn, 1835).

2. Oswald Spengler, *The Decline of the West*, 2 vols. (Oxford: Oxford University Press, 1926–1928).

3. Arnold Toynbee, *A Study of History*, 12 vols., abridged in 2 vols. (New York: Oxford University Press, 1946, 1957).

4. Francis Fukuyama, *The End of History and the Last Man* (New York: Free Press, 1992).

5. Samuel P. Huntington, *The Clash of Civilizations and the Remaking of World Order* (New York: Free Press, 1996).

Now the Bible contains an extensive theology of history, viewed as salvation history.[6] In its Christian canon, the Bible itself is structured as a story which stretches from a beginning (creation and fall), through mid-point (Jesus Christ crucified and risen), to an end (the future coming of Christ in glory, bringing the kingdom of God in its fullness to the new earth). The Bible contains a long history, stretching well over a thousand years. Little wonder then that around the time of Matthew both Jews and Christians tried to find for it a structuring principle or a form of division into historical periods.

The simplest of these is a two-part pattern based on two eons or epochs: "this world (*aiōn*)" and "the world (*aiōn*) to come." "World" is the older translation of a word which has a spatial meaning (= world) but also a temporal sense (= eon).[7] This two-part pattern occurs both in the Gospels and in Paul, but especially frequently in the rabbis. However, there is also a five-part pattern based on the visions in Daniel 2 and 7. It is developed from the scheme of four ancient Near Eastern empires known to the author of Daniel (Babylonian, Mede, Persian, and Greek), with the addition of a final age.[8] This five-part scheme was received in the Book of Revelation and has a long history of influence.[9]

A SEVEN-PART DIVISION OF HISTORY

The most developed scheme of biblical periodization is, however, a seven-part "system." There are variants of this scheme, especially in Judaism,[10] but in Christian writings the seven ages or periods usually run as follows:

1. From Adam to Noah;

2. From Noah to Abraham;

3. From Abraham to David;

4. From David to the Exile;

---

6. Oscar Cullmann, *Christ and Time* (Philadelphia: Westminster, 1964; orig. 1946).

7. The Greek word *aiōn* often represents the Hebrew term *'ōlām*.

8. The earliest Christian commentator on Daniel, Hippolytus of Rome (third century), replaced the Greek empire with the Roman one, and this became the common interpretation until the nineteenth century.

9. Mariano Delgado, Klaus Koch, and Edgar Marsch, eds., *Europa, Tausendjähriges Reich und Neue Welt* (Freiburg: Universitätsverlag, 2003).

10. Hermann L. Strack and Paul Billerbeck, *Kommentar zum Neuen Testament aus Talmud und Midrasch*, 6 vols. (Munich: Beck, 1922–1961), 3:824–27.

5. From the Exile to Jesus;
6. From Jesus to his Second Coming;
7. From the Second Coming to the End of the World.

This seven-part scheme calls for a number of comments, but let us come to the point at once. This scheme seems to be known to the evangelist Matthew. In my view, he presupposes it as known to the more learned of his readers.[11] He proceeds to extract three or four of the seven stages, and he insists upon them in several ways. He begins with two christological titles that structure the whole Gospel in some sense, but certainly structure the genealogy: "The book of the origin of Jesus Christ, son of David, son of Abraham" (Matt 1:1). Matthew then goes on to give a list of names (from the third, fourth, and fifth ages in the seven-part scheme), running from Abraham to David, from David to the Babylonian exile, and from the exile to Joseph, Mary, and Jesus. He concludes with a summarizing verse, already cited, that is decisive for our argument. "Therefore all the generations from Abraham to David [are] fourteen generations, and from David to the exile of Babylon [are] fourteen generations, and from the exile of Babylon to the Christ [are] fourteen generations" (Matt 1:17).

Repetition is a biblical form of emphasis. Matthew is insisting on something, but he does not say explicitly what it is. To be sure, readers have always understood that the genealogy relates Jesus to (and roots him in) the history of Israel, the chosen people of God. (They may not always have rejoiced in this fact but they have understood it.) Our thesis, to repeat, is that Matthew is also providing a theology of history. In this theology each stage of biblical revelation has its place and meaning. With the coming of Jesus called Christ (1:16), a new stage of salvation history has begun. While mentioning only the middle three stages, Matthew presupposes the early stages from Adam to Noah to Abraham as known, and elsewhere he names Noah (24:37–38), although he never mentions Adam by name.

IMPLICATIONS OF THE SEVEN-AGE SCHEME

Now that the main point has been made, there is a place for some comments on the scheme in seven stages, and then for some of its implications as these have been worked out by early Christian exegesis. Particular attention will be given to ancient writings that divide sacred history into thousand-year periods, beginning with Revelation (20:1–10) and Second Peter (3:8–13).

---

11. On the reader's task of filling the gaps in a story, see Meir Sternberg, *The Poetics of Biblical Literature* (Bloomington, IN: Indiana University Press, 1985), 186–90.

This approach is called chiliasm (Greek *chilia* = thousand) or millenarianism (Latin *mille anni* = a thousand years). Such an approach has often had a bad reputation in the Catholic Church. It is widely thought to be an area reserved for crackpots, but that may be unfair.

The scheme of thousand-year periods was constructed by the authors of Second Peter and Revelation through a combination of two biblical passages: the seven days of creation as recounted in Genesis 1, plus the Psalmist's concept: "A thousand years in your sight are like yesterday when it is past, or like a watch in the night" (Ps 90:4). By combining these two elements, each day of creation was taken to refer to a thousand-year period of history. The fact that the intervals between each of the periods did not always amount to a thousand years exactly (e.g., the time between David and the exile, or between the exile and Jesus) did not seem to trouble some of those who adopted the scheme. Nevertheless, Matthew is cautious in speaking of fourteen *generations*, not of thousand-year periods.[12]

Matthew 1:2-17 is perhaps an original fusion of two different schemes: (a) a world week of seven millennial "days," that is, seven thousand-year periods of salvation history; (b) a scheme of generations grouped or broken up by major figures or events: Adam, Noah, Abraham, David, the Exile, Jesus. The major figures or events give historical labels to each of the millennial "days" and thus make them more concrete and meaningful.

The three sets of names in Matthew's genealogy should yield a total of 42 names. (For why they do not, see below.) If we add the ten generations from Adam to Noah (Gen 5:3-31) and the ten generations from Noah's son Shem to Abraham (Gen 11:10-26), plus the forty-two generations from Abraham to Jesus (Matt 1:2-17), we arrive at a total of sixty-two generations from Adam to Jesus.[13] This total figure calls to mind the sixty-two weeks mentioned in Dan 9:25. One hesitates to pursue this link for a number of reasons. First, there is the evident difference between generations of named figures and weeks. Second, the sixty-two weeks of Daniel 9 come in a larger context of seventy weeks, divided into sixty-two, seven, and one, all part of Gabriel's visionary message (Dan 9:24-27). In its original intent, this passage, renowned for its difficulties, probably refers to the period between the return from exile under Zerubbabel (along with the high priest Joshua) and the death of Onias III, the deposed high priest murdered in 171 BCE. The

---

12. Alfred Wikenhauser, "Das Problem des tausendjährigen Reiches in der Johannes-Apokalypse," *Römische Quartalschrift* 40 (1932) 13-25; Wikenhauser, "Die Herkunft der Idee des tausendjährigen Reiches in der Johannes-Apokalypse," *Römische Quartalschrift* 45 (1937) 1-24; Wikenhauser, "Weltwoche und tausendjähriges Reich," *Theologische Quartalschrift* 127 (1947) 399-417.

13. See below for St. Augustine's understanding of this point.

sixty-two weeks are a round number to describe the period from the return down to Antiochus IV. As such, this scheme does not fit perfectly with Matthew's text. He deals with the same period in the fourteen generations of the third section of his genealogy.

JESUS AND MOSES

Matthew does not mention Moses in this genealogy, even to locate the lifetime of "Nahshon son of Aminadab" (Num 1:7; 2:3; cf. Matt 1:4). From a Jewish viewpoint this is a breathtaking omission. After all, Moses is traditionally regarded as the human author of the Torah, the instruction divinely revealed on Sinai. The Torah or Pentateuch remains to this day the canon within the canon for observant Jews, and the main reading at the weekly service. The Torah is by far the most important part of the Hebrew Bible in the traditional Jewish scale of values. Thus, for Matthew to omit Moses here could seem to Jewish readers as leaving out the most important human figure in biblical history. To be sure, Matthew is offering a genealogy of a Judahite, a son of David, not of a Levite. But the genealogy is also trying to shape a view of salvation history. In this context the omission of Moses has a decentering effect. This is so, even though Matthew's Gospel shows no hostility to the Torah of Moses (5:17-20; 23:23).[14] Indeed, Moses is named seven times in Matthew (8:4; 17:3, 4; 19:7, 8; 22:24; 23:2). Moreover, the Law is mentioned nine times, but it is often associated with the prophets, as if to soften the legal focus.[15] But the genealogy's emphasis is elsewhere, on David and Abraham as forebears of Jesus.

Some scholars believe that the structure of Matthew's Gospel suggests that he presents Jesus as a new Moses. In a short essay published almost a century ago, Benjamin W. Bacon noted that after each of five major discourses in Matthew (7:28; 11:1; 13:53; 19:1; 26:1) a phrase occurs which marks the end of the discourse.[16] The phrase runs: "Now when Jesus had finished saying these things . . ." (*kai egeneto hote etelesen ho Iēsous tous logous toutous*). The last time the phrase occurs (26:1), the word "all" is introduced before "these things," as if to suggest that the time for speaking is over. Now begins the final combat (suffering, death, and victory over death), after which there is a short but important parting statement, the Great

---

14. Dale C. Allison, *The New Moses: A Matthean Typology* (Minneapolis: Fortress, 1993), 182.

15. Alexander Sand, *Das Gesetz und die Propheten* (Biblische Untersuchungen 11; Regensburg: Pustet, 1974).

16. Benjamin W. Bacon, "The Five Books of Matthew against the Jews," *The Expositor* 15 (1918) 56–66.

Commission (28:18-20). The closing formula of the five discourses reminds us of Deuteronomy's description of Moses (Deut 31:1; 32:45), and suggests that Jesus was in some respects like Moses.[17] From these textual facts, Bacon developed the hypothesis that Matthew intended to write a Christian Pentateuch in which narrative preceded each of the five discourses. This hypothesis was well received for a long time, but it left readers uneasy that this structure left out Matthew's final chapters (26—28), dealing with the death and resurrection of Jesus. Most scholars could not imagine that Matthew intended such a thing.[18]

Although scholars after Bacon tried various makeshift solutions, with Pierre Benoit proposing a seven-act drama[19] and Edgar Krentz suggesting a three-part division,[20] the best proposal so far is a chiastic one based on the alternation of narrative and discourse, thereby building on the insight of Bacon:

Chapters 1–4: Birth and beginnings (narrative = N)
    5–7: **Sermon on the Mount** (discourse = D)
        8–9: Authority and invitation (N)
            10: **Mission** (D)
                11–12: Rejection by this generation (N)
                    13: **Seven parables of the kingdom** (D)
                14–17: Acknowledgement by the disciples (N)
            18: **Community rules** (D)
        19–22: Authority and invitation (N)
    23–25: **Woes and apocalypse** (D)
26–28: Death and resurrection (N)

---

17. Allison, *New Moses*, 192.

18. Even if a few daring scholars (influenced by redaction criticism) might have thought that Matthew did indeed intend a decentering or shift of accent from the paschal proclamation to a semi-Pelagian works righteousness, they were careful not to say this in print.

19. Pierre Benoit, "Matthieu," *Bible de Jérusalem* (Paris: Cerf, 1950; rev. ed. 1961). The seven acts are listed in Benoit's *Jerusalem Bible* translation annotations: the preparation (chaps. 1-2); the formal proclamation (chaps. 3-7); preaching by signs and missionaries (chaps. 8-10); the obstacles to the kingdom (11:1—13:52); the Church in embryo (13:53—18:35); the crisis (chaps. 19—25); the coming of the kingdom through suffering and resurrection (chaps. 26—28).

20. Edgar Krentz, "The Extent of Matthew's Prologue," *JBL* 83 (1964) 409-14. Krentz's three-part division is based on the repeated phrase "from then Jesus began" (*apo tote ērxato ho Iēsous*: 4:17; 16:21). This gives the division: 1:1—4:16; 4:17—16:20; 16:21—28:20. This division dissolves the five discourses into the paschal message.

In this analysis all 28 chapters are embraced in a meaningful whole, centered on the parables of the kingdom.[21] But this chiastic solution, like the solutions of Benoit and Krentz, has failed to impose itself on many scholars.[22]

JESUS AND JOSHUA

Meanwhile, in the neighboring field of Old Testament studies, James A. Sanders had a brilliant intuition, which he set down in a brief book, *Torah and Canon*.[23] He thereby launched a whole new approach to the Bible called canon criticism. In his little book, his strongest idea was this. Originally, the Hebrew foundation story was a Hexateuch, a six-part work that concluded with Joshua and the conquest of the Promised Land by force. Sometime later, the rabbis decided to divide the sacred books differently. Genesis to Deuteronomy became the Pentateuch, while Joshua was placed with the early prophets. For Sanders, this was a blessing for both Judaism and Christianity. It provided them with a foundational text that was not essentially bound up with a violent conquest of a particular territory. This new arrangement was better suited to a Judaism which, for millennia, had to survive outside the land—like Moses. And it suited Christianity better with its sense of universal mission, its emphasis on non-violence and love of enemies, its orientation toward the future eschatological gift of the kingdom of God and toward eternal life with God in heaven.

So far, so good. But what if Matthew had another idea? What if he accepted the Hexateuch as his model? That is my suggestion. To accept this proposal, that Matthew intended to structure his gospel book into six sections, it would be important to remember first that Joshua in Greek is spelled Jesus. For Matthew, on this view, the new Joshua (Jesus), by his suffering and death, by his mortal combat, conquered the great enemy (death), and entered the promised land of the risen life with the heavenly Father. Matthew's sixth book would consist in his chapters 26—28, which conclude with the Great Commission (28:18–20). These compact final verses affirm that Jesus is the Son of Man to whom all authority on heaven and earth has been transmitted (cf. Dan 7:13–14; Matt 11:27). He (the Emmanuel) will

---

21. Charles H. Lohr, "Oral Techniques in the Gospel of Matthew," *CBQ* 23 (1961) 403–35.

22. William D. Davies and Dale C. Allison, *A Critical and Exegetical Commentary on the Gospel according to St Matthew*, 3 vols. (ICC; Edinburgh: T&T Clark, 1988–1997) 1:61–72.

23. James A. Sanders, *Torah and Canon* (Minneapolis: Fortress, 1972; 2nd rev. ed., Eugene, OR: Cascade, 2005).

be with us in this, the sixth age, as well as in the final seventh age (Matt 1:21; 18:20). That is why these verses have been called an anticipated second coming of Jesus (cf. 27:51–53).[24]

A possible objection to this proposal is that we do not know enough about the currency of the Hexateuch model at the time of Matthew. After all, some have proposed an Enneateuch model, carrying the Torah through three more books for a total of nine, adding to the previous six the Books of Judges, Samuel and Kings. (The last two are reckoned as single books in the Hebrew computation.) Both Hexateuch and Enneateuch offer multiples of Matthew's beloved triad, and a normal reckoning counts six contrasts between the Law of Moses and Jesus' teaching in Matt 5:21–48. However, Joshua son of Nun, Moses' successor, seems to play no role in Matthew (contrast Acts 7:45; Heb 4:8; 11:30–31), and so the suggestion is not without its difficulties.

On the other hand, almost as soon as the Christian Church began to enter into polemical debate with the Synagogue, the story of Joshua (Jesus son of Nave in the Septuagint spelling) became an ideal type of Christ. Joshua was contrasted with Moses in his victory over Amalek, in his crossing of the Jordan (a prefigurement of baptism), in his receiving the second law (Deuteronomy), and in his conquest of the land (the fall of Jericho was interpreted as a symbol of the end of the world).

Matthew in fact does not mention Joshua in the genealogy, even though "Nahshon son of Aminadab" (Num 10:14; cf. Matt 1:4) was his contemporary (Num 11:28). He does, however, include mention of Rahab in Matt 1:5. Rahab became a type of the Church, especially as a type of the pagans who are incorporated into the *ecclesia*, the people of God, and thus spared in the destruction that befell Jericho. In the New Testament she is an ancestor of Jesus (Matt 1:5), and then is contrasted as a model of salvation by works (Jas 2:25) and as a model of salvation by faith (Heb 11:30–31).[25]

The fact that Rahab is mentioned in Matthew's genealogy (1:5) is the anchor for the basic idea that Matthew was well aware of the contents of the Book of Joshua. The fact that he chose not to render the Joshua-Jesus typology more explicit matches his general literary discretion. He does not use footnotes—they had not yet been invented. He is telling a story and giving

---

24. John P. Meier, *Matthew* (Wilmington, DE: Glazier, 1980).

25. The Joshua typology, already found in the *Letter of Barnabas* (12:7–10; 17:14), is greatly developed by St. Justin Martyr (*Dialogue with Trypho* 49, 70, 75, 89–90, 113–14), St. Irenaeus, Tertullian, St. Hippolytus, St. Clement of Alexandria, Origen (who devoted a commentary to the Book of Joshua), Eusebius, St. Cyril of Jerusalem, and St. Zeno of Verona. Cf. Jean Daniélou, *From Shadows to Reality: Studies in the Biblical Typology of the Fathers* (Westminster, MD: Newman, 1960) 227–28.

instructions to the church. With regard to structure he leaves discreet hints in the five conclusions to the great discourses (7:28; 11:1; 13:53; 19:1; 26:1), but he does not hit the reader over the head. Even more is this discretion and restraint present in the last three chapters of the gospel. The biblically literate reader is, however, free to interpret the silences.

FROM THE COMING OF JESUS TO THE END OF THE WORLD

In the seven-stage scheme the sixth age (between the first and second comings of Christ) is sometimes called the time of the Church, the time of the Holy Spirit, the time in which we live now. In the Acts of the Apostles the risen Christ gives the apostles the Spirit as a foretaste of the full realization of the Kingdom, as the gift for this interval (Acts 1:6-8). To be sure, theologically the Spirit is present at all periods of history, from creation (Gen 1:2) to the end of the world and beyond. But the New Testament presents the time after Easter as a period of a special outpouring of the Spirit (Pentecost). On the other hand, the number six can suggest a time of evil just before the fulfillment, which is thus associated with the number seven. This could account for some of the disappointing, even sinful, aspects of the last two thousand years.

In the seven-part scheme, the seventh age would involve the coming (*parousia*) in glory of the Son of Man. His coming involves judgment (Matt 25:31-46) and governing the world in justice and peace (Matt 24:3, 27, 37, 39; 1 Cor 15:23; 1 Thess 2:19; 3:13; 4:15; 5:23). Judging here includes the Hebrew sense of the verb *shāphat*, as in the Book of Judges, where the charismatic leaders like Deborah, Gideon, and Samson do indeed judge cases, but also lead in battle and govern the people.

Readers may reasonably ask where this seventh age is suggested in the genealogy. The answer is surprising. If we return to our key structuring verse (1:17), we recall that Matthew insists on the number fourteen three times. Now when we actually count the names we do find fourteen names (or generations) in the first two lists but only thirteen in the third list. Why is this? Several suggestions have been made, but only one is of major theological significance. It was cautiously made by the late Swedish scholar Krister Stendahl in 1962. The thirteenth name is Jesus, "who is called the Messiah [or Christ]" (1:16, 17). For Stendahl, the missing fourteenth name is also Jesus Christ but now as Son of Man in his glory, "at his coming (*parousia*) at the end of time. We . . . have here the strong futuristic eschatology of the early church."[26] This suggestion would seem farfetched and improbable if it

26. Krister Stendahl, "Matthew," in *Peake's Commentary on the Bible*, ed. Matthew

did not fit so well with Matthew's Jewish-Christian outlook, which includes an interest in eschatology, apocalyptic, and salvation-historical thinking. Matthew's broad outlook points to the universal significance of Jesus as he comes first in humility and suffering and then in his glory in the future, anticipated already by his Easter resurrection.

FROM ADAM TO ABRAHAM

There is another perplexing omission in Matthew's genealogy. If Matthew knew the seven-part scheme (as we assume he did), why did he omit the first two parts: from Adam to Noah, and then from Noah to Abraham? What is clear from Matt 1:1 and 17 is that Matthew is striving for a christological concentration on Abraham and David as ancestors of the Jews. Matthew makes no mention of Jesus as a second Adam (cf. 1 Cor 15:45) or as son of Adam (Luke 3:38).[27] There is also no developed Christian tradition of calling Jesus son of Noah, but both Noah and Adam count as ancestors of Jesus in Luke's genealogy (Luke 3:36, 38).

We may note here a significant salvation-historical statement concerning the virtuous, murdered, son of Adam (= Abel), found in Matt 23:35 and Luke 11:51, that is, in the Sayings Source (Q): ". . . so that upon you may come all the righteous blood shed on earth, from the blood of righteous Abel (Gen 4:8, 10) to the blood of Zechariah son of Barachiah".[28] This verse

---

Black and H. H. Rowley (Edinburgh: Nelson, 1962), 769-98, here 770-71. For this futuristic eschatology see Matt 24:29-31 (and its parallels in Mark and Luke), as well as Acts 2:20; 3:20-21.

27. Admittedly there is an allusion to Adam and Eve (unnamed) in Matt 19:4: "Have you not read that the one who made (*ktisas*) at the beginning 'made them male and female'?" However, the idea of Christ as second man or last Adam is a Pauline notion (1 Cor 15:45, 47).

28. Here we may briefly notice some of the problems connected with the reference to "the blood of Zechariah son of Barachiah, whom you murdered between the sanctuary and the altar" (Matt 23:35). There is some debate as to which Zechariah is meant. Zechariah son of Berechiah son of Iddo is the eleventh of the twelve minor prophets (Zech 1:1; cf. Ezra 5:1), but he is not known to have been slain except in the diffuse post-biblical tradition that all the prophets suffered violent ends; cf. Odil Hannes Steck, *Israel und das gewaltsame Geschick der Propheten* (WMANT 23; Neukirchen-Vluyn: Neukirchener, 1967). Zechariah, the son of the priest Jehoiada, may be the person meant (2 Chr 24:20-22), because he was stoned to death in the court of the Temple by order of the king who had been offended by his preaching. Some commentators think that it is a third Zechariah, son of Baris (or in some manuscripts, Baruch), known from Josephus, *J.W.* 4.5.4 §§334-344. Of these three options, probably the first fits best here, since Matthew refers twice in this chapter (23:30, 37) to the tradition that the prophets were killed. Note finally that in the Septuagint of Isa 8:2, two reliable witnesses support

is an extract from the climax of the woes (Matthew 23; Luke 11) and very likely goes back to the historical Jesus. The verse reflects a perspective of eschatological judgment in which the whole human history of unjust suffering, from the first to the last murder of the innocent in the Hebrew Bible, will be set right by God. The verse tries to embrace the whole of biblical history. In this respect it represents a precedent in the preaching of Jesus himself for the comprehensive historical perspective that Matthew attempts in his genealogy. But it takes its start from the story of Adam, Cain, and Abel at the beginning of Genesis. So Matthew knows the story too, even though he chooses not to mention it in his genealogy.

As we continue to answer the question, why did Matthew omit the first two stages in the scheme (Adam and Noah), we may also suggest a pedagogical reason. Adding the first two steps, even with only ten names in each of these two sections, would have made the genealogy too long for Matthew's taste. It would have damaged his pattern of fourteen names per section, as well as the triadic pattern. As the adage says, "All good things come in threes" (*omne trinum perfectum*), so Matthew loves triads.[29] Moreover, brevity is the soul of wit, and many regard the genealogy as too long even in this briefer form.

Another reason for the omission of the first two stages might be Matthew's literary coquetry. Like other biblical authors, of both testaments, he employs what has been called the "foolproof method" of biblical composition.[30] This means that he has written his gospel in plain prose, with much narrative that any reader or hearer can understand. This ready intelligibility provides the basis for the measure of truth in the old Calvinist doctrine of the perspicuity of Scripture. This doctrine holds that any believing reader can and should read the Scriptures daily; with the help of the Holy Spirit, the reader will derive spiritual profit from the reading. This is well and good but it is not the whole truth. The biblical authors added subtle tests of skill for their more learned readers and copyists—those initiated into the professional secrets of the guild of scribes. These tests have proven a source of endless delight and fascination to studious readers down through the centuries. These readers are asked to apply their background knowledge of the Bible and its accompanying tradition to a particular composition.

Isaiah: the priest Uriah (cf. 2 Kgs 16:10-16) and Zechariah son of Barachiah (whereas in the Hebrew he is the son of Jeberechiah).

29. Davies and Allison, *St Matthew*, 1.62; cf. Dale C. Allison, "The Structure of the Sermon on the Mount," *JBL* 106 (1987) 423-35.

30. Sternberg, *Poetics*, 50-56. We can compare what has been said of the novelist Anthony Trollope's style: "plain British boiled beef."

APOCALYPTIC ORIGIN OF THE SEVEN-PART DIVISION OF HISTORY?

This last point leads us naturally to the difficult question: how old is the seven-age scheme of history? Could Matthew have known of it? Was it sufficiently well known that he could reasonably expect some of his readers to know about it and to see an allusion to it in his genealogy?

Already in the 1920s, Paul Billerbeck proposed that *1 Enoch*'s Ten Week Apocalypse was the closest pre-Christian parallel to Matthew and his most probable source.[31] We will proceed as though this were correct, but with fear and trepidation, given the difficulties in dating and determining the text and translation of *1 Enoch*. To be sure, what is properly characteristic of the apocalyptic theology of history is *numbered* periods as parts of the divine plan. Apart from Genesis 1 and the history by generations in the Pentateuch and in the historical books of the Hebrew Bible, this reckoning of numbers may be said to begin already with Jeremiah's prophecy of a seventy-year exile (Jer 25:11-12; 29:10; Zech 1:12). This figure of seventy years is then reflected on in 2 Chr 36:22-23 and in the influential Dan 9:24-27. The latter passage in Daniel teems with ambiguities of translation, but these are concerned with the Messiah rather than the numbered periods.[32] It is from this background that *1 Enoch* most likely takes its start.

The Apocalypse of Weeks appears in *1 Enoch* 93:1-10; 91:11-17 — where the Ethiopic text has these sections in reverse order.[33] The Qumran Aramaic fragments provide textual evidence for the scholarly rearrangement.[34] In this case the basis for the rearrangement is simple. It is based

---

31. Strack and Billerbeck, *Kommentar zum Neuen Testament*, 1:43-45 (on Matt 1:17).

32. D. S. Russell, *The Method and Message of Jewish Apocalyptic* (Philadelphia: Westminster, 1964), 224-29; Paul Volz, *Jüdische Eschatologie von Daniel bis Akiba* (Tübingen: Mohr/Siebeck, 1936); Joseph Bonsirven, *Palestinian Judaism in the Time of Jesus Christ* (New York: Holt, 1964), 205-25. On the implications of Dan 9:24-27 for messianism, see Joseph A. Fitzmyer, *The One Who Is to Come* (Grand Rapids: Eerdmans, 2007), 60-64.

33. Most of *1 Enoch* has been dated anywhere from 250 BCE to 50 CE. This long book is not a unity that was written at one date by one author but the product of an Enoch "school" that continued into two more works known as *Second Enoch* and *Third Enoch*. The parts of *First Enoch* that most concern us are found in considerable fragments in Aramaic at Qumran, so certainly before 70 C.E., and probably composed around 50 BCE. The Aramaic fragments are important because the complete text, preserved only in Ethiopic (Ge'ez) has suffered some textual disturbance in the crucial chapters 91 and 93. Scholars have long suspected this dislocation and rearranged the chapters accordingly.

34. J. T. Milik, *The Books of Enoch: Aramaic Fragments* (Oxford: Clarendon, 1976);

on a list of ten "weeks" or historical periods in the history of Israel. Seven refer to Israel's past history, three to the present messianic age and to future judgments. However, in 91:15, the text speaks about "the tenth week in the seventh part." This can be taken to mean that the author thinks of the last three weeks as part of a seventh age. If this interpretation is correct, we would have in *1 Enoch* the earliest trace of a seven-age scheme. Even if this is correct, we are still compelled to note that the scheme is not here explicitly based on the seven days of creation, nor on Ps 90:4, nor on named biblical heroes. What is in play is the explicit use of the term *week*, itself derived from the seven days of creation in biblical revelation (Gen 1:1–2:4a).

We come closer to our goal when we turn to the *Second Book of Enoch* (also known as *Slavonic Enoch*). This work also bristles with difficulties—linguistic, textual, and chronological. Though the existing manuscripts are medieval, the priestly concerns evident in the text lead some scholars to date the original composition to the time when the temple was still standing in Jerusalem, that is, some time before Matthew's Gospel was written. The book exists in two forms or recensions. In one of these we find at the beginning of chapter 33: "God shows Enoch the epoch [age] of this world, the existence of 7000 years, and the eighth thousand is the end . . ." (opening of 2 *Enoch* 33).[35] This seems like a chapter heading, perhaps added by a scribe to clarify and to introduce what follows: "On the 8th day I likewise appointed, so that the 8th day might be the 1st, the first-created of my week, and that it should revolve in the revolution of 7000, so that the 8000 might be in the beginning of a time not reckoned and unending" (2 *Enoch* 33:1–2).

If this text is part of the original work, composed before 70 C.E., it would be a valuable predecessor of Matthew's scheme, because it contains the world week of seven millennia, seven historical periods, followed by an eighth day of eternal rest. It implies the influence of Genesis 1 and Ps 90:4, but it still does not link the seven ages with biblical figures or events like the Babylonian exile.

George W. E. Nickelsburg, *1 Enoch 1: A Commentary on . . . 1 Enoch, chaps. 1–36; 81–108* (Hermeneia; Minneapolis: Fortress, 2001), 434–50; Loren T. Stuckenbruck, *1 Enoch 91–108* (Commentaries on Early Jewish Literature; Berlin: de Gruyter, 2007), 49–152.

35. This quotation and the next are from Francis I. Andersen, "2 (Slavonic Apocalypse of) Enoch," in *OTP*, 1:91–213, here 1:156; cf. Andrei Orlov, *From Apocalypticism to Merkabah Mysticism: Studies in Slavonic Pseudepigrapha* (JSJSup 114; Leiden: Brill, 2007).

EARLY CHRISTIAN USE OF THE SEVEN-AGE SCHEME

Outside of the New Testament, the earliest Christian attestation of the seven-age scheme occurs in a curious work of the mid-second century, the letter attributed to St. Barnabas (*Let. Barn.* 15:4).[36]

> Pay attention, children, to what he says: "He finished in six days" (Gen 2:2 LXX). He is saying that in six thousand years the Lord will finish everything. For with him the "day" signifies a thousand years. And he bears me witness (on this point) saying: "Behold, a day of the Lord shall be as a thousand years (cf. Ps 90:4). Therefore, children, "in six days"—in six thousand years—"everything" will be finished" [i.e., the universe will arrive at its term].

Here once again we see the seven-age scheme, based on the same combination of biblical texts, but without the labeling of the ages according to biblical figures or events. We almost have the impression that Matthew is original in his connecting the biblical periods with *named* figures and events.

But at least one major church father, St. Augustine of Hippo (354–430), understood the full scheme underlying Matthew's genealogy. In the time of testing after Alaric had sacked Rome (410 C.E.) and the Empire in the West was tottering toward its collapse, Augustine wrote his enormous, rambling meditation on ancient history in the light of Christian faith. He tried to make sense of it all in his 900-page *City of God*. Augustine refers explicitly to Matthew's scheme and completed it with the first two stages, from Adam to Noah and from Noah to Abraham. In Books 19 to 22 of *The City of God*, Augustine treats carefully the major eschatological texts of the Bible and tries to work out a synthesis of the data, from the days of creation to the four kingdoms of Daniel 7, through the Antichrist and the Millennium, to the beatific vision and the eighth day of the eternal Sabbath in heaven. This all builds up to a magnificent finale, the last paragraph of the entire work (*De civitate Dei* 22.33.5).[37]

---

36. Robert M. Grant et al., *The Apostolic Fathers* 6 vols. (New York: Nelson, 1965), 3:128. A similar scheme appears in St. Justin, *Dialogue with Trypho* 81.4; St. Irenaeus, *Adversus Haereses* 5.28.3; St. Hippolytus, *Commentary on Daniel* 4.23; St. Clement of Alexandria, *Stromateis* 6:137–45.

37. St. Augustine, *The City of God*, trans. Marcus Dods (New York: Modern Library, 1955), 867. Cf. *Oeuvres de St Augustin*, tome 37, *La cité de Dieu*, livres 19–22, ed. Gustave Bardy (Paris: Desclée de Brouwer, 1960); R. A. Markus, *Saeculum: History and Society in the Theology of St. Augustine* (Cambridge: Cambridge University Press, 1970); W. G. Most, *Saint Augustine's De Civitate Dei* (Washington, DC: Catholic University of America Press, 1949).

This Sabbath shall appear still more clearly if we count the ages as days, in accordance with the periods of time defined in Scripture, for that period will be found to be the seventh. The first age, as the first day, extends from Adam to the deluge; the second from the deluge to Abraham, equaling the first, not in length of time, but in the number of generations, there being ten in each. From Abraham to the advent of Christ there are, as the evangelist Matthew calculates, three periods, in each of which are fourteen generations—one period from Abraham to David, a second from David to the captivity, a third from the captivity to the birth of Christ in the flesh. There are thus five ages in all. The sixth is now passing, and cannot be measured by any number of generations, as it has been said, "It is not for you to know the times, which the Father hath put in His own power" (Acts 1:7). After the period God shall rest as on the seventh day, when He shall give us (who shall be the seventh day) rest in Himself. But there is not now space to treat of these ages; suffice it to say that the seventh shall be our Sabbath, which shall be brought to a close, not by an evening, but by the Lord's day, as an eighth and eternal day, consecrated by the resurrection of Christ, and *prefiguring* the eternal repose not only of the spirit, but also of the body. There we shall rest and see, see and love, love and praise. This is what shall be in the end without end. For what other end do we propose to ourselves than to attain to the kingdom of which there is no end? I think I have now, by God's help, discharged my obligation in writing this large work. Let those who think I have said too little, or those who think I have said too much, forgive me; and let those who think I have said just enough join me in giving thanks to God. Amen.

Augustine, we observe, reckons ten generations in the first two stages, and (following Matthew) fourteen in the next three.[38] We may also note here in passing that the great age of Adam, 930 years according to Gen 5:5, almost amounts to a millennium in itself.

With regard to this concluding passage from Augustine, two main comments are in order, one positive, one negative. We see first that this great Latin church father was able, thanks to his concern, to understand the events of history, including events during which he was living (like the Vandals' siege of his city of Hippo), in the light of faith guided by biblical

---

38. George Foot Moore, "Fourteen Generations: 490 Years: An Explanation of the Genealogy of Jesus," *HTR* 14 (1921) 97–103, here 196. Moore mentions the view of Cornelius Jansen that one goal of the genealogy is to show that the Messiah arrived at the right time, foreseen by biblical prophecy.

revelation. Hence he was able to comprehend the full sense of Matthew's genealogical scheme better than any other early Christian known to me. To his credit, he saw that Matthew implied the first two stages even if he did not say so explicitly. On the negative side, due to his neo-Platonic exaggerated spiritualization, and despite his best efforts to overcome his neo-Platonism through faith in the incarnation of the Word, he developed, toward the end of his life, a horror in regard to a millennial kingdom on earth (*De civ. Dei*, 20.7). That is why he blurs so subtly the seventh day in the scheme with the eighth day.

In fairness let it be added that, by including the phrase "*prefiguring* the eternal repose" he meant to say that the seventh day on earth, the millennial kingdom, *prefigures* the eternal rest of the eighth day in heaven, thanks to its fulfillment of God's intention for human history—namely, justice, peace, and joy (Rom 14:17). If that is Augustine's meaning, then no criticism is called for. Certainly in his earlier preaching (Sermon 259, PL 38:1197–98), Augustine does hold for a millennial Kingdom on earth. It is usually thought that he dropped this view in *The City of God*.[39] But this may not be correct. If so, then no negative criticism applies.

To be sure, Augustine was also a genius of human developmental psychology and Christian spirituality. It is not surprising, therefore, that he also applies the seven-age scheme to his own life and thus to the lives of others: infancy, childhood, adolescence, young adulthood, mature adulthood, decline, and old age. This seven-age scheme underlies the thirteen books of Augustine's *Confessions*.[40] It also underlies the structure of Books 15 to 22 of *The City of God*.[41]

This double use of the seven-age scheme, for personal growth and development as well as for understanding world history, shows its fundamental fruitfulness. In this way Matthew's genealogy becomes meaningful even for our spiritual lives. At least since Denis the Areopagite (6th century CE), Christian spirituality has presented the life of the graced soul according to a three-age scheme: purgative, illuminative, unitive—or, more biblically, beginners, proficient, perfect. This scheme has influenced both Christian and Jewish believers.[42]

---

39. Jean Daniélou, *The Bible and the Liturgy* (Notre Dame, IN: University of Notre Dame Press, 1956), 275–86.

40. D. Doncet, "L'ars memoriae dans les Confessions," *Revue des Etudes augustiennes* 33 (1987) 49–69.

41. Auguste Luneau, *Histoire du salut chez les Pères de l'Eglise: La doctrine des âges du monde* (Théologie Historique 2; Paris: Beauchesne, 1964). The main passages in Augustine are *De civ. Dei* 16:43; 15:1 and 9; 12:12; 20:19 and 23; 22:7.

42. Benedict T. Viviano, "Synagogues and Spirituality: The Case of Beth Alfa," in

COMMENTATORS FROM 1907 TO 2007

My thesis is clear: Matthew in 1:17 is providing an extract from a larger preexisting world week scheme of seven thousand-year periods as an outline of a theology of history. Let us now look at some commentaries published 1907–2007 (mostly German), to see how they understand Matthew's genealogy.

Johannes Weiss, at the beginning of the twentieth century, proposes that Matthew's three sets of fourteen generations can be understood as describing a preparation, a splendor, and a decline. The task of the genealogy is to bring forth the Messiah.[43] Erich Klostermann recognizes a principle of a week (*Hebdomadenprinzip*) or set of sevens. He observes that there are ten generations from Adam to Noah according to Gen 5:1–32 and ten generations from Noah to Abraham according to Gen 11:10–26. This is picked up by the rabbinic text *m. Abot* 5:2–3, and later by Augustine, as we have seen.[44] Billerbeck states that what earlier generations thought and taught about the time of arrival of the Messiah is fulfilled in Jesus.[45]

Adolf Schlatter remarks that the numerical rhythm for Matthew is a sign of the divine government of all events. Such thinking had been encouraged by Daniel who described the time between the Exile and the Promise as 70 weeks (Dan 9:24–27). Schlatter also notes that the rabbis emphasize that major events in salvation history often occur on the same day of the year. For example, in their interpretation of Exod 12:42, the rabbis and Targumists say that on the 14th day of the month of Nisan the creation, the binding of Isaac, the exodus from Egypt, and the future arrival of the Messiah all occur. On the 9th of Ab the two destructions of Jerusalem and its temple occur.[46]

Joachim Gnilka also verifies that behind the artificially constructed symmetry lurks a plan of God. The play with numbers means that God guides history to its intended goal. *Christologically*, Jesus born of Mary is the awaited Christ. *Ecclesiologically*, the history of the People of God is to be conceived as a history of promise. Gnilka recognizes the role of Enoch's world week, but adds consideration of the twice fourteen days of the lunar

---

Jesus and Archeology, ed. James H. Charlesworth (Grand Rapids, MI: Eerdmans, 2006), 223–35.

43. Johannes Weiss, *Matthäus-Kommentar* (Göttingen: Vandenhoeck & Ruprecht, 1907) 232–34.

44. Erich Klostermann, *Matthäus-Kommentar* (Tübingen: Mohr/Siebeck, 1927) 1–6.

45. Strack and Billerbeck, *Kommentar zum Neuen Testament*, 1:43–45.

46. Adolf Schlatter, *Der Evangelist Matthäus* (Stuttgart: Calwer, 1929), 6–7.

calendar as well as of the Hebrew gematria value of fourteen as the number for David.[47] The characteristic feature of Matthew's genealogy is the penetration of the messianic promise fulfilled in Jesus with the history of the people of Israel: "This penetration validates the universality of the messianic promise, because of its start with Abraham and because of its mention of the four women, but also it points to the traces of God's guidance of history. Despite many oppositions and low points, it reaches its goal."

The historical descent of Jesus from the Jewish people is today largely undisputed. Whereas Nazi-era exegesis tried in vain to prove that Jesus was of "Aryan" descent, today we acknowledge that Jesus was Jew, a son of Abraham. For Matthew it is self-evident and theologically necessary that salvation comes from Israel. Jesus' Davidic origins are widely attested in the New Testament (e.g., Rom 1:3; Heb 7:13). These origins are traced legally through Joseph, not biologically through Mary. Joseph was from a lateral branch of the Davidic line, not from the direct royal line. Nevertheless, Gnilka observes that the genealogy had relatively little influence on later Christian life, perhaps because it was not considered very edifying.[48]

The recent commentary on Matthew by Peter Fiedler reflects the interests of the younger generation, with its focus on narrative literary criticism and the role of the reader. For Fiedler Matt 1:17 is the narrator's commentary on the genealogy to help the reader interpret the lists of names in a deeper sense, as a theology of history. The periods are a means to see God's guiding hand at work in the chaos of events. This apocalyptic historical determinism has deeply marked Matthew (cf. Dan 11:36). There is a "providential design" (in the words of Donald Hagner). Matthew 1:17 invites the reader to pause and to reflect before the next phase is told. The next phase is going to be the special time of Jesus and the Church. We should react, not with hopelessness due to the perceived chaos, but with the confidence which comes from seeing the orderly plan of God. From the verse we can derive comfort and stability as we interpret the present.

According to Fiedler, the genealogy is an ideal (i.e., unreal) table of ancestors to legitimize someone formally as Messiah. Jesus is the messianic Son of David because he fulfills the genealogical presuppositions precisely. Israel's whole history flows to him, and he is the selection filter for the genealogical sequence. But the sense of Matt 1:1 (Jesus as son of David, son of Abraham) will only become clear in the course of the whole narrative.[49]

47. In Hebrew reckoning, the name David (D-V-D) may be understood as a series of numbers: $D = 4$; $V = 6$; $D = 4$; total = 14.

48. Joachim Gnilka, *Das Matthäusevangelium*, 2 vols. (Freiburg: Herder, 1986-1988), 1:11-14.

49. Peter Fiedler, *Matthäus* (Stuttgart: Kohlhammer, 2005).

For Ulrich Luz the point is to present Jesus as a human, historical figure. He cites St. Irenaeus: the meek and humble human being was preserved (*Adv. Haer.* 3.11.8).[50] W. D. Davies and Dale Allison note that, besides 1:17, Matthew likes to write summary verses, such as 4:23 and 9:35.[51] Like Luz, Davies and Allison know of but show little interest in the scheme of the seven ages of the world week because they seem not to be very interested in a theology of history or in an apocalyptic kingdom of God coming in the future.

In last place we may note an article by Karl-Heinrich Ostmeyer. He makes two points that are rarely found in the earlier literature. The first point is that the three sections of the genealogy each represent a different aspect of the biblical record. The first section speaks of the patriarchal era, with pagan or foreign wives. The second offers the royal descent. The third is actually *priestly*. Matthew thereby wishes to include the priestly-temple aspect of the biblical tradition as does the Letter to the Hebrews, even though both know that Jesus is of the tribe of Judah, not of Levi. (This is probably a correct perception of Matthew's intention.)

Ostmeyer's second point is that if you add up the three sets of fourteen generations it gives you approximately 40 generations. Now 40 weeks is about the time of a full pregnancy. So it took 40 generations for salvation history to gestate the Promised One. Jesus was born "in the fullness of time," as Paul says (Gal 4:4). Matthew does not explicitly mention the number 40 here because it was common knowledge. Ostmeyer's two ideas are interesting and fresh contributions, but it is not self-evident that Matthew had them sharply in view.[52]

CONCLUSIONS

From these gleanings in the works of earlier commentators, we may draw a few main conclusions. The first is christological. The genealogy not only presents Jesus as true king and son of David, but also as priest in some sense (if Ostmeyer is to be trusted). Jesus as prophet is not so clearly emphasized here. Jesus is rather presented as the fulfillment of the prophets' hopes for an anointed savior. To be sure, Jesus as prophet will come later in Matthew

---

50. Ulrich Luz, *Matthew 1–7* (Hermeneia; Minneapolis: Fortress, 2007), 85-88.

51. Davies and Allison, *St Matthew*, 1:185-88.

52. Karl-Heinrich Ostmeyer, "Der Stammbaum des Verheissenen: Theologische Implikationen der Namen und Zahlen in Mt. 1.1–17," *New Testament Studies* 46 (2000) 175-92.

(e.g., Matt 12:17-21, 39-41)—and especially in John's envoy Christology and in his development of Jesus as the prophet like Moses (Deut 18:18).

Is Jesus implicitly the Danielic divine Son of Man in the genealogy? This depends upon the missing fourteenth name in the third set of the genealogy. Theoretically this omission could be due to error or carelessness or due to the fact that Matthew only found thirteen names in his source and he was too scrupulous to invent a fourteenth.[53] It is better, however, to respect the intelligence and competence of the author Matthew who elsewhere shows signs of meticulous care in composition. That is why Stendahl's solution is so attractive. His suggestion is that the missing fourteenth name is the future coming Son of Man. It is theologically satisfying because the title may be understood as a divine one and it corresponds to a documentable interest by Matthew in the Son of Man as linked with the Kingdom of God.

Ecclesiologically, the two dominant titles Son of David and Son of Abraham (Matt 1:1) can be unpacked in this way. The Son of David title connects Jesus with a historic people, the united kingdom of Judah and Israel, the south and the north. (The quest for the reunion of the two kingdoms is the ecumenical problem specific to the Hebrew Bible.) Jesus comes with a people, the people of God, and at the moment of his arrival he is largely confined to the Jewish people. But the title Son of Abraham suggests an expanding horizon whereby the people of God are widened to include all the nations as they receive Jesus' message and become his disciples. This is the progressive expansion that occurs in the Gospel itself. The restriction of the mission only to the lost sheep of the house of Israel (Matt 10:5-6; 15:24) finally gives way to the great commission to all the nations (Matt 28:18-20).

---

53. Davies and Allison, *St Matthew*, 1.185-88.

Acknowledgments

The author and publisher gratefully acknowledge the journals and publishers where many of these essays first appeared.

"The Normativity of Scripture and Tradition in Recent Catholic Theology." In *Scripture's Doctrine and Theology's Bible: How the New Testament Shapes Christian Dogmatics*, edited by Markus Bockmuehl and A. J. Torrance, 125-40. © 2008 by Baker Academic, a division of Baker Publishing Group. Used by permission.

Review of William S. Kurz and Luke Timothy Johnson, *The Future of Catholic Biblical Scholarship: A Constructive Conversation*, Review of Biblical Literature [http://www.bookreviews.org/] (2004). Used by permission.

"The Renewal of Biblical Studies in France 1934-1954." In *Ressourcement: A Movement for Renewal in Twentieth-Century Catholic Theology*, edited by Gabriel Flynn and Paul D. Murray, 305-17. © 2012 by Oxford University Press. Used by permission.

"The Dogma of the Prophetless Time in Judaism: Does Prophecy Cease with Christ for Christians? Some Explorations" first appeared in *L'Ecrit et l"Esprit: Etudes d'histoire du texte et de theologie biblique en hommage a Adrian Schenker*, edited by Dieter Boehler, I. Himbaza, and P. Hugo, Orbis Biblicus et Orientalis 214. 418-31. © 2005 by Academic Press Fribourg, 2005), Used by permission.

"Eschatology and the Historical Jesus." In *The Oxford Handbook of Eschatology*, edited by J. L. Walls, 73-90. Oxford Handbooks in Religion and Theology. © 2008 by Oxford University Press. Used by permission.

ACKNOWLEDGMENTS

"The Adoration of the Magi: Matthew 2:1–23 and Theological Aesthetics." *Revue Biblique* 115 (2008) 546–67. Used by permission.

"The Christian and the State." In *The Reception of Paulinism in Acts*, edited by Daniel Marguerat, 227–38. Leuven: Peeters, 2009. Open-access policy.

"Hakeldama, the Potter's Field, and the Suicide of Judas (Matt27:-10; Acts 1:16-20)" In *Jerusalem und die Laender*, edited by Gerd Theissen et al., 203–10. NTOA 70. © 2009 by Vandenhoeck & Ruprecht. Used by permission.

"A Woman's Quest for Wisdom and the Adoration of the Magi." In *The Gospel of Matthew at the Crossroads of Early Christianity*, 683–70. BETL 243. Leuven: Peeters, 2011. Open-access policy.

"Making Sense of the Matthean Genealogy: Matthew 1:17 and the Theology of History." In *New Perspectives on the Nativity*, edited by Jeremy Corley, 91–109. © 2009 by T. & T. Clark, a division of Bloomsbury Publishing. Used by permission.

Abbreviations

AAS	*Acta apostolicae sedis*
AB	Anchor Bible
ABD	*Anchor Bible Dictionary*. Edited by David Noel Freedman. 6 vols. New York: Doubleday, 1992
ABR	*Australian Biblical Review*
AnBib	Analecta Biblica
ATD	Das Alte Testament Deutsch
ATANT	Abhandlungen zur Theologie des Alten und Neuen Testaments
Bib	*Biblica*
BETL	Bibliotheca ephemeridum theologicarum lovaniensium
BEvTh	Beiträge zur evangelischen Theologie
BFCT	Beiträige zur Förderung christlicher Theologie
BKAT	Biblischer Kommentar, Altes Testament
BTB	*Biblical Theology Bulletin*
BWANT	Beiträge zur Wissenschaft vom Alten und Neuen Testament
BZ	*Biblische Zeitschrift*
BHT	Beiträge zur historischen Theologie
BZNW	Beihefte zur Zeitschrift für die neutestamentliche Wissenschaft
CBA	Catholic Biblical Association

CBQ	*Catholic Biblical Quarterly*
CSEL	Corpus scriptorum ecclesiasticorum latinorum
DBS	*Dictionnaire de la Bible: Supplément*, edited by L. Pirot and A. Robert. Paris, 1928–
EBib	Ètudes bibliques
EncBrit	*Encylcopaedia Britianica*
ETL	*Ephemerides theologicae lovanienses*
ETR	*Etudes théologiques et religieuses*
ExpT	*Expository Times*
EvTh	*Evangelische Theologie*
FRLANT	Forschungen zur Religion und Literatur des Alten und Neuen Testaments
FZPhTh	*Freiburger Zeitschrift für Philosophie und Theologie*
GCS	Die griechischte christliche Schriftsteller der ersten [drei] Jahrhunderte
HNT	Handbuch zum Neuen Testament
HTG	*Die Humanisierung des Mythos bei Thomas Mann: zu seinem neuen Buch "Der Erwählte,"* by Alois Winkelhofer. Stuttgart, 1951
HTKAT	Herders theologischer Kommentar zum Alten Testament
HTKNT	Herders theologischer Kommentar zum Neuen Testament
HTR	*Harvard Theological Review*
ICC	International Critical Commentary
ITQ	*Irish Theological Quarterly*
JBL	*Journal of Biblical Literature*
JJS	*Journal of Jewish Studies*
JSem	*Journal of Semitics*

ABBREVIATIONS

JSNTSup	Journal for the Study of the New Testament: Supplement Series
JSJSup	Journal for the Study of Judaism in the Persian, Hellenistic, and Roman Periods: Supplement Series
JSOT	*Journal for the Study of the Old Testament*
JSOTSup	Journal for the Study of the Old Testament: Supplement Series
JSPSup	Journal for the Study of the Pseudepigrapha: Supplement Series
KEK	Kritisch-exegetischer Kommentar über das Neue Testament (Meyer-Kommentar)
LCC	Library of Christian Classics
LCL	Loeb Classical Library
LD	Lectio divina (Commentaries)
LTK	*Lexicon für Theologie und Kirche*
NICNT	New International Commentary on the New Testament
NPNF1	*Nicene and Post-Nicene Fathers*
NTOA	Novum Testamentum et Orbis Antiquus
NTS	*New Testament Studies*
OBO	Orbis biblicus et orientalis
OTL	Old Testament Library
OTP	*Old Testament Pseudepigrapha.* Edited by James H. Charlesworth. 2 vols. New York, 1983
PG	Patrologia graeca. Edited by J.-P. Migne. 162 vols. Paris, 1857–1886
PL	Patrologia latina [= Patrologiae cursus completus: Series latina]. Edited by J.-P. Migne. 217 vols. Paris, 1844–1864
QD	Quaestiones Disputatae
RB	*Revue biblique*

ABBREVIATIONS

RBL	*Review of Biblical Literature*
RHPR	*Revue d'histoire et de philosophie religieuses*
RQ	*Römische Quartalschrift*
RSR	*Recherches de science religieuse*
RTL	*Revue théologique de Louvain*
SANT	Studien zum Alten und Neuen Testament
SB	Sources Bibliques
SBFLA	*Studii biblici Franciscani liber annus*
SBLDS	Society of Biblical Literature: Dissertation Series
SC	Sources chrétiennes
SHAW	Sitzungsberichte der heidelberger Akademie der Wissenschaften
SJ	*Studia Judaica*
SJLA	Studies in Judaism in Late Antiquity
SNTSMS	Society for New Testament Studies Monograph Series
ST	*Studia Theologica*
TDNT	*Theological Dictionary of the New Testament*. Edited by Gerhard Kittel and Gerhard Friedrich. Translated by Geoffrey W. Bromiley. 10 vols. Grand Rapids, 1964–1976
ThTo	*Theology Today*
TQ	*Theologische Quartalschrift*
TRE	*Theologische Realenzyklopädie*. Edited by G. Krause and G. Müller. Berlin, 1977–
TRev	*Theologische Revue*
TS	*Theological Studies*
TU	Texte und Untersuchungen
TWAT	*Theologisches Wörterbuch zum Alten Testament*. Edited by G. Johannes Bottweck and Helmer Ringgren. Stuttgart, 1973–77

ABBREVIATIONS

TZ	*Theologische Zeitschrift*
VTSup	Vetus Testamentum Supplements
WBC	Word Biblical Commentary
WMANT	Wissenschaftliche Monographien zum Alten und Neuen Testament
WUNT	Wissenschaftliche Untersuchungen zum Neuen Testament
ZAW	*Zeitschrift für die alttestamentliche Wissenschaft*
ZNW	*Zeitschrift für die neutestamentliche Wissenschaft und die Kunde der älteren Kirche*
ZTK	*Zeitschrift für Theologie und Kirche*

Index of Names

Abelard, x,
Achtemeier, P. J., x
Akiba, 69
Albright, W. F., 38, 48, 49, 51
Alexander the Great, 57
Allison, D. C., 117, 118, 136, 176, 180, 182, 184, 196, 198, 206, 207, 208, 212, 220, 221
Alter, R., 126
Althaus, P., 111, 118
Anthony of the Desert, x
Antiochus IV, 57, 206
Arendt, H., 59
Aristotle, x, 26, 58, 125, 126, 141, 148
Aron, R., 37
Assman, J., 137, 152
Athanasius, 22
Attridge, H. W., 51
Augustine, x, xi, 23, 31, 42, 60, 71, 104, 165, 179, 205, 215-18
Aus, R. D., 132
Averroes, 58

Balthasar, H. U. von, 90, 124-25, 127-28, 141
Barfield, O., 124
Barnett, P. W., 76
Barr, J., 54, 191
Barrett, C. K., 129
Barth, G., 184, 190
Barth, K., 24, 84, 87, 111, 112, 114, 125, 166, 168, 171, 172, 173, 180, 182, 184

Bassler, J. M., 129
Batiffol, P., 45-46
Baum, G., 94
Baur, F. C., 24, 160-61, 179-80
Bea, A., 7, 15
Beethoven, L. von, 72, 163
Begg, C. T., 185, 191
Benedict XVI, Pope, ix, 57, 89, 98, 149
Benedict, St., 24
Benoit, P., 41, 87, 176, 182, 207, 208
Berkeley, Bishop, 130
Berkley, G. E., 159
Bernard of Chartres, 93
Bernard of Clairvaux, 32
Billerbeck, P., 93, 203, 213, 218
Billot, L., 17, 18
Blackburn, S., 130
Bland, K. P., x
Bloch, E., 114, 118
Bloom, H., xi
Boff, L., 114, 119
Boismard, M.-E., 87
Bonhoeffer, D., 84, 112, 119, 146
Bonsirven, J., 36, 113, 119, 213
Borg, M. J., 115, 119
Bornkamm, G., 112, 119, 143, 184, 190
Bossuet, J.-B., 34
Bousset, W., 110-11, 119, 158, 162, 163
Bouyer, L., 15, 41
Braun, F.-M., 87
Braun, H., 112
Bridget of Sweden, 84

INDEX OF NAMES

Brown, R. E., 32, 49, 51, 52, 53, 54, 87, 89, 119, 129, 133, 176, 182, 184, 185, 199
Brueggemann, W., 193, 195
Brunner, E., 111
Bruns, J. F., 185
Buber, M., 136
Buis, P., 195
Bultmann, R., xii, 23, 75, 111–12, 119, 125, 129, 157, 164, 168–73

Caird, G. B., 113, 115–16, 119
Callan, C. J. 47
Carlin, G., 46
Carter, W., 114, 119
Catherine of Siena, 24, 84
Celsus, 2, 104
Cerfaux, L. 36–37
Chaine, J., 38
Chenu, M.-D., 5, 15, 41
Clement of Alexandria, St., 58, 104, 209, 215
Clements, R. E., 140
Clifford, R. J., 51
Collins, A. Y., 51, 185
Collins, J. J., 51, 119, 185, 191
Congar, Y.-M., 5, 15, 20, 36, 41, 84
Conzelmann, H., 112, 119, 157, 158, 171, 173, 174
Coppens, J., 38
Cormier, H., 15
Creighton, M., 11
Crossan, J. D., 52, 115, 119
Cullmann, O., 19, 87, 112, 113, 114, 119, 151, 153, 168, 185, 203

Dahood, M., 49
Daniélou, J., 15, 19, 34, 41–44, 125, 184, 209, 217
Darwin, C., 2, 5, 10
Davies, W. D., 87, 93, 94, 95, 158, 176, 180, 182, 208, 212, 220, 221
Deissmann, A., 166, 173
Descartes, R., 59

Dewey, J., 46
Dhorme, P.-E., 6
Dietrich, W., 189
di Lella, A., 51
Dodd, C. H., 113, 115, 116, 119, 129
Donfried, K. P., 143, 170
Driver, G. R., 55
Droge, A. J., 180, 182
Duhm, B., 162
Duling, D. C., 184, 192
Dupont, J., 143, 165

Eichhhorn, J. G., 7
Einstein, A., 65
Elliott, M. W., xv
Emerson, R. W., 110, 149
Erasmus, 106
Eugene of Savoy, 67

Faraday, M., 65
Feldman, N., 71
Fiedler, P., 219
Filastrius, 74
Fishbane, M., 81
Fitzmyer, J. A., 32, 43, 49, 51, 55, 87, 143, 213
Fogarty, G. F., 5
Fonck, L., 36
Francis of Assisi, St., x, 24
Frederick II, 62
Freud, S., ix, 38, 92
Fritz, V., 189, 193
Fukuyama, F., 60, 98, 202
Fuller, R. H., 53
Furnish, V. P., x

Gadamer, H.-G., xi
Galbiati, E., 184, 185, 196–97
Galton, F, 57, 59, 161
Garbe, G., 185
Gasparri, P., 15, 36
Geiselmann, J. R., 19–21
Gelin, A., 41
Gelineau, J., 40
Gerhardssohn, B., 148
Ghazzali, al-, 58

232

INDEX OF NAMES

Gibbon, E., 2, 60
Gilson, E., 40
Glazier, M., 51
Gnilka, J., 117, 153, 176, 182, 218, 219
Gore, C., 53
Graves, R., 139
Greenspahn, F. E., 76–78, 80
Gregory XI, 84
Gregory, A. F., 153
Gregory Nazienzen, St., 70
Grimm Brothers, 2, 191
Grobel, K., x
Grotius, H., 6, 106
Guardini, R., 125
Guitton, J., 7, 15, 37
Gunkel, H., 19, 40, 110, 119, 155, 161–63, 173
Gutierrez, G., 114, 119

Hadfield, G. A. C., x
Haenchen, E., 143
Hamann, J. G., 60
Hanson, P. D., 190
Harnack, A., xv, 66, 75, 97, 109, 111, 119, 120, 161, 168
Harrington, D. J., 55
Harrisville, R. A., 150
Hart, D. B., 57
Hauret, C., 38
Hay, D., x
Headlam, A. C., 147
Hegel, G. W. F., 2, 3, 60, 64, 131, 160, 162, 163, 202
Heidegger, M., xi, 57, 112
Heitmueller, W., 162, 164
Held, H. J., 184, 190
Hengel, M., 119, 153, 164, 167, 190
Herder, J. G., 2, 3, 17, 60, 107
Herodotus, 3
Hick, J., 68
Hippolytus, 105, 203, 209, 215
Hobbes, T., 6, 106, 107
Hochhuth, R., 169
Hodge, B. J., 159
Hoenig, S. B., x
Hoepfl, H., x

Hofbauer, C. M., 72
Holl, Karl, 111
Holtzmann, H. J., 109
Homer, ix, x, 2
Hoppe, L. J., 187
Horsley, R. A., 114, 119
Hummel, R., 184
Huntington, S. P., 60, 202
Husserl, E., 64
Hyvernat, H., 45–46

Irenaeus, St., 2, 22, 104, 114, 209, 215, 220

Jaeger, W., 87, 148
James, H., 35
Jedin, H, 11
Jeremias, J., 93, 113, 120, 185
Jerome, St., x, 25
Jewett, R., 152
Joachim of Fiore, 105
John Paul II, Pope, 26, 62, 69, 84, 120, 131
John Damascene, 66, 97
Johnson, L. T., 29–32, 51, 55
Josephus, 38, 74, 76, 77, 78, 79, 134, 138–39, 185, 191, 198, 199, 211
Jungmann, J., 15
Justin, St., 22, 77, 84, 209, 215

Kant, I., 2, 56, 60–62, 109–10, 136, 161
Käsemann, E., 24, 112, 120, 164, 169–70
Kermode, F., 126
Klassen, W., 179, 182
Klauck, H.-J., 179, 182
Kloppenborg, J. S., 52, 115, 120
Klostermann, E., 218
Koester, H., 87, 148
Koester, M. D., 37
Konradt, M., 185
Kraemer, R. S., 133, 134
Kramer, P., 65
Küchler, M., 175, 182

INDEX OF NAMES

Küng, H., 66, 120, 125, 130, 170
Kurz, W., 29, 32, 55

Lacordaire, H. D., 4
Ladin, O. bin, 68
Lagrange, M.-J., xiii, 4–7, 14–15, 17, 18, 30, 32, 35–36, 38, 40–42, 44, 45–46, 52, 86, 93, 113, 120, 125, 152, 164, 197
La Potterie, I. de, 87, 129
Larcher, C., 120, 148, 191
Lavigerie, C. M. A., 35
Lavoisier, A. 64
Legasse, S., 152
LeGuin, U., 84
Lehmann, K., x
Leibniz, G. W. F. von, 59
Leivestad, R., 73
Leloir, L., x
Leo XIII, Pope, xii, 14, 15, 34, 35, 36, 45, 46
Leo, F., 162
Lessing, G. E., 3, 59, 66, 107
Levenson, J. D., 97, 126
Levi-Strauss, C., 87
Lewis, C. S., 84, 124
Lieberman, S., 148
Lietzmann, H., 157, 166, 168, 171–73
Loennrot, E. 2
Lohfink, N., 7, 87
Lohmeyer, E., 13
Lohr, C. H., 208
Loretz, O., 9
Lortz, J., 11
Lotze, H., 162, 163
Lowth, R., 7
Lubac, H. de, 15, 32, 34, 41–44, 125
Ludolf of Saxony, 105
Luneau, A., 217
Luther, M., x, 24, 111, 168, 170, 179
Luz, U., xiv, 133, 176, 182, 185, 220
Lyell, C. 10

Macquarrie, J., 65
Maimonides, M., 58, 62, 106

Marcion, 24, 42, 64, 116
Marcus, J., 95
Marguerat, D., 117
Marrou, H. I., 40
Martel, C., 67
Marx, K, ix
Matera, F., 50
Mathew, G., 124, 135
Maurras, C., 42
May, H., 59
McCullough, D., 59
McHugh, J. A., 47
McKenzie, J. L. 38, 50, 52
Meeks, D., 114
Meier, J. P., 51, 53, 117
Menken, M. J. J., 133, 134, 180, 182, 196
Menocal, M. R., 99
Merry del Val, R., 7, 15, 35
Mersch, E., 15, 37
Merz, A., 121
Metz, J. B., 109, 114
Michaelis, J. D., 7
Michel, O., 181, 182
Miles, J. A., 52
Mill, J. S., 57
Moltmann, J., 109, 114
Montagnes, B., 55
Montalembert, C. F. R., 4
Montesquieu, C., 2, 107
Moore, G. F., 216
Morgan, J. P., 45
Murphy, R. E., 52
Murphy-O'Connor, J., 64, 87

Narcisse, G., 125, 14l
Neuhaus, J. R., 65
Newman, J. H., 2
Newton, J., 59, 65, 83
Neyrey, J. H., 121
Nickelsburg, G. W. E., 214
Niebuhr, H. R., 121
Nietzsche, F., x, 57, 58
Nolan, B. M., 184

Origen, 44, 69, 77, 104

INDEX OF NAMES

Ostermeyer, K. H., 220

Pahlavi, Reza 68
Pannenberg, W. 97, 114
Pasteur, L. 65
Peli, P, 43
Perrin, N. 114–15, 121
Pesch, R. 137
Petain, H. P. 42
Peterson, E. 149
Philo, 38, 44, 58, 80, 96
Pine, Msg., 47
Pius IX, 130
Pius X, 15, 36, 47
Pius XI, 15
Pius XII, 15, 19, 37
Plato, 26, 58, 126, 140, 148, 151
Popper, K. R. 131
Powell, M.A. 199
Priestly, J.B. 65
Pritchard, J. B. 185
Proksch, O., 167
Propp, W. H. C., 146
Proust, M., 35

Quinn, J. D., 153

Rad, G. v., 81, 114, 130
Rahner, K., 15
Ramee, P. de la, 64
Ramsay, B., 140
Ranke, von, L., 11
Reed, D. A., 180, 182
Reimarus, H. S., 111
Reiser, M., xv
Renan, E. 111, 125
Ricciotti, G., 93, 113
Ricoeur, P., ix, 80
Ritschl, A., 111
Robinson, J. A. T., 113

Said, E., 17
Sailer, J. M., 72
Sanday, W., 147
Sanders, E. P., 117

Sanders, J. A., 208
Sarpi, P., 11
Sato, M., 180
Satran, D., 140
Sayers, D., 84
Schalit, A., 134
Scheil, V., 5
Scheler, M., 61
Schenker, A., 73
Schillebeeckx, E., 30, 71, 184
Schlatter, A., 66, 97, 171, 218
Schedl, C., 66
Schiller, F., 72
Schlegel, F., 17, 60, 131.
Schleiermacher, F., xi, 17, 107, 160
Schlier, H., 150
Schmidt, K. L., 23
Schnackenburg, R., 113, 121, 129, 151
Schneider, G., 143, 151
Schoeps, H. J., 66
Schreiber, S., 152
Schürer, E., 134
Schwab, R., 40
Schweitzer, A., 111, 113, 118, 121, 157, 160, 161, 164, 166–68, 171, 173
Seitz, C., xv
Senior, D., 176, 182
Siegman, E., 50
Simon, R., 7, 34, 125
Skehan, P., 49
Smith, M., 49, 153
Smith, M. S., 52
Soederblom, N., 168
Solages, B. de, 37
Sommer, B. D., 76
Spalding, J. L., 46
Spencer, F. A., 47
Spengler, O., 60, 202
Spinoza, B., 6, 59, 106
Stein-Schneider, H., 179, 182
Stendahl, K., 170, 196, 210
Sternberg, M., 132, 204, 212
Stone, M. E., 140
Strack, H. L., 93, 218
Strauss, D. F., 107, 125
Strecker, G., 194

INDEX OF NAMES

Strugnell, J., 49
Stuckenbruck, L., 214
Suggs, M. J., 184
Suhard, E. 38
Sullivan, K., 49, 52
Surenhusius, 106

Tacitus, 2, 11, 60
Taubes, J. 152
Taylor, J.J. 143
Teilhard de Chardin, P. 37
Theissen, G., 117, 121
Theresa of Calcutta, 84
Thomas Aquinas xi, xii, 3, 5, 18, 23, 32, 58, 106
Thucydides 3
Tillich, P., 62, 65
Tischendorff, C., 45
Tolkien, J. R. R., 84, 124
Torrey, C. C., 49
Tournay, R. J., 40
Toynbee, A., 60, 131, 202
Trilling, W., 184
Tromp. S., 37
Tuckett, C.W., 153, 196

Ugolini, 106
Ulrich, E. 49
Urbach, E.E. 77, 78

VanderKam, J. C., 49
Vaux, R. de 34, 38, 44
Vawter, B. 38
Vermes, G., x, 134
Vico, J. B., 2, 3 60
Vielhauer, P. 169
Viviano, B. T. 136, 188, 198

Voltaire, 2
Voste, J., 7, 15, 38

Wagner, R., 136
Wainwright, E. M., 188
Walesa, Lech, 84
Wedgwood, C. V., 71
Weingreen J., x
Weiss, J., xv, 110, 111, 113–14, 116–18, 121, 152, 157–58, 162, 164–65, 171–73, 218
Weisse, C. H., 109
Wellhausen, J., 5,10, 15, 40, 44, 76
Westermann, C., 74–76
Wettstein, J. J., 106
Whelan, C. F., 180, 182
White, H. V., 63
Wick, P., 180, 182
Wielandt, B., 98
Wikenhauser, A., 121, 205
Willits, J., 185
Wilson, E., 38
Wink, W., 2, 30
Winston, D., 148, 191
Wischmeyer, O., xv
Witherup, R., 55
Wolff, H. W., 59, 194
Wrede, W., 111, 160, 162, 165, 173
Wright, N. T., 116–17
Würthwein, E., 194

Yonge, C., 84

Zeno, 58
Zia, M. J., xii
Zimmerli, W., 185

Index of Scripture and Other Ancient Sources

Genesis

	10, 32, 38, 44, 110, 167, 208, 212
1–11	7, 18
1–3	5, 15, 37, 38, 129
1	36, 103, 205, 213, 214
1:1—2:4a	83, 214
1:2	210
2:2	215
3:17–19	155
4:8	211
4:10	211
5–9	5
5:1–32	218
5:3–31	205
5:5	216
6–10	14
11:10–26	205, 218
28:12	102
28:17	102
28:22	102
41–50	137

Exodus

	44, 189
1–15	137
1	138
1:17	146
1:22	196
2	138
4:5–8	189
4:19	196
7:8—11:10	146
12:42	218
14:31	146
15:27	44
20:7	71
23:2–3	146
23:2	11
23:15	136
24	108
32–34	146
34:20	136
34:29–34	108

Leviticus

	189
19:15	9
19:18	95, 99
19:34	95

Numbers

	189
24:17	76
33	31
33:9	44

Deuteronomy

	208, 209
1:17	9, 146
4:5–8	189
6:5	95, 99
6:6	129
6:7	129

Deuteronomy (continued)

11–27	6
15	1
16:16	136
16:18–20	11, 129, 146
16:20	146
17:14–20	146, 196
18:15–19	76, 81
18:15	74
18:18	74, 221
31:1	207
32:45	207
34	18

Joshua

	6, 209
22:5	95
24:31	78

Judges

	6
2:7	78
13:5	133, 139
13:7	133, 139
16:23–30	139

1 Samuel

	38
3:1	76
6	177
8:11–18	10
9:1—10:16	10
10:17—24:12	10
24	95, 146
24:6	146
26	95, 146
26:11	146
31:4–5	180

2 Samuel

5:2	135, 196
9–20	43, 146
11	127
12:7	129
15–17	180
17:23	180

1 Kings

	10, 183, 188
1–11	185, 189
1–2	43, 146, 198
1	186
1:37	186
1:47	186
1:48	189
1:49	186
1:52–53	186
2:24–25	186
3	186
3:1	186
3:3	186
3:5	198
3:16–28	193
4:29–34	193
4:33	193
5:8	186
4	186
4:1	186
4:7	186
4:20	186
4:29–34	186
5:1–18	193
5:6	186–87
6:7	187
6:16	187
6:19	187
6:23	187
6:37–38	187
8	187
9	187
9:2	198
10	197
10:1–23	88
10:1–13	183, 188, 190, 192, 196, 199
10:1–29	133
10:1–3	192
10:1	194
10:2	193, 194
10:3	194
10:4–9	192
10:5	194
10:6–9	193
10:6	194
10:7	194

INDEX OF SCRIPTURE AND OTHER ANCIENT SOURCES

10:8	194
10:9	194
10:10–13	192, 193
10:10	195
10:12	190
10:13	193, 198
10:14	190
10:20	188
10:23–25	188
11	188
16:18	180
18:28	74
19	108
21	129

2 Kings

	10
5:18–19	71
9:11	74
16:10–16	212

1 Chronicles

	10
1–9	189
10:4	180
11:2	135
22:8	183, 192
22:9	188

2 Chronicles

	10, 188
1–9	185
1	186
9:4	195
24:20–22	211
36:22–23	213

Ezra

5:1	211
7:29	171
10	129

Nehemiah

2:1–10	57

6:7–14	76
6:12–14	74, 76, 77

1 Maccabees

	20
1:1–18	57
4:42–46	77
4:44–46	74
9:27	74, 77, 78, 83
14:41	74, 77

2 Maccabees

2:1–8	74

Psalms

1	130
12:6	195
19:1	123
90:4	103
77:19	xiii, 12
23	25
139	25
29	36
23:	25
74:9	73, 74
104	130, 140
109:1	154
110:1	155

Proverbs

3:18	10
3:5–6	56
7:17	190
8:15	147
8:19	195
8:22–30	200
9:1–6	195, 200
9:13	195
20:27	56
23:1–3	193
25:1–7	193
25:21–22	144
29:18	76
31:30	123, 140

Canticles

3:6	136, 190
4:6	136
4:14	136
5:1	136
5:5	136
5:15	136

Wisdom

2:16	190
6:1–11	147
6:22—10:21	190
7:27	77, 83
8:7	58, 128, 190
10:10	102
10:17	136
11:1—19:22	190
13–15	2
13:5	58, 190
18:1–3	190
18:3	136

Sirach

10:45	147
15	20
24	200
24:15	195
38:34b	130
39:1–11	130
39:12–35	83
42:15–25	129
43:1–33	129
47:12–22	190

Isaiah

	133
2:1–4	70
2:2–5	133
7:14	196
8:2	211
11:1	133
13:6	102
13:9	102
13:13	102
40–55	82
40:3	104
45:7	145
60	189
60:1–7	189
60:3	123
60:6	136, 202

Jeremiah

	38, 74, 79, 133, 138, 177
7:11	187
18:2–3	175, 177
19:1–2	178
19:4	178
19:6	178
19:7–8	178
20:9	75
23:29	14
23:9–22	74
25:11–12	213
27:5–7	147
29:5	147
29:10	213
31:5	196
32:7–9	177

Lamentations

2:9	74, 77

Baruch

1:11–12	147

Ezekiel

34:1–10	10

Daniel

	5, 20, 66, 75, 79, 102, 105, 112, 116, 117, 118, 203
2	203
2:37	147
2:44	155
3:38	74
4:17	147

INDEX OF SCRIPTURE AND OTHER ANCIENT SOURCES

7	36, 151, 203, 215
7:2	151
7:4	151
7:5	151
7:7	151
7:8	151
7:10	151
7:12	151
7:13–14	70, 76, 102, 103, 105, 155
7:14	151
7:15	151
7:24	155
9	79, 205
9:24–27	205, 213, 218

Hosea

	133
2:17	74
7:3–7	10, 13
8:4	147
11:1	137, 196
13:9–11	10

Joel

3:1–5	82
3:1	77

Amos

1	129
3:8b	75
7:14	74
8:11	74, 77
5:18–20	102

Jonah

	36

Micah

	133
3:1–4	147
3:5–7	77
3:9–12	147

4:1–4	133
4:1–3	70
4:5	70
5:1–2	196
5:2	135

Zephaniah

1:4	74

Haggai

	74–75, 79

Zecheriah

	74–75, 79
1:1	211
1:12	213
2:1–14	79
4:1	79
3:5	79
11:13	177
13:2–6	74, 77

Malachi

20, 74–75, 79

PSEUDEPIGRAPHA

2 Baruch

85	74
85:1	78
85:3	78

1 Enoch

91	213
91:11–17	213
93	213
93:1–10	213

INDEX OF SCRIPTURE AND OTHER ANCIENT SOURCES

2 Enoch

33	214
33:1–2	214

1 Esdras

4:41	122

4 Ezra

7:29	171

Letter of Aristeas

	147

NEW TESTAMENT

Matthew

	xiii, 21, 27, 58, 67, 86–100, 104, 108, 115, 179
1–2	183, 199
1:1–18	xiv, 103
1:1	134, 183, 204, 211, 219, 221
1:2–17	205
1:4	206, 209
1:5	209
1:6	183
1:17	201–21
1:18–25	132
1:19	135
1:21	139, 209
1:23	96
2	xiv, 123, 132, 134
2:1–23	91
2:1–13	196
2:1–12	122–41
2:1–8	132
2:1–2	134
2:1	134
2:2	134, 135, 190, 199
2:3	134, 186
2:4	134
2:7	123, 134, 135
2:8	123
2:9–12	132
2:9	134, 135
2:10	135
2:11	136, 188, 200
2:12	134, 135, 198
2:13–23	132
2:13–15	132
2:13	200
2:14	200
2:15	134
2:16–18	123, 132
2:16	135
2:19–23	132
2:19	134, 200
2:21	200
2:23	131
3:3	104
2	xiv
2:7	123
2:8	123
2:16–18	123
4:18–22	186
4:25	186
5–7	x
5:17–20	x, 23, 88, 94
5:18	104
5:19	165
5:21–48	187, 209
5:37	9
5:44–45	95
6:10	110, 112
6:9–13	116, 187
6:33	103, 110
7:12	110
10:1–4	186
10:5–6	221
10:34–36	184
10:39	181
10:41	81
11:12	184

INDEX OF SCRIPTURE AND OTHER ANCIENT SOURCES

11:19	200
11:20–24	116
11:21–22	187
11:25–30	200
11:25–27	186
11:27	22, 208
11:28–30	187
11:29	96
12:17–21	221
12:28	110
12:32	103
12:39–41	221
12:42	186, 197, 199, 200
13:24–30	41
14:15–21	186
14:23	187
15:2	187
15:24	221
15:32–39	186
16:17–19	165
16:18	197
16:24	61
17:5	187
17:11	102
17:24–27	148, 187
18:14	99, 181
18:20	96, 209
19:4	211
19:28	188
21:12–13	184
21:13	187
22:15–22	187
22:22	148
22:34–40	95, 99, 187
23	94, 95
23:8	96
23:10	96
23:13–36	27
23:27	122, 140
23:34	82
23:35	211
24:3	84, 210
24:27	84, 210
24:29–31	211
24:36	112
24:37	84, 210
24:39	84, 210
25:31–46	71, 101, 181, 210
25:31	186
25:40	99
25:46	71, 101, 178
26:7	198
26:12	198
26:24–25	176
26:26–30	187
27	xiv
27:3–10	175–82, 188
27:3–5	181
27:25	27, 94
27:33–56	187
27:43	190
27:51–53	209
28:18–20	88
28:18	221
28:20	104

Mark

	27–28, 52, 89, 104, 108, 109, 115, 176, 179, 180
1:15	110, 112
3:29	71
6:14–29	133
8:34	61
9:1	113
9:12	102
12:17	148
12:28–31	95
13:24–25	117
13:26–27	149
13:26	112
13:31	104
13:32	103, 104, 112, 117
14:21b	176
14:25	110
15:33–37	128

Luke

	24, 27, 51, 104, 108, 115, 132, 160, 179
1	8
1:2–4	23
1:33	105, 156

Luke (continued)

1:76	104
2	8
3:36	211
3:38	211
6:27–35	95
6:31	110
9:23	61
9:28–36	128
9:32	128
10:1	44
10:13–15	116
10:17	44
10:25–37	43
10:25–28	95
11	212
11:2–4	116
11:20	110
11:31	199
11:37–52	95
11:51	211
12:14	186
12:57	56
20:26	148
22:36–38	150
23:2	143
23:43	106
23:56	136

John

	3, 21, 24, 26, 27, 28, 29, 32, 51, 52, 58, 63, 68, 80, 88, 104, 105, 108, 129, 160, 168, 178, 179, 180, 191, 221
1–20	53–54
1:3	63
1:14	128
1:21	81
3:8	75
4:19	81
5	130
6	29, 180
6:14	81
6:51–58	22
6:70–71	176, 178
7	130
7:40	81
7:52	81
8	130
8:31–32	9
8:32	9
8:44	27, 94, 95
8:52–53	81
9	130
9:22	95
9:28	95
10	130
10:22	20
12:42	95
14:3	84, 113, 149
14:6	9
14:18	113
14:26	24, 26
14:28	113
16:2	95
16:12–13	81, 84
16:13	24
17:12b	176, 178, 179
18:36	129
19:11	150–51
19:39	136
20	29
20:22–23	32
20:22	84
20:30–31	53
20:31	22
21	53–54, 88
21:15–19	179
21:22	113
21:24–25	53

Acts

	24, 160
1:1	23
1:2	82
1:3–7	103
1:5	82
1:6–8	210
1:7	216
1:8	82, 84
1:16–20	175–82
1:16	82

INDEX OF SCRIPTURE AND OTHER ANCIENT SOURCES

1:18–19	175	12:6–8	82, 143
2:1–13	82	12:20	144
2:1–4	84	13	145
2:20	211	13:1–11	143
2:33	82	13:1–7	142–53
3:20–21	211	13:1–3	151
3:21	67, 102	13:1	144, 150
5:29	151	13:2	144
7:45	209	13:3	149
11:27	82	13:3a	144
13:3	82	13:4–5	149
13:6	138	13:4a	144
13:8	138	13:4c	144
15	179	13:4d	144
15:32	82	13:5	144
19:6	82	13:6b	144
21:9	82	13:7	145, 148
21:10	82	13:8–10	88, 165
24	153	13:8	145
24:1–10	142	13:9	144
24:19	142	14:17	93, 103, 217
24:26	143		
24:27	143	## 1 Corinthians	
25:9	143		161, 164, 166
25:16	xiv, 10, 142, 153	2:6–8	149
26	153	6:6	56
26:31–32	143	12–14	84
28:23	143	12:10	82
28:31	143	12:28–31	82
		13	82
## Romans		13:1–13	71, 142
	152, 160, 161, 166, 168, 169	13:2b	xiii
		13:8	82
1	20	13:11	xiii
1:3	219	13:13	128
1:16–17	x	14	81, 82
2:11	146	14:24	82
3:21–31	x	14:31	82
7	92	15	156, 171
8	84	15:9	165
9:6–33	145	15:20–28	84, 149, 154–74
10:15	122	15:22	159
11:1–36	145	15:23	210
12–15	143	15:24–25	149
12:1–2	149	15:24	159
12:2	149, 150	15:25	159
12:3	143	15:27	159

1 Corinthians (continued)

15:27c	159
15:28	159
15:28	159
15:45	211
15:47	211
16:5	56

2 Corinthians

	161, 166
3:6	x
11:32	133

Galatians

	67, 160, 161, 179
1–4	x, 130, 170
1:15–16	165
2–3	23
2:11–14	x, 130
2:14	105
4:4	220
4:24	ix
5:13	150
5:14	88
6:7	72

Ephesians

	25, 161, 170
1:21	103
2:20	82
3:5	82
4:11	82
5:21	150
6:12	150
6:17	150

Philippians

	161
2:6–11	13, 92
2:7	117
3:20	149
3:21	149

Colossians

	161, 181
1:20	102
1:24	181

1 Thessalonians

	161
2:14–16	27
2:19	210
3:13	210
4:13–19	84
4:13–18	149, 158
4:15	210
5:2	103
5:9	149
5:19–20	81, 203
5:21	27
5:23	210

2 Thessalonians

	161

1 Timothy

1:4	108

2 Timothy

3:16–17	22
4:4	108

Titus

1:14	108
3:1	150

Philemon

	161

Hebrews

	24, 161, 179, 220
4:8	209
4:12–13	28
7:13	219
11:30–31	209

James

24, 67, 88, 160, 179

1:13–15	20
2:14–16	10

1 Peter

2:13–17	150
2:16	150
2:21	150
3:13—4:2	150
4:8	71

2 Peter

205

1:4	128
1:16	108
1:19–20	22
3:8–13	204
3:8	103
3:10	159
3:15–16	10, 22
3:10–11	104
3:12	103
3:15–16	22

1 John

53, 54, 88

3:2	159

2 John

53, 54

3 John

53, 54

Jude

24, 179

Revelation

5, 24, 81, 110, 179, 203, 205

1:12–18	128
12	36, 139
13	151
18:6–8	151
20	163
20:1–15	158
20:1–10	84, 103, 149, 171, 204
20:5	158
20:13	158
20:15	158
20:1–10	103

❦

EARLY CHRISTIAN WRITINGS

Augustine

De civitate Dei

60, 215

1:17–18	179
12:12	217
15–22	217
15:1	217
15:9	217
16:43	217
19–22	215
20:19	217
20:23	217
22:7	217
22.33.5	215

Contra Gaudentium Donistarum

179

On the Consensus of the Gospels

104

Sermon 72

71

Sermon 259
PL 38:1197–98   217

1 Clement
5   153

Clement of Alexandria
Stromateis
6:137–45   215

Egerton fragment
115

Gospel of Peter
115

Gospel of the Hebrews
115

Gospel of Thomas
75, 104, 115

Hippolytus
Commentary on Daniel
4.23   215

Irenaeus
Adversus Haereses
3.11.8   220
5.28.3   215

Justin
Dialogue with Trypho
49   209
70   209
75   209
81.4   215
89–90   209
113–14   209

Letter of Barnabas
12:7–10   209
15:4   215
17:14   209

Proto-evangelium of James
104

GRECO-ROMAN WRITINGS

Aristotle
Politics   148

Posterior Analytics   125

Rhetoric   26
I.9, 1366b   148

Josephus
Antiquities
8.1–211   185
13.300   77
15   134
16   134
16.361–394   199
17.1–8   134
17.182–187   199

Bellum Judaicum
1.18–33   134
1.68   74, 77
1.538–551   199
1.661–664   199

Contra Apionem
1.8   74
1.106–115   185

Justinian
Institutiones
I.i:I   148

INDEX OF SCRIPTURE AND OTHER ANCIENT SOURCES

Plato

Apology
29c — 151

Gorgias
479E — 126

Laws
— 148

Republic
— 148

RABBINIC WRITINGS

Babylonian Talmud

Sanhedrin
11a — 78

Sota
48b — 78

Yoma
99b — 78

Canticles Rabbah
8.11 — 78

Jerusalem Talmud

Sota
9:13 — 78

Mishnah

'Aboth
— 96
1:1 — 78, 79
1:3 — 195
1:12 — 96
3:2 — 96
4:5 — 195
5:2–3 — 218
5:22 — 10

Sota
9:9–15 — 74

Seder 'Olam Rabbah
86b — 78

Tosefta

Sota
13:2 — 73, 74
13:3 — 78

QURAN

— 61, 67, 68, 98, 99
27:14–44 — 196
33:41 — 78

www.ingramcontent.com/pod-product-compliance
Lightning Source LLC
Chambersburg PA
CBHW030823230426
43667CB00008B/1352